About the Editors

Amy Eckert is Assistant Professor of Political Science at Metropolitan State College of Denver. Her current research focuses on the growing privatization of war and Just War theory. Her work has appeared in such journals as *International Studies Quarterly* and the *Journal of Global Ethics*. She is President of the International Studies Association–West and a member of the executive board of the International Ethics section of the International Studies Association.

Laura Sjoberg is an Assistant Professor at Virginia Tech in Blacksburg, Virginia. Her research focuses on mainstreaming gender in the field of security studies. She is the author of *Gender, Justice, and the Wars in Iraq* (2006) and (with Caron E. Gentry) *Mothers, Monsters, Whores: Women's Violence in Global Politics* (2007). Her work has been published in the *International Feminist Journal of Politics*, *International Politics*, *International Studies Quarterly*, and *International Studies Perspectives*.

D1522223

Rethinking the 21st Century

'New' Problems, 'Old' Solutions

edited by
Amy Eckert & Laura Sjoberg

ZED BOOKS
London & New York

Rethinking the 21st Century: 'New' Problems, 'Old' Solutions was first published
in 2009 by Zed Books Ltd, 7 Cynthia Street, London N1 9JF, UK
and Room 400, 175 Fifth Avenue, New York, NY 10010, USA

www.zedbooks.co.uk

Designed and typeset in Monotype Jansen
by illuminati, Grosmont, www.illuminatibooks.co.uk
Cover designed by Andrew Corbett
Printed and bound in the UK by the MPG Books Group

Distributed in the USA exclusively by Palgrave Macmillan,
a division of St Martin's Press, LLC, 175 Fifth Avenue, New York, NY 10010

A catalogue record for this book is available from the British Library
Library of Congress Cataloging in Publication Data available

ISBN 978 1 84813 006 7 Hb
ISBN 978 1 84813 007 4 Pb

Contents

Acknowledgments   vii

1   Introduction: 'New' Problems and 'Old' Solutions   1
    Amy Eckert and Laura Sjoberg

    PART I 'New' Issues in War-making and War-fighting

2   Popular Support and Terrorism   22
    Caron E. Gentry

3   Preventive Warfare   46
    Yannis A. Stivachtis

4   Genocide: An Obligation to Fight?   70
    Rebecca Glazier

5   Justifying Changes in International Norms
    of Sovereignty   90
    Jennifer M. Ramos

PART II Apportioning Responsibility and Blame
in the Era of 'New' War

6   Honorable Soldiers, Questionable Wars?   112
    Frances V. Harbour

7   Outsourcing War   136
    Amy Eckert

8   The Problem of Patriotism   155
    Cheyney Ryan

PART III 'New' Additions to the Security Agenda

9   Sanctions as War   173
    Laura Sjoberg

10 Pandemic Influenza and Security   193
    Christian Enemark

11 Natural Disasters   211
    Lisa Burke

    Conclusion   228
    Amy Eckert and Laura Sjoberg

    Notes   237

    References   246

    Notes on Contributors   271

    Index   274

Acknowledgments

The intellectual and personal motivation for this project was a bright, enthusiastic community of scholars who attend the annual conference of the Western region of the International Studies Association. The support of ISA–West, and of the International Studies Association, which funded a workshop on this topic of New Problems and Old Solutions prior to the 2007 ISA–West meeting, was crucial to putting this book together. We are grateful for the comments of audiences at the 2007 Annual Meeting of the International Studies Association–West, particularly our workshop discussant Richard Shapcott, and the 2008 Annual Meeting of the International Studies Association. The contributors to this book inspired the work that we put into it. We would also like to thank our kind, generous, and patient editor at Zed Books, Ellen Hallsworth, who put up with our first attempt at editing a book (which, it appears, just as all of our advisors told us, is not as easy as writing the darn thing yourself – but is, in many ways, more intellectually rewarding). Each essay in this collection, we believe, contributes something unique to the intersection of political theory and security studies, and together they are more than the sum of their parts.

Amy wishes to acknowledge Laura Sjoberg for her friendship, her lively intellect, and for her help in building ISA–West into an academic community oriented around international ethics. For the past several years, ever since I was somewhat misplaced on a panel of hers, Laura has been indispensable to me as a friend, colleague, and intellectual partner. Fran Pilch first encouraged me to attend ISA–West when we met at a workshop on international ethics at Vanderbilt University in 2004. When I did, I found it to be a region characterized by a great deal of energy and collegiality. Thanks to the work and support of Laura and others, including Fran Pilch, ISA–West has become a venue in which work like that contained in this book has flourished.

I would also like to thank the Metropolitan State College of Denver, particularly my department chair Robert Hazan and my dean Joan L. Foster, for support and encouragement of this project. Financial support from the International Studies Association in the form of a workshop grant was key to the creation of this project.

Last but certainly not least, I would like to acknowledge my spouse Rick Prill, for his love and support.

Laura would like to express gratitude, first and foremost, to Amy Eckert, who is one of the most energetic and dedicated scholars she has ever met. I have been so involved in ISA–West (despite not living in the region) for two reasons: vibrant, brilliant people like Amy and the contribution that ISA–West made to my professional development. The summer after my first year in graduate school, I found the ISA–West conference on the website of the American Political Science Association. I decided to apply, because one ought to do things like that, and because a weekend in Las Vegas sounded like fun. That weekend, I met people who would mentor me through the rest of my time at graduate school – Jon Strand, Fran Pilch, and many others – clearly caring about my career and believing in me and my work. I work with and for ISA–West to repay that debt, which is immeasurable.

I am also indebted to the institutional support of the Political Science Department at Virginia Tech, the Political Science Department at Duke, and the International Studies Association.

Personally, my work on this project has been largely completed in the shadow of the tremendous loss of Hayward Alker, who told me that he would like to read this book when I told him that we were planning it. I just hope to spend the rest of my career producing work he might have been proud of, and with a small percentage of his enthusiasm. My spouse, Chris Marcoux, and my younger brother, JD, supported me as I worked long nights putting this together. I also had the support of my (now three) Chihuahuas – April, who solves security problems with violence; Gizmo, who is constantly insecure; and Max, the most adorable source of insecurity in the world.

I also owe a debt to an isolated, but memorable, negative experience, at my first ISA–West in 2002. While the majority of my work addresses gender issues in IR, at that particular conference I presented a paper that proposed a formal modeling approach to analyzing sanctions compliance. The paper won the Graduate Student Paper Award. In congratulating me, someone who did not know me at all told me that 'this is the sort of work young scholars should be doing – instead of silly stuff like constructivism and gender.' It was at that moment that I learned to value the connections across diverse research programs and research methods. This project is very much a reflection of that inspiration.

To Frances Pilch,
who saw us as a team before we knew each other

I

Introduction:

'New' Problems and 'Old' Solutions

Amy Eckert and Laura Sjoberg

> We are in a conflict between good and evil. And America will call evil
> by its name. (President George W. Bush, quoted in Carver 2003: 1)

In response to this new 'conflict between good and evil,' the Bush
administration in the United States implemented a 'new strategic
framework' to address 'the new security threats that we face in the
twenty-first century' (Bolton 2002). Pundits declared the previously
illegitimate tactic of preventive warfare a 'legitimate tool for dealing
with new security threats,' which includes the ability to 'kill terrorists,
prevent weapons proliferation, halt genocidal killing, or stop the spread
of deadly disease' (Daalder and Steinberg 2005). President George
W. Bush reached out to the Russian government to which he had
previously shown hostility, explaining that 'it's time to work together
to address the new security threats that we all face.' These 'new'
threats will require new tools and new tactics, 'new and imaginative
solutions' for the 'threats that freedom-loving people will face in
the near future' (Bush 2001). Bush (2002b) emphasized the newness
of twenty-first-century security problems in the 'National Security
Strategy of the United States,' even though many of the solutions and
strategies contained within that document were borrowed from earlier
security strategies and marked as new. The claimed newness of the
problems, however, allowed the Bush administration to change the

discourse of international security, from a continuous problem with access to both past and new solutions to a 'new' problem that requires radically different strategies.[1] As such, the 'new military-strategic doctrine – sometimes called the Bush Doctrine – contains not a subtle adjustment but rather a radical change that elevates the danger of aggression, militarism, and war to an entirely new level' (Webb 2002). In other words, the new and decontextualized solutions to new security problems have 'frightening' implications for any understanding of international security (Webb 2002). This paradigm of 'newness' has become the dominant way of characterizing and dealing with security problems in the early twenty-first century. The departure of the Bush administration in the United States provides a critical moment to reevaluate and rethink this conceptualization – is newness and decontextualization the right way to think about twenty-first-century security? Or is there another, more fruitful, way?

The Bush administration is not the only government that points to a radical change in the security situation as motivation for a new approach to security problems. Tony Blair called the war in Iraq 'the front line in the battle against terrorism and the new security threat that we face.' He explained that it is 'a new and poisonous evil form of extremism' which threatens the 'basic values of humanity' (BBC News 2004). Russian President Vladimir Putin 'skillfully used a time gap between the [9/11] tragedy and the American retaliatory action to promote a Russian view on how the international community should reorganize itself in the face of a new security threat – thus promoting Russia's status in the international arena' and volunteering a 'new strategic partnership' with a president of the United States who had campaigned on the promise of being tougher on Russia (Chinyaeva 2001). In a 2004 White Paper on national defense, the Chinese government introduced a 'new security concept' which serves as 'the people's call for cooperation and world peace' in times of trouble (*People's Daily* 2004). Additionally, 'Japan has recently begun a process to transform its security strategy and envision a new role for itself' in response to a 'new security environment,' which includes a Chinese threat, ballistic missiles, terrorism, risk of invasion, and North Korea (Hwang 2005).

To be sure, the twenty-first century has quickly demonstrated that it is a century of very different threats to the one that preceded it.

The newness of twenty-first-century security problems is not entirely contrived. The shocking attacks of September 11, 2001, carried out by a terrorist organization, put the US and the rest of the world on notice that the greatest threats could come from unexpected sources. During the Cold War, the United States' attention focused on threats from powerful states like the Soviet Union. The 9/11 attacks, carried out by a handful of individuals armed with box cutters and airline tickets, drove home the realization that the stable, predictable Cold War order had ended. The 1995 sarin gas attack in the Tokyo subway put the world on notice that the daily infrastructure could be used in terrorist attacks (Litfon 2000). The 2004 tsunami (Huxley 2005) and 2005 Hurricane Katrina (Dyson 2006) brought attention to natural disasters as security issues. The genocide in Rwanda in the 1990s was the most efficient killing spree in history (Sjoberg and Gentry 2007). As Mary Kaldor notes, 'in the context of globalization, what we think of as war – war between states in which the aim is to inflict maximum violence – is becoming an anachronism.' This is not to say, however, that security threats are decreasing. Instead, in the place of traditional war is 'new war, a mixture of war, organized crime, and massive violations of human rights. The actors are both global and local, public and private' (Kaldor 1999). In the twenty-first century, threats emanate not only from powerful states but increasingly from less obvious sources; not only from nuclear wars but from terrorism, disease, environmental degradation, military privatization, and other 'new' security issues.

These 'new' problems raise new questions about, and require the adaptation of inherited notions of, justice. A sense that the world is changing has created a state of urgency in politics – to look for *new* answers to these *new* problems. In the search for new answers, scholars and politicians alike often resort to stark and ahistorical, perhaps even anti-intellectual, solutions. The Bush Doctrine began by erasing the distinction between terrorists and those who harbor them, and expanded to 'strength beyond challenge' and 'extending liberty, democracy, and security to all regions' (Dolan 2005; Hayes 2007). This doctrine has been characterized as 'without limits, without accountability to the UN or international law, without any dependence on a collective judgment of responsible governments, and, what is worse, without any convincing demonstration of practical necessity' while 'encroaching on highly dangerous terrain' (Falk 2002). Popular culture in the United States has followed suit, popularizing songs like Toby Keith's (2001) 'Courtesy of the Red, White, and Blue' ('this big dog gets mad when you rattle his cage ... we'll put a boot up your ass, it's the American way') and books like Samuel Huntington's (1996) *The Clash of Civilizations*. While some argue that the Bush Doctrine 'represents the realities of international politics in the post-cold-war, sole-superpower world' (Donnelly 2003), others have characterized it as 'ahistorical and apolitical, and therefore warped strategically' (Blumenthal 2006).

This book is an attempt to reappropriate and recontextualize twenty-first-century security problems within traditions of international ethics that hold clues to their solutions. It is crucial to see twenty-first-century 'new' security discourses as a part of and continuation of discourses that have come before. As Nicholas Onuf observes, 'the ground itself is but the rubble of construction. Truths as we take them to be are inextricable from the arguments offered for them' (1989: 35). A language-based constructivist approach sees the 'newness' of these security problems as a discursive rule which creates a state of social rule in a world where there is not 'a sharp distinction between material and social realities' and 'the material and the social contaminate each other, but variably' (Onuf 1989: 40). The act of constructing these security problems as a radical break, 'the co-constitution of people and society, makes history' (Onuf 1989: 42). Accordingly, 'when we speak of order, we choose a fiction to believe in. "Order" is a metaphor, a figure of speech, a disguise. It is constituted by performative speech and constitutes propositional content for such speech' (Onuf 1989: 155). Such performance, however, does not happen in a vacuum – it creates and defines human perceptions of order. Therefore, rules like the 'newness' of twenty-first-century security dilemmas are 'jointly constitutive and regulative' (Onuf 1989: 45). As such, these rules *make* that newness real, creating space for the perceived appropriateness of solutions unconcerned with political or philosophical history or context.

Scholars have always raised questions about accepted ways of seeing (Onuf 2002). This book questions the accepted way of seeing the twenty-first-century security atmosphere as the political equivalent of a clean break from what came before. It contextualizes new security problems in the problems and practices of previous human experience and analysis. After recognizing 'new' security problems as related in both discourse and practice to the security problems of the past, this volume attempts to rein in the alarmist discourse of newness and to contextualize the analysis of these 'new' problems in a discourse of 'old' solutions, derived from decades and sometimes centuries of ethical analysis and political theory. The book considers twenty-first-century security problems in terms of international ethics, exploring the extent to which ethical traditions can shed light on them, looking for 'old' solutions' to 'new' problems to 're-ethicize' international security. Before we consider these analyses, it is useful to take a few moments to consider the two elements that are the focus of this book: 'new' problems and 'old' solutions.

New Problems

The 'new' problems of the twenty-first century consist both of new variations of old problems and of threats that are emerging, or perhaps being recognized as security problems, for the first time. In other words, some 'new' security situations confront security decision-makers, and some existing problems are, due to increasing severity or increasing visibility, beginning to be considered security threats where they were previously left out of that realm of analysis.

The boundaries of the field of international security have been a question of some contestation in recent decades. In *People, States and Fear* (1991), Buzan critiques the discipline of International Relations (IR) for its treatment of the idea of security. Buzan makes the claim that the discipline's thought concerning the term is 'underdeveloped' and 'simple-minded' (1991: 1–2). The crux of his critique faults the lack of coverage and coherency that the discipline has given to 'security.' Buzan relates the elements of his broader, reconceptualized notion of security, including five sectors – military, political, economic, societal, and environmental – where security had been considered primarily a question of military capacity in the past (Buzan 1991: 19). Buzan claims that this broader interpretation of international security is more reflective of the way the world works, is more likely to reach out to people at the margins of global politics, and is intellectually integrative of different perspectives (1991: 370).

Others throughout the 1980s and 1990s supported Buzan's argument for a wider interpretation of what counts as a security threat. Buzan, Waever, and de Wilde suggest that there are also five levels of analysis at which we can see security: the international system, the international subsystem, the unit, the subunit, and the individual (1998: 6). J. Ann Tickner advances the claim that 'the depersonalization of the discipline ... has been carried to its extreme in national security studies,' which allows 'wider security issues, which threaten the survival of the earth and all of its inhabitants, [to] disappear from the agenda when military crises escalate' (1992: 8, 21). A field of study loosely grouped as 'human security' (McRae and Hubert 2001; Thomas 2001) includes 'the protection of individuals and communities from war and other forms of violence' (Human Security Centre 2007). These approaches share an attempt to move national security discourse from using states as the sole referent, to seeking the security of individuals and groups within states.

In addition to trying to include a wider range of *subjects* of international security, 'wideners' are interested in including a broader understanding of the problems that count as security threats. For example, Tickner contends that feminists see that security means 'safe working conditions and freedom from the threat of unemployment and the economic squeeze of foreign debt ... imperialism, militarism, racism, and sexism' (1992: 35). 'New' security theorists include environmental security (Barnett 2001; Dalby 2002), economic security (Kahler 2005; Cable 1995), health security (Chen and Narasimhan 2004; McInnes and Lee 2006), and food security (Rosegrant and Cline 2003).

There are those who have protested the widening of the definition of security, arguing that individuals and their diverse problems do not belong in the realm of international security discourses. Stephen Walt explains that

> The main focus of security studies is easy to identify, however: it is the phenomenon of war. Security studies assumes that conflict between states is always a possibility and that the use of military force has far-reaching effects on states and societies. Accordingly, security studies may be defined as *the study of the threat, use, and control of military force*. It explores the conditions that make the use of force more likely, the ways that the use of force affects individuals, states, and societies, and the specific policies that states adopt in order to prepare for, prevent, or engage in war. (Walt 1991: 212)

Walt's position is echoed by a number of 'traditional' security theorists, who argue that war is the appropriate focus of security studies. These security theorists argue that 'widening' approaches like human security are 'hot air' and likely to pass while security maintains its focus on war between states (Paris 2001).

Even given these protests, the policy world seems to be going the way of the 'wideners,' globally, and even in the United States. In the 1990s, the Canadian and British governments gave special attention to questions of human security and 'good international citizenship' (Cooper 1997; Stairs 1998). The security webpage of President Bush included terrorism, democracy, health, food, and weapons security. Recent resolutions of the United Nations Security Council cover issues of women's health, children's participation, environmental security, and food scarcity.[2] The pages of security studies journals are more and more frequently populated by issues of health, disease, gender, environment, and political structure. This book considers the security agenda as it is presented to the public eye today: as 'widened,' but still centered on state interests.

It is within this context that this book comes to evaluate 'new' security problems. These are of three types: problems labeled as new despite significant continuity with the recent past; re-manifestations of security problems that have been historically significant; and additions to the security agenda. Problems labeled as new despite significant continuity with the past include terrorism, military pre-emption, genocide, and state sovereignty. These are the sort of problems addressed by the first section of the book.

Some 'new' problems are re-manifestations of problems that have been historically significant, but their historical roots are downplayed in policy rhetoric. The discourses about these problems reflect both *actual* newness (changes to the security environment) and *representational* newness (as they are described as quantitatively and qualitatively different from *all* analogical situations), even though there are situations with which they can be compared. Questions of soldiers' responsibility for war, the role of non-state military actors employed by states, and the relationship between citizenship and responsibility for war can be seen in this light.

For example, we can see one dimension of the attacks of September 11, 2001 on the World Trade Center in New York City as a re-manifestation of the problem of individual and non-state actor influence in global politics. The ability of a small decentralized organization like al-Qaeda to strike the international system's hegemonic power reflects broader changes within the international system. While the state may still be the most significant actor within the international system, other actors are playing an increasingly important role. The state faces competition from private actors not only in terms of economic activity but also with respect to the use of force. To some extent, this diffusion of force – the monopoly of which once defined the state – is consistent with globalization and its premium on privatization. In some cases, states have voluntarily ceded some of their authority to private actors. In other cases, these private actors have carved out their own political space. These transformations within the international system have created an environment in which a private actor can strike a powerful state and that state goes to war with a still more nebulous network of private actors.

At the same time, the September 11 attacks were not the only time that individual actors mattered in global politics (Byman and Pollack 2001). Individuals such as Adolf Hitler and Napolean Bonaparte played key roles in the construction of security landscapes during their lifetimes (Byman and Pollack 2001). Political theorists from Augustine to E.H. Carr have explored questions of the transgression of state power, state boundaries, and state supremacy. The apparent newness of the problem of non-state actors is accentuated by states' security concerns in response to the September 11 attacks. It is also directly linked to the desire to 'solve' the problem with new answers, rather than by reference to historical precedent or relevant work in international ethics. These are the sorts of problems addressed by the second section of the book.

In addition to changes in traditionally defined security issues, 'new' security analyses 'widen' the scope of the concept of international security. 'New' threats are also emerging and collapsing the distinction between security and issues previously categorized as 'low politics,' including environmental problems, economics, and pandemics. While they have been previously significant in other policy arenas, they are new to the security realm. These new threats, exemplified by the potential avian flu pandemic, natural disasters, and environmental degradation, fall outside the definition of security as interstate warfare.

Many of these threats do not go through the traditional channels of military hierarchy and require specialized knowledge and innovative tactics for response. Unquestionably issues of human security that threaten individual well-being, these new threats have also come to be seen as problems of international security. These are the sort of issues addressed by the third section of this book.

Though these threats are new to the security agenda, they can be linked to issues that have been traditionally classified as security, and to past ethical reasoning about security specifically and politics generally. There is an element of newness to the consideration of these issues, but not the radical newness described by partisans of the 'new' security debate. Instead, these issues need to be considered in the context of what already compiled knowledge can tell us about them, and what ethical work remains to be done. Without context, the likelihood that these issues are considered unreflectively and dealt with dangerously increases exponentially. Still, the ethical norms of the international arena, including human rights standards and laws pertaining to armed conflict, evolved in that era of great power threat. While they have continued relevance to this new international land-scape, they need to evolve with the new realities of the international system. These issues, then, cannot be considered without both context and innovation. Although traditions of international ethics do not specifically address several of the security threats discussed in this book, this should not be taken to mean that this context does not apply. The chapters in this book explore the contributions that this ethical context – consisting primarily of 'old' thinking – can make to understanding these security problems, despite their 'newness.'

Treating these emerging security problems as new makes it easier to think of them as if they have no connection to the past, or specifi-cally to ethical traditions. Making this break from the past suggests, consciously or not, that the principles arising out of these traditions do not apply to the new and radically different problems. This move has the effect of freeing states from the restrictions that these norms would impose on them, and of appearing to justify increasingly radical and ahistorical methods for dealing with 'new security threats' (Bush 2001a). For their part, scholars of international security have been so caught up in the *newness* of their current dilemmas that they are failing to take advantage of older ethical literatures that make a real contribution to understanding 'new' problems. This volume reintroduces 'old' solutions to contextualize and begin to understand the debate about twenty-first-century security problems.

Old Solutions

The contributions to this volume seek to advance our understanding of these 'new' ethical dilemmas by applying the insights of the past to the moral problems of security within the contemporary international system. Many of these approaches come from inside political science, in the field of political theory, while others borrow from diverse fields such as economics and psychology. The application of political theory approaches to international relations generally has at times encountered obstacles. Artificial dichotomies between political theory and international relations prevented dialogue between the two fields on important issues of concern to both. These dichotomies stem from the misperception that political theory depends on the existence of a state and can therefore not contribute to questions that cross borders because international society lacks a central authority. This dichotomy fails to recognize both that the international system, though lacking a government, contains important components of governance and that the domestic sphere is sometimes more disordered than is often acknowledged. The perception of the two fields as separate has sometimes prevented those in international relations from recognizing the potential contributions of political theory.

Dialogue between international relations and political theory has increased. Martin Wight once suggested that there was no international theory, despite a wealth of domestic political theory (Wight 1966: 18). The divide rested upon the premiss 'that one can differentiate and contrast an orderly and pacific domestic realm and an anarchic and bellicose inter-state realm' (Ferguson and Mansbach 2004: 84). As such, domestic politics could be the subject of political theory while international politics could not be. If this proposition were ever true, it certainly is no longer so. Growing order within international society and growing disorder within domestic societies belie a sharp distinction between these realms. This convergence has fueled the growth of the field of international political theory. One scholar has suggested that strong evidence of this growing interaction is the fact that some scholars – Chris Brown, Charles Beitz, and Andrew Linklater, among others – cannot easily be identified as primarily political or international theorists (Schmidt 2002: 117). Their work, part of a growing body of international political theory, exists in the intersection of political and international relations theory and draws upon both. This convergence between these academic fields suggests a growing recognition that normative considerations do not stop at national borders, but instead permeate international relations, security issues included. While security studies will benefit from the insights of political theory, political theory will also benefit from a re-engagement with the new realities of the international system.

The supposed 'gulf' between political theory and international security may have something to do with the two fields' interpretation of the meaning of the word 'security.' Here, Robert Cox's dichotomy between problem-solving theory and critical theory is instructive. According to Cox (1986), problem-solving theory is an attempt to explain international interaction within the current understanding of the international system, while critical theory questions both the vision problem-solving theorists have of the international system and their perceived inability to change that framework. Following Cox's analysis, theory does not have to be purely descriptive. Instead, theory can be explanation, critique, and practice (Zalewski 1996; Tickner 2001). Both theory and action are necessary to clear and change political space: each alone is insufficient (Flax 1987: 623). On this level, it is not only possible for political theory and international security studies to have conversations; it is necessary.

Still, the treatment of the challenges in this book as 'new' problems raises the question of whether these and other 'old' approaches can contribute anything to the understanding of contemporary issues. Some would say that, because they did not anticipate the exact nature of the security situations of the world as it is today, 'old' political theory, psychological, and economic approaches have little if any utility. This position is best captured by the Bush administration's multiple insinuations that the security world is now entirely different to how it has ever been before, and thus requires a radically different strategy. In the president's public speeches during his term in office, as chronicled on the White House website, we count that he has characterized the security environment as 'new' 215 times. This occurs in 10 percent of his published speeches under the heading 'defense,' and is the most frequently used adjective to describe the security situation. The word 'dangerous' is the second most frequently used adjective. Others would be blind to the nuances of today's security atmosphere and the changes it goes through in order to insist on the strict applicability of theoretical approaches. This position is best shown in the work of international political theorists like Hans Morgenthau (1948), who emphasize the unchanging nature of their suppositions about how states act and interact.

The central claim of this book, as explored with respect to the diverse security issues that it confronts, is that the 'old' approaches rooted in established ethical traditions can make contributions to addressing them, no matter how new they might seem. Just as the divide between political theory and international relations is narrower than is often perceived, so the gap between old and new is not as wide as is often claimed. Not only can ethical traditions provide normative guidance to states and other international actors, but these actors would be well advised to heed the counsel they offer. These 'old' ethical traditions, to the extent that they are embedded within the international system, help to constitute the identities of states and frame their interactions. When viewed in this light, making a sharp break with traditional norms threatens not only those served by those norms but the structure of the system itself that relies on them.

In international security theory and practice, it is not that there are no norms but that 'normativity is conventionalized out of sight' (Onuf 1989: 195). As 'security is a derivative concept … to have any meaning, *security* necessarily presupposes something to be secured; as a realm of study it cannot be self-referential' (Krause and Williams 1997a: ix). As Krause and Williams explain, 'Stephen Walt seems to argue that one of the biggest threats to security is the seductive appeal of contrary methods of understanding it' (1997a: ix). The questions of what it is that needs to be secured and how to secure it are both important; 'the concept of security is not empty – it implicitly invokes and relies on a series of accepted prior visions of what it is to be secured' (Krause and Williams 1997a: x). Whatever definitions of security are used, political theory analyses 'together raise the question of the political functions of security discourse and the role of academic study of international security' (Dalby 1997: 18). The issues in this book are

not only security issues but *securitized* – that is, discussed in terms of
security in the international arena (Buzan et al. 1998: 5). Looking at
them 'means to look at the ways in which the objects to be secured,
the perceptions of threats to them, and available means of securing
them (both intellectual and material)' remain constant or change over
time (Krause and Williams 1997b: 49). In other words, political theory
is an essential part of the study of international security.

Not only are 'old' solutions an essential part of the study of international security, this book argues that they are needed now more
than ever. As R.B.J. Walker notes, 'whether analytically or rhetorically,
claims about security increasingly have an air of slovenly imprecision.
A word once uttered in hard cadences to convey brutal certainties has
become embarrassingly limp and overextended' (1997: 63). As such, the
term 'security' can be not only used but appropriated in insidious,
ahistorical ways. As Ken Booth explains:

> It is not simply an academic dispute over professional turf – about the
> boundaries of a subfield and how it should be studied. Fundamentally, it
> is part of a debate about the focus, direction, and meaning of … Inter-
> national Relations … security is what we make it. It is an epiphenomenon
> intersubjectively created. (Booth 1997: 83, 106)

If security is to any extent what we make it, then we have a scholarly
responsibility to evaluate both the content and context of our security
messages. Like Karin Fierke, we are concerned with 'the public nature
of the rules themselves and how these rules provide a tool for mapping
moves in a changing game in order to gain knowledge of the nature
of the game and its transformation over time' (1997: 225). The public
nature of the claimed newness of the security agenda, especially
coming from the Bush administration, has established newness as
the operative analytical frame for the security agenda of the United
States. This framework is now informing global security practice
and its study. This book, then, combines the analytical merging of
'old' solutions and 'new' problems as part of a scholarly and activist
attempt to recapture and recontextualize the security agenda. Some
of the current discourses of security prioritize newness; this project
shows their links with the theories and practices of the past. Those
partial discourses create and influence the security practice; this book
provides security practice with alternative analytical frameworks,
ethical directions, and policy suggestions.

Rethinking the 21st Century

The pairing of 'old solutions,' be they in political theory or drawn from insights from other fields, with 'new problems' is an exercise in rethinking the twenty-first-century security discourse. This book proposes that the new and decontextualized approach to security led by the Bush administration that has dominated early-twenty-first-century politics is not the best approach to maintain. Instead, it proposes that we rethink this approach by applying the theoretical insights of the past, with adaptations for the degree to which the security problems in the twenty-first century have evolved since the theoretical insights of Augustine, Clausewitz, and Machiavelli. This process of rethinking, this book argues, is a key to positing alternative futures for the twenty-first-century world. A reformulated approach to twenty-first-century security could serve as a strategic intervention in the dominant discourse of newness and decontextualization in security politics today.

Spike Peterson and Anne Sisson Runyan describe feminist theories as strategic interventions in dominant discourses in order to demonstrate the incapacity of traditional theories to deal with the real (1999). In other words, they use words, metaphors, comparisons, and conversations in order to show others what they are missing in the making of and study of politics. Nancy Huston argues that these dominant discourses are an indispensable part of understanding politics because political events follow the direction of the dominant narratives in their historical context (1983: 271). If the radical newness of the security agenda is the dominant discourse, this book is a discursive intervention in that dominant narrative to question its validity and implications. If the dominant discourse is problematic, it can be interrupted on both the discursive and operative levels.

That there is a dominant discourse of international security implies, as this introduction has argued, that subordinated discourses exist. In a world of competing stories, dominant discourses often 'win' despite the fact that they are often 'gendered and colonizing,' not to mention ahistorical and inaccurate (Peterson and Runyan 1999, Hussain 2000). A project of discursive destabilization looks for and points out the silences in the dominant narrative (Gibson-Graham 1994: 216; Sjoberg 2006).

Scholars can intervene in dominant discourses with a number of different tools. First, they can interject counter-narratives which tell different stories with different priorities (Sjoberg 2006). In this book, chapters by Sjoberg and Gentry use existing political theories to retell the event of economic sanctions and the organization of terrorist groups. Second, scholars can 'analyze the content of what is said in politics to find what is neglected, searching for silences' (Charlesworth 1999; Sjoberg 2006). Chapters by Stivachtis, Ramos, Glazier, Ryan, and Eckert examine what is missing from current accounts of pre-emption, humanitarian intervention, genocide, the 'war on terror,' and military privatization. Finally, scholars can present a compelling argument that the narrative which currently dominates is either empirically or theoretically inaccurate (Risse 2000). Chapters by Burke and Enemark demonstrate a compelling reason to alter the discourse of current security politics in order to include and address the issues that they take up in both the theory and practice of international security.

The 'New' Problems and their 'Old' Solutions

This book, then, takes on the dual task of starting a dialogue between political theory and international security and examining that dialogue's meanings and strengths, shortcomings and inadequacies. It is at once a theoretical evaluation of and a discursive intervention in security studies. The first section addresses 'new' dimensions of problems that fall within the traditional purview of international security, but that have been altered by the contemporary conditions of the international system. This section seeks to find 'old' solutions to new problems of terrorism, pre-emption, and military intervention, recontextualizing the security debate that has spiraled into a self-reproducing obsession with its own newness since the September 11 attacks in the United States.

To this end, in Chapter 2, Caron Gentry examines the (il)legitimacy of terrorism in light of Lockean political thought. To the extent that the post-9/11 era is characterized by a 'war on terror,' identifying terrorism assumes special urgency. In place of the platitude that 'one man's terrorist is another man's freedom fighter,' Gentry offers a framework, drawing on Locke's 'right of revolution,' that can help distinguish between legitimate acts of rebellion and illegitimate terrorism. The 'right of revolution,' a central concept from Locke's Second Treatise, underlies the idea that 'whenever any Form of Government becomes destructive of these Ends, it is in the right of the People to alter or abolish it, and to institute a new Government' (Declaration of Independence). Locke's 'right of revolution' may give the international community a fresh, albeit classic, look at terrorism within certain contexts. This framework raises additional questions. How does one determine when the government has become too tyrannical and people have the right to rebel? What signifies legitimate violence (as terrorism is by definition illegitimate violence)? Who in the international system gets to answer these questions? These classic questions of political theory are at the crux of the debate concerning what it means to be a terrorist and how terrorists interact both with each other and with the international community writ large. Gentry argues that 'old' solutions show the political context of the 'new' problem of terrorists as actors to be contiguous with, rather than split from, the history of political organization and political violence.

Chapter 3, by Yannis Stivachtis, deals with the question of preventive warfare. It argues that the 'new' security rhetoric employed by the Bush administration is a deliberate tool to escape past debates about the ethical viability of preventive warfare. This chapter contextualizes the Bush discourse on preventive war within the Just War debate on the subject, and then employs the preventive war theorizing of Sun Tzu, Augustine, and Vattel to measure the Bush Doctrine position on the issue. While these theorists have very little in common in terms of the time, place, and context of their work, each proposes a detailed framework for understanding preventive warfare. Sun Tzu argues that, when possible, a criminal should be attacked before the crime is even committed, but still requires benevolence, justice, and righteousness in the preventive attack. Augustine permits preventive warfare in some situations, but contends that it is not just to attack preventively to seek freedom from fear or vulnerability. Vattel's approach argues that while preventive war is *always* strategically beneficial it is only morally appropriate when the level of risk the potential victim is exposed to is reasonably certain and unacceptably high. The chapter demonstrates that the Bush preventive war doctrine, as outlined in the National Security Strategy of the United States, fails each of these three tests, but has been able to ignore them because of its radical decontextualization. It encourages a rethinking of current preventive war strategies in line with these theoretical insights of the past.

In Chapter 4, Rebecca Glazier takes up the issue of the reaction to genocide in the international arena. Looking at the post-Cold War jump in ethnic wars and genocidal conflicts, Glazier asks if there are theoretical precedents to help the international community deal with this 'new' and urgent problem. In particular, she notes, while the end of the Cold War has made international cooperation for humanitarian intervention in genocide possible to a greater extent than ever before, states have yet to commit universally to such intervention. The case of Rwanda and the unfolding tragedy in Darfur, Glazier notes, represent genocidal conflicts in which states failed to intervene. She finds an 'old' solution in the tenets of Just War theory, which she argues can provide a basis for a theory of obligatory intervention. Glazier proposes changes to the general *jus ad bellum* approach as well as to individual standards which would guide states to an obligation to intervene in genocide. Glazier argues that Just War theory can be used not only to restrain states from fighting unjust wars, but to obligate them to fight necessary ones.

Jennifer Ramos, in Chapter 5, looks at a different sort of military intervention: the United States' intervention in Afghanistan. Ramos is interested in when violations of state sovereignty are seen as acceptable, but unwilling to accept the reductionist answer that the rise of ethnic conflict and terrorism in the post-Cold War era has fundamentally changed the nature of state sovereignty. Instead, she notes that norms of sovereignty in the international arena fluctuate between absolute and contingent based on the behaviors of powerful states and explores the motivations behind those actions. Turning to the 'old' social psychological theory of cognitive dissonance, Ramos explains norm evolution as the by-product of military intervention. The norm of sovereignty that has evolved in the 'war on terror' is that state sovereignty is a privilege contingent on compliance with international counterterrorism conventions. While this iteration of contingent sovereignty is 'new,' Ramos argues, the theory of cognitive dissonance helps to contextualize and explain it in terms of the processes that have changed norms of sovereignty in modern history.

The second section of this volume addresses the question of appropriating responsibility and blame in the era of 'new' war. In Chapter 6,

Frances Harbour addresses the just soldier's dilemma. Recently, the media and politicians have paid substantial attention to the choice a soldier faces when his or her country has elected to fight an unjust war. The soldier is obligated to fight in the war by his or her contract for military service, but obligated not to do so by the principles of Just War which instruct that only a just war may be legitimized. Harbour argues that this problem has actually been dealt with substantially in the Just War literature, but that the recent attention to the just soldier's dilemma paves the way for a reevaluation of the Just War tradition's tendency to assign no blame to individual soldiers. To this end, Harbour finds another tool in the Just War tradition, the principle of double effect, which normally distinguishes between the intended and unintended effects of state conduct in war. She applies this framework to the actions of individual soldiers to produce a more nuanced understanding of individual responsibility for the making and fighting of wars. Using the positions of hypothetical soldiers in real conflicts of various types, Harbour seeks to distinguish among individual actions based on the effects of those individual soldiers' contributions to the overall war effort. By focusing on individual intent and causal effect, Harbour argues that it is possible for an individual to participate justly even in an unjust war. Through the use of the principle of double effect, however, Harbour demonstrates that the 'old' solution of Just War theory has the tools to deal with this and other problems of modern war-fighting.

In Chapter 7, Amy Eckert takes up the question of the privatization of force. While the state's monopoly on the legitimate use of force is a hallmark of the Weberian understanding of the state, states themselves are increasingly relying on private military firms for a multitude of functions ranging from supplying the state's military to engaging in combat. The activities of these private military forces, which occur primarily outside of public view and state control, skew the application of Just War principles. To the extent that private military casualties are not counted as a cost of war, for example, assessing the proportionality of a particular conflict becomes difficult if not impossible. Though they are not part of the public sphere, or the 'basic structure' of the international system, private military forces pose real problems for state actors seeking to apply Just War principles. These difficulties, however, are not because the problem is totally new, but instead result from treating the problem as new. Elements of the problem are 'old,' pre-dating the state system that is threatened by the privatization of force, as are components of the potential solution. The use of mercenaries in medieval and early modern Europe provoked reactions from Just War theorists, as have recent difficulties distinguishing civilians and combatants (Sjoberg 2006: 90). As Eckert demonstrates, though the analysis needs to be rethought, the 'old' solution of the Just War theory can be brought to bear on the 'new' problem of private military corporations in global conflict, which, she suggests, is analogous to the problems of mercenary participation in pre-modern wars.

Cheyney Ryan, in Chapter 8, takes a different approach to the question of who participates in war, focusing on the changes to war-making and war-fighting that have resulted from the recent end of conscription in the United States military. He argues that, while the post-Cold War attraction to 'humanitarian intervention' is indeed nothing new, the marked absence of debate about who fights and dies in those interventions is notable. Ryan notes that, without conscription, there is an increasing disconnect between those who suggest fighting wars and those who end up fighting in them. Invoking the work of American anti-war critic Randolph Bourne, Ryan identifies this phenomenon as 'alienated war,' which, he contends, makes states *freer* to choose violent solutions to their international problems than they would be under conscription. This is because, as Ryan argues, conscription increases the possibility that the war's advocates will have to fight in it. Using his own insights as well as Bourne's and work from Rousseau, Ryan proposes an ethical solution to the 'new' problem of alienated war: that unwillingness to fight in a war should be seen as objection, and, the flip side of the coin, that we should only favor wars that we would be willing to fight in. He proposes this standard as a bridge to re-establish the connection between war's advocates and its fighters.

The third section concerns 'new' additions to the security agenda in the post-Cold War world. While these issues appear new to Security Studies as a discipline, the chapters in this section reveal that there is a substantial amount of theorizing – even security theorizing – relevant to the evaluation of these 'new' issues. In Chapter 9, addressing economic sanctions, Laura Sjoberg draws on Clausewitz's definition of war and Bentham's utilitarianism to make sense of economic sanctions. In the 1990s, advocates of economic sanctions argued that they were a peaceful solution to problems which otherwise would have required military intervention. Citing the successful use of economic coercion to end apartheid in South Africa, advocates saw sanctions as a way to keep dangerous states in check and to coerce reasonable states' interests into coincidence with those of the international community more generally. While sanctions as a problem of domestic and international security are considered relatively new in the twenty-first-century security discourse, ancient and modern strategic theorists have considered economic sanctions as a weapon of war. Through the lens of Bentham's theory of sanctions, this chapter evaluates the new and continuous security elements of economic sanctions through the eyes of 'old' ethical theories. It argues that 'old' solutions frame and contextualize the nuances of the problem of economic sanctions and show them as properly analyzed within the realm of international security and, indeed, war proper.

In Chapter 10, Christian Enemark takes a different 'new' security threat, the problem of a potential influenza pandemic. In contrast to other disease pandemics, the effects of an influenza pandemic would be swift and unfamiliar. The resulting social disruption would pose a greater danger to any given individual than would the potential of becoming infected and dying. Enemark's chapter assesses the nature and extent of the threat posed by the H5N1 avian influenza virus and the value of measures currently under way or under consideration to prevent or mitigate a global human influenza outbreak. At the national and international levels, this pandemic threat could be securitized by implementing emergency responses beyond what would normally be politically acceptable. The imperative to contain the outbreak poses a problem of balancing the need to prevent the disease's spread while minimizing the harm to affected populations. Using historical context and example, Enemark demonstrates that avian flu is a new virus that threatens a new pandemic with different dimensions, but it is one that poses several 'old' problems, concerning state power, public health, and privacy.

In Chapter 11, Lisa Burke takes up the problem of natural disasters as a security threat. Recent events have highlighted the interrelationship and mutual construction of the natural and the social. The construction and selection of which 'events' that occur 'out there' qualify as natural disasters is a political process that is historically constituted by debates about sovereignty and security which employ definitions of statehood that necessitate alienating nature and culture. Burke argues that one justification for sovereign authority and power is the ability to provide security for those within the defined boundaries of the nation-state, regardless of the character of the threat. Machiavelli justified and opposed the *virtù* of the founder of the state to create institutions able to withstand and protect against the ravages and unpredictability of *fortuna*. This account of political community has shaped an understanding of action as militarized intervention, an account which has been problematized by the occurrence and politics of natural disasters.

The Conclusion reflects on the issues raised in the volume and situates them within the divide between old solutions and new problems. It provides a means to bridge the divide between 'old' ideas and 'new' fears, and between those who would ignore context and those who would ignore change in the theory and practice of international security. It reflects on the chapters in this volume as critiques and reconstructions of dominant narratives which focus on the 'newness' of twenty-first-century security. It characterizes these chapters as intellectual and political interventions. It argues that, whether (apparently) 'new' problems represent real shifts in the security environment, re-manifestations of 'old' dilemmas, or no real change at all, they cannot be solved effectively with analysis that treats the twenty-first century as a clean break from the past. Instead, 'new' problems require both 'old' solutions and creative policy analysis. Given this need, it navigates the middle path between acontextual and static analysis through the use of a diverse array of theoretical approaches, from political theory to psychology, from ancient to modern times. It suggests an alternative approach to thinking about security which is recontextualized and rethought, providing a better basis to address security dilemmas, old and new. Rethinking twenty-first-century security through these lenses can open up crucial dialogues about the theoretical and practical bases of security policymaking in the new millennium.

Popular Support and Terrorism

Caron E. Gentry

Immediately following 9/11, the Bush administration proclaimed that 'freedom and democracy are under attack. ... [W]e [Americans] are facing a different enemy than we have ever faced' (Fleischer 2001). It was not just the US's fight against al-Qaeda, the new enemy and the latest incarnation of 'murderous ideologies [fascism, and Nazism, and totalitarianism] of the twentieth century' – '[this] is the world's fight. This is civilization's fight' (Bush 2001a). In President Bush's 2002 State of the Union Address, he continued his insistence that this was a new security era, claiming that 'the civilized world faces unprecedented dangers.' The decade, he predicted, 'will be a decisive [one] in the history of liberty, [because] we've been called to a unique role in human events' (Bush 2002a).

Before the 'war on terror' emerged in action, a war of discourse was already being waged. 'Civilization' and 'unprecedented' are both loaded terms used to connote the US's place in the international hierarchy above that of the 'uncivilized' terrorists. This rhetoric of the uncivilized strives to identify al-Qaeda as such a fearsome and brutal enemy that this group must be stopped at all costs. The fear is expounded upon by proclaiming al-Qaeda's violence as a completely new phenomenon, which is, of course, untrue. The use of such rhetoric is highly suspect and propagandistic.

This discourse was being used to foment support for what would emerge as the 'war on terror,' but it also serves to identify al-Qaeda as a wholly original, uncivilized, and singularly threatening entity. This chapter argues that, on the contrary, terrorism is not a new phenomenon; nor is religious terrorism. The 9/11 attacks have been used by the US government and some academics to define a new era: that of 'global terrorism.' Global terrorism is distinguished by the use of information technology in the planning and implementing of attacks. This element identifies the era of global terrorism as in one sense without precedent; however, al-Qaeda is not the only group to have used information technology. Historically, many terrorist organizations have taken advantage of the latest technology for recruiting, planning and implementing events, and indeed for disseminating ideology. This is closely related to 'propaganda of the deed,' and as the trajectory of terrorism has unfolded, actions identified as terroristic have become more and more extreme (Rapoport 1984: 60). This chapter will argue that the problem posed by global terrorism is not entirely new; nor should our analysis of it ignore the contributions of 'old' theoretical perspectives.

It may seem odd to use John Locke, foundational theorist of the Western democratic state, as a way to approach the concept and problem of radical Islamic terrorism. The power of the citizenry, popular sovereignty, is the basis of Lockean theory. In the Second Treatise, Locke formulated the 'right of revolution,' which articulates a people's right to dissolve their government if it becomes tyrannical or if another government has usurped power. Even though Locke is a Western political theorist, popular sovereignty focuses on the relationship between the people and the government, especially on extending the social contract to include 'the consent to be governed.' The Bush administration's discourse about the 'war on terror' revolved around the idea of extending liberty and democracy – key ideas in Lockean theory – to the world as a means of fighting terrorism. On the other hand, some of the stated goals of al-Qaeda seem to be in keeping with both the fight against tyranny and usurpation and the desire to foster popular support. Therefore, the respect for popular support and liberty as it is perceived by both sides is critical to understanding the 'war on terror.'

Before being able to examine al-Qaeda in light of Lockean theory, we must begin by examining the supposed unprecedented nature of the organization's violence. To argue that the world does not find itself in a radically new era of terrorism, it is important to compare al-Qaeda with historical terrorist group the Assassins. Furthermore, it is critical to look at how the past deeds of terrorist organizations have relied upon the technology of the day – which allows a more productive assessment of al-Qaeda's dependence upon technologies that provide global capabilities.

Terrorism: Not New but Now Global

Al-Qaeda reflects a fascinating mix of long-standing radical Islamic[1] theology that articulates political goals and new technology that permits a globalized strategy. Radical Islamic thought existed previously and can be seen in a group identified as one of the earliest terrorist organizations. The Assassins were a group who selectively killed elites perceived to be blocking the creation of an earlier Islamic caliphate between 1090 and 1275 AD (Hoffman 2006: 84; Rapoport 1984: 664). When we compare the ancient Assassins with contemporary al-Qaeda and register their shared awareness of the need for popular support, we learn that al-Qaeda's belief system is not new, and therefore does not require a wholly new response.

Today there are elements of the 'new,' the 'global,' evident in radical Islamic terrorism: as terrorism has evolved from assassinations to mass murder, terrorists have relied upon modern technology of the day to act and to spread their message. Since the French Revolution, when the word *terrorisme* was coined to describe this style of political violence, there have been three distinct and largely agreed-upon eras of terrorism: (1) modern, from the late 1800s through the world wars and post-colonialism; (2) international, from 1968 to 2001; and (3) global, which began around the turn of the century (see Miller 1995; Hoffman 2006). Each era is tied to and dependent upon contemporaneous forms of technology for ideological dissemination. The differentiations between the eras is important to understanding that al-Qaeda, though it uses unprecedented technology, is not new or unique, inasmuch as its tactics are shared by other groups historical and contemporaneous.

Defining the subjective

Before looking at the specifics of al-Qaeda, however, the definition of 'terrorism' must be addressed, for it is a subjective and loaded term. Schmid and Jongman (2006) examined 109 definitions of terrorism, in which they found a repetition of key terms. Five of the most frequently cited terms are: (1) terrorism is political in scope; (2) it is a method; (3) it is intended to induce psychological trauma on the larger population; (4) the violence is meant to be coercive; and (5) it deliberately targets noncombatants (Schmid and Jongman 2006: 4–5).

The most important characteristic is that the violence is *political* in aim, scope, and reasoning (Hoffman 2006: 2; Wilkinson 2000: 12; Rapoport 1984: 659). Terrorism is also a *method* and is 'identified as the act itself, and the ends towards which violence is directed are de-emphasized' (Cronin 2002: 121).[2] As such, terrorism is not an ideology (Ganor 2002: 297; Wilkinson 2000: 11) but 'a method ... in which random or symbolic victims' are the 'target[s] of violence' (Schmid and Jongman 2006: 2, emphasis removed). The randomness or symbolic quality leads to the *psychological* dimension of terrorism; it is meant to create fear both in the immediate target and in an audience at large (Hoffman 2006: 40; Wilkinson 2000: 12). According to Jenkins, terrorism is 'aimed at causing widespread disorder, demoralizing society, and breaking down the existing social and political order' (2003: 22). 'Terrorism is the systematic use of *coercive* intimidation' (Wilkinson 2000: 12, emphasis added), where the political violence is instrumental to 'either ... immobilize[ing] the target of terror in order to produce disorientation and/or compliance, or to mobiliz[ing] secondary targets of demands' (emphasis removed) (Schmid and Jongman 2006: 2). The deliberate *targeting of civilians and noncombatants* is especially emphasized. To numerous other scholars, the targeting of civilians is one of the main determinants in whether political violence is terrorism (Schmid and Jongman 2006: 6; Cronin 2002/3: 33; Ganor 2002: 288).

The subjectivity and instrumentality of the term is revealed in various states' and IGOs' struggles to define it. In the US, definitions of terrorism vary from the State Department to the FBI (Hoffman 2006: 31–2). These differing definitions from agency to agency reveal each department's jurisdictions, agendas and priorities. Internationally, there is no agreed-upon definition of terrorism (Hoffman 2006: 32). Dugard argues that the UN's failure to find a permanent definition of terrorism in the 1970s is emblematic of the North–South divide. Essentially, the global North wanted the definition to reflect the criminality of terrorism while the global South preferred a definition that recognized an ethnicity's post-colonial right to self-determination (Dugard 1974: 72–3). Complicating this deeply entrenched difference of opinion is the fact that some actors who were once labeled as 'terrorist' 'have achieved legitimacy in the international system' – including Nelson Mandela. Mandela was labeled a terrorist in his role as leader of the African National Congress and later became the president of South Africa (Cronin 2002: 121). Conversely, some groups that were once defended are now considered illegitimate, like the Chechens (see Lapidus 1998: 8). All of this ultimately frames terrorism as a matter of perception.[3]

Paramilitaries, guerrilla groups, and terrorist organizations are divided into typologies based upon the various groups' belief systems. These belief systems are important because they help groups and members decide upon strategy, target selection, and appropriate activity and scale; all of these should be in keeping with the political goals of the groups (see Fromkin 1974; Drake 1988). These typologies include state (Stalin), state-sponsored (Iran), left-wing (West Germany's Red Army Faction), right-wing (neo-Nazis), ethno-nationalist (the Irish Republican Army), and religious (the Aryan Nations). Many terrorist groups fall into more than one category, as they are not mutually exclusive. For example, Stalin's terrorism fits into the category both of 'state' terrorism and of 'left-wing' terrorism. The Aryan Nations, on the other hand, can be seen as both 'religious' and 'right-wing' (see Sharpe 2000). Regardless of its belief system, to be identified as 'terrorist' a group must have goals that are political. For example, the Aryan Nations wants to overthrow the US government and reveal the hidden Jewish international conspiracy (the Zionist Occupation Government) (Aryan Nations 2008). Al-Qaeda's goals are based on religious belief, but the organization also has political goals: to create the Caliphate and to end US presence in Saudi Arabia and Iraq.

The Assassins and al-Qaeda: between 'old' and 'new'

This section argues that radical Islamic terrorism is not the new phenomenon that the Bush administration would like the general

public to believe it is. First, religious terrorism is not new; second, it
is not limited to Islam. Christian extremist groups that use theology
to justify their political violence include the aforementioned Christian
extremist group the Aryan Nations, the Order, the Ku Klux Klan, and
the Army of God (Sharpe 2000; Hoffman 1995; Sargent 1995). There
are messianic Jewish groups in Israel and far-right Hindu nationalist
groups in India (Narula 2003; Hoffman 1995). Rather than argue that
radical Islamic terrorism operates in a religious terrorism vacuum, my
aim is to engage critically with the discourse that insists the threat
posed by al-Qaeda is 'unprecedented.' To do this, we must look at
the historicity of radical Islamic thought.[4]

In 1984, David Rapoport published a study on three ancient terrorist groups, the Thugs, the Assassins, and the Zealots–Sicarii.[5] With
reference to his history of the Assassins, one can draw five direct
comparisons between this group and al-Qaeda, in terms of their
organizational purpose, propaganda, martyrdom, state-based support,
and organizational structure. Most importantly, and connecting these
five parallels, is the creation of mass support through their actions for
the jihad movement, ancient and contemporary respectively.

The political goal was and is is the establishment of an Islamic
state or *ummah*.[6] The Assassins' organizational 'purpose was to fulfill
or purify Islam,' in part through undermining the governments of
the Turkish Empire (Rapoport 1984: 664; see also Stern 2003: xxii).
They wanted to 'reconstitute Islam into a single community' and
'organiz[ed] an international conspiracy' to do this according to their
doctrine (Rapoport 1984: 666). This is eerily similar to the goal of
al-Qaeda. Al-Qaeda's purpose is to be '"the solid base" – *qaeda* – "for
the hoped-for society",' an Islamic caliphate (Wright 2006: 149). The
caliphate would encompass 'the southern [former] Soviet republics,
the Philippines, Kashmir, central Asia, Somalia, Eritrea, and Spain
– the entire span of the once-great Islamic empire' (Wright 2006: 149).
Al-Qaeda was formed with the intention of undermining the Soviet
empire's presence in Afghanistan, but it is now focused on removing
Muslim apostates from Arab countries and, at the very least, forcing
the US out of the Middle East (Darling 2007; Wright 2006: 199; Kepel
2004: 85–9; Henzel 2005: 76).

In common with the earlier group, al-Qaeda depends upon publicity to rouse mass support. The Assassins thrived on publicity

(Rapoport 1984: 666). In order to deliver a moral message, they assassinated non-believers in a way 'that evoked attention' and sympathy from the greater Islamic community (Rapoport 1984: 664–5). Al-Qaeda believes its 'duty [is] to awaken the Islamic nation' to the threat of Western secularization (Wright 2006: 196; see also Gunaratna 2005a). Many of al-Qaeda's declarations and letters cite the Prophet Muhammad to underscore their theological intentions in the hope of reaching out successfully to devout Muslims (see Ibrahim 2007). Ayman al-Zawahiri[7] believes operations must be 'exemplary' and 'decipherable by targeted populations' to raise the mass awareness that will lead to the fall of the apostates and the rise of the *ummah* (Kepel 2002: 98).

For both groups, martyrdom is an essential outcome of mass support and the means to generate more. The Assassins took great risks in the manner in which they assassinated their intended targets (Rapoport 1984: 666). The assassinations had to take place in public in order to maximize attention and '[o]ne who intends his act to be a public spectacle is unlikely to escape,' which led to martyrdom (Rapoport 1985: 665). Martyrdom, therefore, was 'central' to demonstrating the faith of the Assassins, who were rewarded with 'entry into paradise,' and with drawing people to the cause (Rapoport 1984: 665). Since the jihad in Afghanistan, martyrdom-seeking has been central to the al-Qaeda subculture. That martyrdom is acceptable is witnessed in the 9/11 attacks, which bin Laden praised: 'By their very deeds they produced a great sign, demonstrating that it was the belief in their hearts that urged them to such things' (in Ibrahim 2007: 267–8).

In recent years, state-sponsored terrorism has received substantial attention. Rapoport observes that the Assassins benefited from state sanctuary in the Middle Ages (1984: 666). The state fostered an efficient means for the organization 'to create a quasi-monastic form of life and to train leaders, missionaries, and [martyrs]' (Rapoport 1984: 666). This, again, strongly foreshadows elements of the organization of al-Qaeda, especially with regard to its relationship with the Taliban. The Taliban both welcomed al-Qaeda, knowing of the money bin Laden had poured into Sudan, and gave it a base for its operations (Wright 2006: 261). It also decreed a quasi-monastic lifestyle, including forcing men to grow their beards and women to wear the burqa (Wright 2006: 261–2).

Finally, like the organizational structure of the Assassins, that of al-Qaeda is designed to cultivate the crossing of territorial boundaries (Wright 2006; Gunaratna 2005b;Takeyh and Gvosdev 2002: 97; Rapoport 1984: 665). The Assassins created 'an extensive network of supporting cells in sympathetic [areas]' (Rapoport 1984: 666). Furthermore, they would place a young member in the household of a target, who would 'at the appropriate time ... plunge a dagger into his master's back' (Rapoport 1984: 666). Thus, the Assassins also foreshadowed 'sleeper cell' attacks. Al-Qaeda is ultimately borderless. It uses the Internet and television to 'politici[ze] and radicali[ze] Muslims both in the territorial communities of the Middle East and Asia and in the migrant and diaspora communities in the West' (Gunaratna 2005a: 33). These newly mobilized individuals may or may not have contact with the network of cells placed throughout the world (Gunaratna 2005a: 33; see also Hess 2003: 351; Takeyh and Gvosdev 2002: 101).

Rapoport's study draws important parallels between two groups separated by 800 years. Al-Qaeda has ties to the distant past (see Kepel 2004: 95). Yet it has taken full advantage of modern innovations. For example elements of the organization are dependent upon technology, such as its high-tech infrastructure and actions planned and implemented through the Internet. This technology is also used to recruit and communicate among members as the foundation for mass support.

The inevitability of 9/11: propaganda of the deed

When the term *terrorisme* was introduced during the French Revolution, it referred to state terrorism. Yet, the term, as described above, is used now to refer to many different actors from states, such as Nazi Germany, to sub-state actors, such as the FARQ in Colombia, to non-state actors,[8] such as al-Qaeda. These different actors, existing in different times and places, have used varying tactics and technology, reflecting both ideology and innovation. Al-Qaeda is certainly no different. Behind this evolution is the need to draw attention to the cause, which is best defined as 'propaganda of the deed' (see Miller 1995). Politically violent groups believe in the need to create an attack that will match or outperform the last in order to capture the public's attention (see Hess 2003: 354). This strategy is pursued with varying degrees of success. The events of 9/11 were followed by the Madrid and London bombings, which, though smaller, were in their own way no less horrific, and produced worldwide media coverage. Subsequently, of course, in August 2006 al-Qaeda planned to bring down airplanes over the Atlantic.

'Propaganda of the deed' is a phrase coined by anarchists in Europe during the latter part of the 1800s. The Russian anarchist Peter Kropotkin wrote that 'Terror ... [is] propaganda by the deed' (Rapoport 1984: 660). Johann Most, a German anarchist, subsequently developed the concept in his writings (Miller 1995: 43). 'Action is propaganda,' Most wrote, and encouraged other anarchists to place posters and flyers in the location in which violence had occurred, explaining their position (Miller 1995: 44). This signified an important realization: terrorism relies upon the use of violence to gain attention and thereby to propagate the ideology (see Cronin 2002/3: 35). All terrorist organizations want 'maximum publicity to be generated by [their] actions' – in this way both attention and fear are generated (Hoffman 2006: 173). The different eras of latter-day terrorism – modern, international and global – have all relied upon propaganda of the deed, which is itself reliant upon the means of contemporary technology to captivate an audience.

Modern terrorism rose with the random violence of the anarchists and the targeted assassinations of the Serbian Black Hand (Miller 1995). Johann Most advocated killing people because it would have a 'greater impact: "The more highly placed [is] the one shot or blown up, the more perfectly executed the attempt, the greater the propagandistic effect"' (Miller 1995: 44; see Cronin 2002/03: 35). The ultimate act of this era was the assassination of Archduke Franz Ferdinand of Austria in 1914 (Cronin 2002–03: 35). The anarchists utilized the technology of the time to produce their paper leaflets and posters: the steam-powered printing press (Hoffman 2006: 177). Nevertheless, there is a 'saturation point' in the public's attention to terrorist violence; it becomes complacent regarding certain tactics. Thus, terrorist groups constantly seek out new ways to garner attention from their audience, a factor that is key to understanding the evolution from the modern terrorism of the anarchists to international terrorism.

It was the 22 July 1968 Palestinian hijacking of an El Al flight from Jerusalem to Rome that heralded international terrorism (Hoffman 2006: 63). Terrorism 'became "significant" for the first time in the 1960s when it "increased in frequency" and took on "novel dimensions" as an international ... activity' (Rapoport 1984: 658). Hoffman argues that international terrorism was made possible by the rapidity of communication and accessibility of television time:

> the US satellite launch was the first, critical step in facilitating the American news media's worldwide predominance through its ability to reach a ... vast audience. Ironically, it was also this development that made the same audience exponentially more attractive to terrorists. (Hoffman 2006: 178)

It was this technology and the modern transportation system that 'allow[ed] [people] to coordinate activity quickly' (Rapoport 1984: 659). The technology of the time directly impacted the choices that terrorist groups made – a time of faster movement of information and people required politically violent actions that took advantage of this pace of life. The differences between groups in the two eras of modern and international terrorism can be attributed to the technological advances of their day that enabled them to spread their messages efficiently. Modern terrorism utilized print and the steam-powered printing press; international terrorism manipulated commercial airliners in an age of mass transport and mass communications. What they showed was secular ideology and the desire to rally mass support.

The shift from international to global terrorism is frequently defined by the emergence of al-Qaeda in the 1990s. 'With the events of 9/11, both the frequency and scale of the threats posed by terrorist groups dramatically changed' to encompass both 'mass destruction and mass disruption' (Gunaratna 2005b: 14). While global terrorism cannot be defined simply with reference to ideology, the fact that al-Qaeda has been granted such prominence in terrorism research has an important bearing on the concept. The violence of al-Qaeda, as a religious extremist group, is considered to be more dangerous than that of groups motivated by secular concerns (see Hess 2003: 347). According to Ranstorp (1996: 41), when a politically violent individual or group acts in the name of their deity, then their violence knows no bounds (Hoffman 2006: 83; Jurgensmeyer 2000: 11; Rapoport 1984: 659, 660).

However, these assumptions should be critically examined. It should not be enough to define an era based on the activities of one group, as Gunaratna and Hess do. Al-Qaeda is reified as *the* threat of *this* era. While the diffuse nature of the al-Qaeda network does allow for multiple attacks on multiple fronts, it has been argued that the US government and the media nevertheless pay a disproportionate amount of attention to the organization – magnifying the threat in order to command consent for the 'war on terror' (Berger 2007; Grier 2006). Further, researchers' claims that religious terrorism is the 'bloodiest' ignore the state terrorism of Stalin, Hitler, Pol Pot, Milosevic. To single out one typology (religious), and one group (al-Qaeda), creates a discourse that serves to subordinate al-Qaeda and place the US and its allies in a superior position.

Global terrorism is defined by its reliance upon current information technology: such 'terrorist network[s] ... utilize the existing global economic, transportation, and communications systems to organize and manage far-flung subsidiaries and to move funds, men, and material from one location to another' (Takeyh and Gvosdev 2002: 97). Never before have terrorist organizations used business tactics and information technology so efficiently (Hoffman 2006; Kepel 2004: 73; Cronin 2002/03: 45). In consequence they operate seamlessly across international borders – employing the technologies that define globalization work to the advantage of their groups.

While al-Qaeda has been described as 'an unlikely marriage between Wahhabism and the Silicon Valley' (Kepel 2004: 112),[9] this ignores its political message and the fact that it is not alone in using information technology to further its objectives (Hoffman 2006, 197). A variety of groups have their own websites to recruit membership and solicit funding; one can visit Aryan-nations.org to learn about the organization, how to print and distribute pamphlets, and how to send money – all with legal advice. The Liberation Tigers of Tamil Eelam use their website to provide information on attacks by the Sri Lankan government and to gain financial support from the Tamil diaspora (Tamil Eelam 2008).

Due to the disproportionate amount of attention al-Qaeda receives, its attacks have been a successful means of raising awareness and popular support for its cause. Like the Assassins before it and in common with the two previous eras of terrorism, al-Qaeda is well aware of the need for popular support. Popular support and the will of the people are also foundational to Locke's 'right of revolution.' In order to consider how Locke's ideas might contribute to an understanding of global terrorism, the concepts of popular sovereignty and the right of revolution must be understood in their original context.

John Locke's Right of Rebellion

John Locke was an English political theorist who extended Hobbes's conception of the social contract to include the need for popular sovereignty and the consent of the governed. Locke witnessed the Glorious Revolution, when parliamentarians overthrew King James II and replaced him with William of Orange – an important event in the shaping of British parliamentary democracy. Locke, whose work influenced the liberal construction of the state system, argued that in specific situations sub-state actors – the people – had the obligation to rise up against tyrannical governments, 'the right of revolution.' In order to understand this concept, one must first establish what Locke understood as a good state and then look at how states, by putting themselves at war with their people, become tyrannical, thereby breaking the monopoly on violence, allowing the people who make up a state to channel popular support to revolt and use violence against the tyrant.

The state as part of the Social Contract provides for and protects the 'common good' (Locke II §131).[10] The ideal form and purpose of the state is revealed 'in a constituted commonwealth, standing upon its own basis, and acting according to its own nature, that is, acting for the preservation of the community' (Locke II §149). The state is ultimately based on popular sovereignty: 'Men enter into society' for the 'preservation of their property' and therefore citizens 'chose and authorise a legislative' to make laws and set rules 'to limit the power ... of every part and member of society' (Locke II §222). In other words, citizens, in return for protection of rights and liberties, give 'all power ... with trust' to the state 'for the attaining an end, being limited by that end' (Locke II §149). That this power is limited is important to an understanding of Locke's conception of the monopoly on violence.

The monopoly on violence is an outcome of the Social Contract. Creswell claims that in 'Lockean theory, the right of force has been given up to the state' (2004: 636). The state should only use the entrusted power

> at home, only in the execution of such laws, or abroad to prevent or redress foreign injuries, and secure the community from inroads and invasion. And all this to be directed to no other end, but the peace, safety, and public good of the people. (Locke II §131)

The manipulation of the monopoly on violence is 'the use of 'Force without Right' (Locke II §19) (Ward 2006: 694). The 'exercise of power beyond right' results in 'tyranny' and this happens when the ruler 'makes not the law, but his will, the rule' (Locke II §199). The 'greatest crime' is for 'a ruler or subject' to use force 'to invade the rights of either prince or people, and lays the foundation for overturning the constitution and frame any just government' (Locke II §230). Both tyranny and the rule by force of invasion (usurpation) are important justifications for the right of revolution.

Traditionally, the right of revolution is a response to tyranny: 'nothing else justifies revolt but the excessive wrongdoings of the rulers' (Seliger 1963: 554). According to Strauss, '[t]yranny at its best is … rule without laws' and 'seems irreconcilable with the requirement of justice' (2000: 73). King James I of England declared that the 'Tyrant doeth thinke his Kingdome and people are onely ordained for satisfaction of his desires and unreasonable appetites' (as quoted in Zaller 1993: 589). A tyrant uses 'exorbitant … power … for destruction, and not the preservation of the properties of the people' (Locke II §229). Tyranny occurs more specifically when people are 'persuaded in their consciences, that their laws, and with them their estates, liberties, and lives are in danger' (Locke II §209) and that the 'legislative, or the prince, either of them, act contrary to their trust' as given by the people (Locke II §221).

'Usurpation' is another form of tyranny: 'As usurpation is the exercise of power, which another hath a right to; so tyranny is the exercise of power beyond right, which no body can have a right to' (Locke II §199). Locke, not believing in aggression, wrote that those who had usurped power through invasion and domination did not have a right to rule over the next generation. Domination through conquest and invasion was only applicable to those directly conquered; for

> the conqueror, even in a Just War, hath by his conquest, no right of dominion [over the future generations]: they are free from any subjection to him, and if their former government be dissolved, they are at liberty to being and erect another to themselves. (Locke II §185)

The second generation of a conquered country is allowed to re-establish its government – in modern terms, the conquered country has the right to be self-determining.

Thus, there are two reasons for revolt: tyranny and usurpation. In both cases, the state has reverted back to or instigated a state of war and thus forgoes its monopoly on violence. At this point, the people can withdraw their consent and seek a new government. The right of revolution is the prerogative of the people (Seliger 1963: 551).[11] Locke says:

> Whenever the legislators endeavour to take away, and destroy the property of the people, or to reduce them to slavery under arbitrary power, they put themselves into a state of war with the people, who are thereupon absolved from any farther obedience, and are left to the common refuge, which God had provided for all men, against force and violence. Whensoever therefore the legislative shall transgress this fundamental rules of society; and either by ambition, fear, folly, or corruption, endeavour to grasp themselves, or put into the hands of any other, an absolute power over the lives, liberties, and estates of the people; by this breach of trust they forfeit the power the people had put into their hands, for quite contrary ends, and it devolves to the people. (Locke II §222)

In short, when a government becomes tyrannical or when a ruler has usurped power, the people have the right to revolt against this illegitimate power. Because of its actions, the state has given up its sovereign power and has put itself and its people into a state of war. Wherever 'war is made upon ... sufferers, who having no appeal on earth to right them, they are left to the only remedy in such cases, an appeal to heaven' (Locke II §20). With the two differentiated reasons for revolt, there are two separate groups who can act against the government. Only the citizens of a tyrant can withdraw their consent and revolt. Under an invading force, Locke makes it clear that only future generations of the conquered people can revolt.

While these standards provide a way to evaluate terrorist organizations, Locke would find the use of violence that targets noncombatants as problematic. Indeed, he would be against it. The central premiss of the right of revolution rests in the protection of the people's safety and the rights of the community; to reiterate, 'all this [power] is to be directed to no other end, but the peace, safety, and public good of the people' (Locke II §131). The use of power should come when other options have been exhausted, because the rule of law is clearly important to Locke. A citizen should only use force against a transgressor ('the one using force, which threatened my life'), if s/he has no time to appeal to the law:

> The law could not restore life to my dead carcass: the loss was irreparable; which to prevent, the law of nature gave me a right to destroy him, who had put himself into a state of war with me, and threatened my destruction. (Locke II §207)

Terrorism forces the people into a state of war, because, by definition, it intends to cause fear in a larger population and it targets noncombatants. The people should not be the target of the right of revolution, because it is only the people who can 'remove, or change the legislative' and only the people have the right to 'des[troy] the authority' (Locke II § 227). There are some terrorist groups[12] that 'introduce a power which the people hath not authorized,' which introduces a 'state of war' (Locke II § 227). As terrorism is a method, the targeting of noncombatants, both civilians and non-uniformed soldiers, is viewed as reprehensible, which weighs heavily in the negative view of politically violent organizations. Thus, while Lockean theory can be viewed as being in accordance with some of al-Qaeda's objectives, the fact that al-Qaeda uses extreme and horrific violence against its Western targets, and indeed sometimes Muslim populations (see Pillar 2004: 106), ultimately brands it as a terrorist organization rather than as an agent expressing Locke's notion of legitimate revolutionary activity.

A Lockean Approach to Global Terrorism

Al-Qaeda's use of 'new' technologies does not render Locke's standards for legitimate revolutionary activity irrelevant to evaluating the terrorist group; nor do the new impacts of global terrorism render the

insights of Lockean theory unavailable to the victims and opponents
of al-Qaeda's violence. Instead al-Qaeda articulates its purpose as a
fight against tyranny and usurpation – the keys to Locke's 'right of
revolution.' The right of revolution, according to Locke, is dependent
upon popular support. Consequently, my purpose here is to examine
whether al-Qaeda has such support, for its conflict with the West is
clearly contingent upon it.

Bruce Hoffman reported to the US House of Representatives
that after 9/11 al-Qaeda can be seen to be composed of four different
pillars: al-Qaeda central, al-Qaeda affiliates and associates, al-Qaeda
locals, and the al-Qaeda network (Hoffman 2005: 4). Al-Qaeda central
is what is left of the pre-9/11 bureaucratic organization, which was
weakened by the war in Afghanistan; in 2005 it was said to have
only a few hundred members (Gunaratna 2005b: 11). The leadership
is located in Pakistan and has some control, 'if not actual command
capability,' over the planning and implementation of attacks, among
other functions (Hoffman 2005: 4). While the central pillar's claim to
the 'right of revolution' is weak at best (not least because it is a tactical
center rather than a popular movement), the three other pillars claim
mass support and are thus key to the conflict between al-Qaeda and
its adversaries.

Al-Qaeda's vision of tyrants and usurpers

The ideology created by al-Qaeda's leadership (al-Qaeda central)
can be related, in part, to Lockean theory. Osama bin Laden and his
peers, including al-Zawahiri, were brought together by their shared
desire to push the Soviet army out of Afghanistan in the 1980s. This
tightly knit and radicalized group of primarily 'Arab Afghans' sought a
new reason for jihad after the Soviet Union withdrew in 1988 (Wright
2006: 158–9). When the US used Saudi Arabian soil to launch the Gulf
War, bin Laden condemned the troops as 'foreign "crusaders"' on the
soil of Islam's most sacred places (Wright 2006: 182; see also Kepel
2002: 87). From here, bin Laden and al-Qaeda began to fight against
the US as a tyrannical and usurping power and against the Middle
Eastern rulers, who failed to support their cause.

The rhetoric of al-Qaeda describes the US and the West as having
characteristics similar to the Lockean tyrant. After the Coalition

invasion of Iraq in 2003, bin Laden released a statement to the American people, describing the tyrannical nature of the Bush administration:

> You elect the wicked from among you, the greatest liars and most depraved... Bush and his gang, with their heavy sticks and cruel hearts, are an evil to [all] mankind. (bin Laden 2007: 210)

Al-Zawahiri took up this argument, but extended it to include Middle Eastern apostates (those rulers who have betrayed Islam), 'This point in Islamic history is witness to a furious struggle between the powers of the infidels, tyrants, and haughtiness, on the one hand, and the Islamic *umma* and its *mujahid* vanguard on the other' (2007a: 66). Al-Zawahiri called for jihad against rulers who have seemingly abandoned the Muslim faith (al-Zawahiri 2007b: 128). This fight against the apostates is closer to Locke's standard for legitimate revolutionary activity as it aims at those persons who actually have a say in the government.

Al-Qaeda's descriptions of the US as a tyrant fit well with its portrayal as a usurping force. Not only was the US characterized as an oil thief or swindler; it was criticized as a military occupier, first of Saudi Arabia then Afghanistan and Iraq (see Darling 2005; Lav 2007: 2). Al-Qaeda's 'Declaration of War against Americans' (1998) creates several arguments against the perceived US usurpation of Arab and Muslim rights:

> For over seven years American has been occupying the lands of Islam in its holiest places, the Arabian Peninsula – plundering its riches, dictating to its rulers, humiliating its people, terrorizing its neighbors, and turning its bases in the Peninsula into a spearhead with which it fights the neighboring Muslim peoples. (bin Laden 2007: 12)

The fight against aggression and invasion continues to have importance in regards to the war in Iraq. In a 2005 letter to Abu Musab al-Zarqawi,[13] al-Zawahiri 'stresses that Zarqawi [in Iraq] has the right to defend ... against either aggression or the threat of aggression' (Darling 2005: 5).

Yet bin Laden's response to this perceived tyranny contradicts Lockean notions of the people's sovereignty and natural rights. The al-Qaeda leadership sees itself as a vanguard which must rouse the masses; it believes the best way to do this is violent action against other peoples – which in turn means violation of the sovereignty and security of those people. Furthermore, Lockean theory, based in natural rights, is diametrically opposed to sharia law:

> Muslims ... should spread *sharia* law to the world – that and nothing else. Not laws under the 'umbrella of justice, morality, and rights' as understood by the masses. (attributed to bin Laden, in Ibrahim 2007: 33)

There is also the issue of popular support. Locke is clear that only certain populations have the 'jurisdiction' to revolt: the people to whom the government belongs and the people who have been conquered. The motivation of the al-Qaeda movement, and consequently the key to the fight against the organization, is the appeal to popular support.

Post-9/11 al-Qaeda and the struggle for popular support

Al-Zawahiri is clear that al-Qaeda needs popular support to keep up its momentum. This struggle is not one for security alone, but to win the goodwill of the people. Yet Al-Zawahiri's vision includes the politicizing of the appropriate populations, led by a vanguard elite, against the apostates and Western invaders (Kepel 2002: 96).

Furthermore, the idea of Muslim unity is very important. Instead of being limited by Western ideas of delineated states and citizens, 'national ... origin should not become a source for division. Islamic unity dictates that Muslims should not be divided according to race, sects or national of origin' (Islamic Center of Beverly Hills 2007). Along with this, radical Islam's interpretation of the Prophet's dying words, 'Let there be no two religions in Arabia' (Wright 2006: 180), as the struggle of all Muslims to rid the Middle East of non-Muslims, implies that the al-Qaeda leadership sees the fight against the apostatic tyrants and Western usurpation as inclusive of all who 'truly' believe in Allah and not limited by state citizenship. Thus, mass support must be raised within the Middle East to fight against the governments there, but also to fight against the threat of Western domination globally.[14]

Al-Zawahiri recognizes that the only way al-Qaeda will create their desired caliphate and get rid of the Arab apostate rulers is to win popular support, which 'will be decisive in the difference between victory and defeat' (Darling 2005: 3). Without mass popularity, 'al Qaeda will be crushed in the shadows'; therefore, in keeping with propaganda of the deed, 'al Qaeda planning must seek to enlist the general public in their battle, bring the mujahideen to them, and not to conduct their struggle far away from the public eyes' (Darling 2005: 3). As the jihad movement is gaining members, al-Zawahiri sees 'a new phenomenon ...: young combatants who abandon their families, countries, property to seek a place in which to carry out jihad' (in Kepel 2002: 95–6). It is imperative that the elites take the message of al-Qaeda's vision for Islam to the masses to grow the movements' numbers (Kepel 2002: 97).

Al-Zawahiri is very aware of al-Qaeda's image: he 'argues that they are fighting a media and propaganda war for the hearts and minds of the Muslim world and must avoid giving their enemy any advantage in this struggle' (Darling 2005: 7). In the aforementioned 2005 letter from al-Zawahiri to Zarqawi, al-Zawahiri chastens Zarqawi for beheading hostages: 'the Muslim general population will never accept the scenes of him personally murdering hostages' (Darling 2005: 7). Al-Zawahiri suggested that should Zarqawi need to kill his captives, he 'should use a bullet rather than damaging the broader al-Qaeda movements with his brutality' (Darling 2005: 7).

The last three pillars of post-Afghanistan al-Qaeda, according to Hoffman's conception, are the embodiment of popular support. The affiliates and associates are 'established insurgent and terrorist groups who ... have received training, arms, money, and other assistance from al Qaeda' (Hoffman 2005: 5). The Chechens, Kashmiris, and Bosnians are forces included in this designation (Hoffman 2005: 5). The al-Qaeda locals are former jihadis or mujahideen with fighting experience from the Balkans, Chechnya, or even Iraq, who have moved on to other conflicts (Hoffman 2005: 6). The final category, the al-Qaeda network, comprises the truly home-grown Muslim extremists in both the global South and the global North. They may have been raised Muslim or subsequently converted and 'have no direct connection with al-Qaeda ... but nonetheless are prepared to carry out attacks' (Hoffman 2005: 6–7). This newly 'galvanized ... broad spectrum of Islamist groups' work within the ideology of al-Qaeda, but care very little if they are so designated (Gunaratna 2005a: 32).

Support for al-Qaeda has grown in response to the war in Iraq, the images of torture at Abu Ghraib, and US backing for Israel's policies in the Palestinian Territories (Henzel 2005: 79; Kepel 2004: 7; Pillar 2004: 102). This growth is exponential and is connected to the emergence of new groups in Iraq, Chechnya, and Indonesia, where it is becoming 'difficult to ... separate some of the regional conflicts, which have local grievances and indigenous roots, from the movement of global *jihad*' (Gunaratna 2005b: 12, 15). For example, the popularity of martyrdom in Iraq 'demonstrat[es] the growing localization' of al-Qaeda (Kepel 2004: 40).

It is at this juncture that Lockean theory helps those interested in decreasing the threat of terrorism in the twenty-first century. Al-Qaeda, and thus the fight against it, is dependent upon popular support. Yet there are significant factors that stand in the way of non-radical Muslims trusting the US and its allies (Pillar 2004: 108). Scholars argue that the 'war on terror' and US foreign policy have substantially hindered the achievement of the US goal of combatting global terrorism. For example, Rohan Gunaratna believes that 'the US-led invasion of Iraq has not reduced the threat of terrorism but has increased it significantly' (2005a: 33). Furthermore, the past, and arguably current, dependence upon the 'Rumsfeld model of fighting ... has its limitations' because, while there have been 'tactical successes,' 'the failure to target terrorist ideology and motivations is ensuring the continuity of the threat' (Gunaratna 2005a: 34).

Beyond tactics and strategy, some non-radical Muslims doubt the reasoning behind the US's extension of the 'war on terror' to Iraq. Because many believe it is a war over oil, not terrorism, 'every other time [the US] talks about fighting terrorism' many Muslims distrust US strategy and believe there are 'ulterior motives' (Pillar 2004: 108). Pillar believes that this distrust will 'strengthen the roots of ... Islamist terrorism' (2004: 108). Furthermore, the 'longer this war ... lasts, the greater the long-term strategic risk of radicalizing Muslim sentiment against the United States' (Atran 2004: 69). This is clear from a Program on International Policy Attitudes survey: 70 percent of Iraqis wanted the US-led forces out of Iraq by 2007 and 60 percent supported attacks on the forces. Still, popular rejection of the United States alone does not indicate 'any significant support for al Qaeda' (Program on International Policy Attitudes 2006: 2).

What is not well known is that many Muslims, Arabs and more specifically Palestinians view 'Western' (liberal) governmental style and elements of 'Western' culture in a favorable light. This understanding is key to finding support against al-Qaeda among Muslim populations. Atran argues that there is a 'war of ideas' perpetuated by the Bush administration that articulates the view 'that terrorists and their supporters "hate our freedoms"' (2004: 73). However, Atran highlights surveys showing 'that most Muslims who support suicide terrorism and trust bin Laden favor elected government, personal liberty, educational opportunity, and economic choice' (2004: 73). The same attitude is found among Palestinians (Atran 2004: 74). Even more important, this support for 'Western' ideals is strongly represented among young adults, the population that is most targeted by terrorist recruiters (Atran 2004: 73). Still, these same people resent 'US foreign policies, particularly regarding the Middle East' (Atran 2004: 74).

These sentiments are also apparent among the growing number of Muslims in Europe, whose population 'has more than doubled in the past three decades' (Savage 2004: 26). Many are willing to embrace and assimilate to the culture there, but also want to retain their unique cultural affiliations and traditions (Savage 2004: 31). Herein lies the tension. A cultural issue as seemingly small as Germany and France banning headscarves, linked to the ghettoization[15] and high unemployment among Muslim communities[16] in many European states, suggests that their level of unhappiness is set to increase (Savage 2004: 25). Thirteen European countries do not even recognize Islam as a religion for the purposes of freedom from discrimination based on religion, and often Muslims 'are an unrecognized minority' and are left out of subsequent protections (Savage 2004: 26). Many younger Muslims, who may even be third-generation European citizens, 'generally … do not feel part of the larger society nor that they have a stake in it. Conversely … they often are not viewed as fellow citizens by the general public but are still identified as foreigners and immigrants instead' (Savage 2004: 30). It would appear that certain 'Western' principles, of liberty and property, are being denied to Muslims in the West, against the prescriptions of Locke's notion of popular sovereignty. This is important as more Muslims in the West are being targeted by al-Qaeda recruiting, for the more dissatisfied this targeted population is, the more likely they are to sign up to the cause and fight as citizens of Western states against perceived tyrannies.

If Western states are looking to combat terrorism, they should begin by focusing on overcoming this resentment and alienation.

Though the traditional understanding of Lockean citizenship and popular support is limited to the citizenries of delineated states, Islamic belief, mainstream and radical, states that all Muslims are united across or in spite of borders. Thus, all (radical) Muslims, according to al-Qaeda central, have the right to fight against perceived tyrannies and usurpations of power. Within a Lockean understanding of citizenship, al-Qaeda still has 'jurisdiction' for raising popular support; its fight is against the Middle Eastern apostates, thus it continues to seek and find support in these countries. Its fight is also against *perceived* US and Western usurpation in the Middle East and elsewhere – thus all populations, but primarily the Iraqis, Afghanis and Palestinians (against US-supported Israel), have the right to revolt. And Muslim resentment against the West is growing in the Middle East and among Muslim populations *in the West*; thus, if the US and its allies wish to avoid a protracted war, recognizing and addressing this resentment is vital.

Conclusion

The rhetoric used since the 9/11 attacks has conveyed the premiss that the US and its allies faced a new era in security with a new enemy. Furthermore, this fight encompassed the preservation of Western ideals of liberty and freedom. This rhetoric has oversimplified the threat and the motivation for the violence. Certainly, the world finds itself facing a new era in terrorism. However, the enemy is not in fact that new; nor is the 'newness' all that unexpected. In many ways, the fight does not come down to facing an unprecedented security challenge posed by an enemy deploying unprecedented means. Instead, the rhetoric serves to extend the war to another front – one that allows the alienation to continue and the denial of personal liberty to flourish.

Al-Qaeda as the poster child for global terrorism is not that new and is not without precedence. The comparison of al-Qaeda with the Assassins is not intended to convey the notion that radical Islamic terrorism is the only kind, but rather that it is not unique, nor as new as some would have the public believe. Additionally, looking at the previous eras of terrorism, modern and international, it is clear that al-Qaeda is following in the footsteps of other terrorist groups in its reliance upon the latest technology. The element that is 'new' – al-Qaeda's use of mass destruction, which was planned and ordered via the Internet, using recruits probably found via the Internet – could only have emerged in this period. For all parties in the conflict have access to information technology and the networking facility it provides. Therefore, this aspect of al-Qaeda's infrastructure should not be perceived as anomalous. Further, al-Qaeda is not alone in the use of information technology; it just receives the most attention. This stems from the Americentric discourse on terrorism, which holds 9/11 up as a unique event in world history perpetrated by the most 'uncivilized' persons (who are nevertheless sophisticated enough to use the same technology as the 'civilized' West against it), while ignoring the violence that people in Kashmir, Chechnya, the Palestinian Territories, Israel, Sri Lanka, and so on, experience every day. This allows for an ignorance of conflicts and other politically violent groups where information technology is important.

Al-Qaeda's destructive tendencies are also not assessed relative to other violence. Its highly destructive attacks may be unprecedented for terrorism, but their context is an era of conflict and war where more civilians are being killed during war deliberately (see Kaldor 2006). And this violence does not compare in scale to state violence. Further, it is often forgotten that radical Islamic terrorism accounts for no more than 50 percent of terrorist activity per year (MIPT 2006).

Al-Qaeda's theology insists that the use of mass destruction is a way of clearing the way for the caliphate and for raising awareness of its purpose, and thus of radicalizing the masses. Yet this violence is also alienating those it is trying to appeal to – witness al-Zarqawi's beheadings of Westerners in Iraq or the Riyadh bombing in November 2003 which killed many Muslims (see Pillar 2004). This may lead to a loss of the popular support that al-Qaeda recognizes it is dependent upon in its drive to create the caliphate.

Lockean theory is inherently interested in the will of the people. In the small element examined in this chapter, the right of revolution, its legitimacy is determined by the consent of the governed. The right of revolution is allowed when a government becomes too tyrannical or when an invading force tries to extend its power beyond its right. The only people allowed to participate in a legitimate revolution are those governed by a tyrant or usurping force.

Al-Qaeda's conception of Middle East apostates and of the US and the West as tyrants and/or usurpers ironically falls into an ill-fitting alignment with Lockean theory.[17] Whereas, according to Locke, only Egyptians have to right to revolt against the Egyptian government or Saudis against the Saudi monarchy, al-Qaeda's manipulation of the notion of Muslim unity argues that all Muslims everywhere have the imperative to fight against these tyrannical and/or usurping powers. And this radicalization of Islamic thought is gaining ground, both in the tension-filled Middle East and in the West. Al-Qaeda may indeed be winning in its bid for popular support.

The solution, it seems, lies in Locke. 'Winning hearts and minds' is a phrase much bandied about in the 'war on terror,' often in a way that conveys a manipulative intent on the part of the US to sway Muslim minds. Locke's most elementary belief is in liberty and the rights of individuals. Thus the most apparently radical suggestion, though in reality the least so, might be to suggest that the US practice the protection of the liberty and rights of Muslims in Iraq and at home, and encourage its allies (both friendly and alienated) to do the same. The Bush administration claims that the war in Iraq was necessary to both maintaining US security and creating a magnet in Iraq to draw al-Qaeda there. What this does is value US lives and personal liberty over those of Iraqis. The longer the war in Iraq continues, the longer the 'war on terror' will be seen as an excuse by Muslims for US violence, and the longer the Muslim populations in the West continue to live in an alienated manner, the greater will be the numbers attracted to al-Qaeda's version of Islam. By providing for the rights of the people and respecting their wishes – popular sovereignty – we will perhaps see a marginalization of radical Islam and its associated terrorism.

3

Preventive Warfare

Yannis A. Stivachtis

Throughout the twentieth century, warfare operated on the assumption that an anticipatory strike would usually be immoral. To be in the right morally, states were only to fight wars when they had been attacked. This idea that states should only strike *second* has been credited with the Cold War ending peacefully, and blamed for the strategy of appeasement Western Europe took towards Germany in the late 1930s, as well as the United States' late entry into World War I and World War II. Israel, an exception, launched a pre-emptive strike that technically started the Six Day War. Had Israel delayed its response until it was actually attacked, self-defense as a response to an armed attack would likely have been inadequate, the argument goes. Although no one doubted that an attack on Israel by its opponents was imminent, that certainty did not prevent a cloud of moral ambiguity complicating the international reaction to Israel's action. If preemptive strikes (in response to the certainty of imminent attack) were both rare and frowned upon in the twentieth century, preventive strikes (in response to a more nebulous threat) were almost universally condemned. When in 1981 Israel attacked a site in Iraq largely thought to have housed the country's nuclear weapons development program, a United Nations resolution condemning the action passed with an overwhelming majority (Bradford 2004: 1410). The Security Council acted swiftly in 'unanimously condemning the military attack by Israel in clear violation of the Charter of the United Nations and the norms of international conduct' in Resolution 487.

Previous United States foreign policy was much in agreement with the idea that wars should be fought for defense of self and allies, but not for pre-emption. George Washington warned Americans that they should not become militarily entangled in foreign affairs. Woodrow Wilson refused on several occasions to become involved in World War I, despite the Allies' need for military assistance, on the grounds that the United States had not been attacked. An aversion to first strikes came in handy for both sides of the Cuban Missile Crisis. In the first Gulf War, President George H.W. Bush deliberately stopped the United States military at the Kuwaiti border with Iraq, arguing in part that a preventive strike against the Saddam Hussein government was not morally or politically defensible.

Modern Just War theory had little to say about these questions before the terrorist attacks of September 11, 2001 and the new security problems of the 'war on terror.' Michael Walzer, in *Just and Unjust Wars*, argued that preventive war is unjust because the threat cannot possibly rise to the level of determinacy required for just cause with a remote attack scenario – in other words, that it presupposes a standard of danger which does not exist (1977: 76). Walzer contends that it is pre-emption, not prevention, which could be just, and even then pre-emption should only be acceptable if the anticipated injury is clear and real (1977: 80). For example, Walzer defends the Israeli first strike in the Six Day War, arguing that Israelis were certain that they were about to be attacked, and acted to counteract that attack only hours before it was going to happen (1977: 85). He does not defend, on the other hand, the Japanese attack on Pearl Harbor, despite the consensus opinion that the United States was likely to enter the war on the side of the Allies at some point. The threat to Japan was not clearly identifiable and immediate.

International law also reflects the stringent standards applied to pre-emptive attacks. The standard for a justifiable pre-emptive attack is reflected in the correspondence between US Secretary of State Webster and his British counterpart Privy Counsellor Alexander Baring, Lord Ashburton, regarding the *Caroline* incident in the 1840s. Canadians loyal to Britain destroyed the steamship *Caroline*, which they believed was being used to supply the Canadian rebels with arms and volunteers, by setting it on fire and cutting it adrift over Niagara Falls. Following the destruction of the *Caroline*, Daniel Webster and Lord Ashburton addressed the issue of whether the destruction of the ship fell within the scope of legitimate anticipatory self-defense. While both men agreed that such a right existed, Webster criticized this particular action as outside its scope, arguing that this right only existed in light of a danger that was 'instant, overwhelming, leaving no choice of means, and no moment for deliberation.'[1] This is still the relevant legal standard for assessing the legality of anticipatory attacks and underscores the rigid standard to which pre-emptive attacks are held. The comparison between the treatment of self-defense and anticipatory self-defense is illustrative of the skepticism with which the international community assesses claims of anticipatory self-defense, a skepticism which has been essential to limiting the proliferation of pre-emptive self-defense claims by states. Preventive attacks, which respond to a speculative rather than an imminent harm, have no chance of satisfying this stringent test as they respond to a danger that cannot be instant and leaves adequate time for deliberation.

The post-9/11 era seems to have ushered in a new debate about the validity of preventive warfare. The Bush administration in the United States explicitly declared a National Security Strategy (NSS) that endorsed not only pre-emptive but also preventive warfare (Cook 2004; Gaddis 2002). Based on his argument that we have entered a 'new world' with the 'war on terror,' Bush argued that new times call for new measures, and that preventive warfare was the only way to protect the United States from the unprecedented threats posed by terrorism. In the NSS, Bush explains:

> We will cooperate with other nations to deny, contain, and curtail our enemies' efforts to acquire dangerous technologies. And, as a matter of common sense and self-defense, America will act against such emerging threats before they are fully formed. We cannot defend America and our friends by hoping for the best. So we must be prepared to defeat our enemies' plans, using the best intelligence and proceeding with deliberation. History will judge harshly those who saw coming this danger but failed to act. In the new world we have entered, the only path to peace and security is the path of action. (Bush 2002b)

The NSS was 'the single most authoritative statement of any administration's view of the world from the perspective of national security' (Cook 2004: 797). Several scholars have identified this NSS as a major shift in United States security policy, the likes of which has not been seen since 'a major shift of this kind occurred between the Reformation and the Peace of Westphalia, which created the current international system of sovereign independent states' (Cook 2004: 799). John Lewis Gaddis (2002: 51) contends that this NSS is markedly different from others, and, by justifying both pre-emption and hegemony, introduced a new era of both American foreign policy and international security. In response to the nature of these threats, the Bush administration treated pre-emption and prevention as the rule rather than the exception.

This chapter argues that the 'new world' rhetoric employed by the Bush administration was a deliberate tool to escape past debates about the ethical viability of preventive warfare. The NSS justification for preventive warfare is markedly different than the justifications in traditional Just War theory, international law, and political philosophy. The Bush NSS statement blurs the distinction between the category of pre-emptive war, which is justifiable within a carefully limited range of circumstances, and the category of preventive war, which has never been treated as justified by traditional approaches to anticipatory self-defense. Further, there is an argument to be had that the United States' current understanding of what counts as a just preventive war is much more expansive than those that the Bush administration could ignore by differentiating our 'new world' from their 'old world.' This chapter first introduces the Just War theory debate about preventive war, and then compares that debate to the legal and ethical justifications discussed in the prosecution of preventive war in American foreign policy. It then argues that comparing the Bush NSS position on preventive war to those of 'old' theorists, including Sun Tzu, Augustine, and Vattel, can give us substantial insight into the ethical guidelines states *should* reference when considering or planning a preventive war. These three theorists are chosen because each holds a permissive position on the question of preventive war. Still, this chapter contends that each theorist expresses important concerns that the Bush NSS overlooked. It argues that 'old' theory could help contextualize and explain the 'new world' in which Bush could advocate preventive war.

The Just War Debate on Preventive War

Michael Walzer, mentioned briefly above, is not the only Just War theorist who has paid attention to the question of preventive war. Those in Just War theory who defend preventive war classify it as fundamentally defensive in nature. They take the argument that aggression constitutes just cause, and ask if that aggression must be *actual* or *expected*. In other words, if a states knows that it will be attacked, does it have to lose the strategic advantage of striking first to be just? In this view, preventive war can be defensive – defending from future attacks (Nichols 2003). This view sees pre-emption as 'anticipatory self-defense' (Rivkin et al. 2005). Walzer argues that states who know about an impending attack plan do not have to take that risk, so pre-emptive war can be just. As per preventive war, however, he contends that any scenario of threat that is more remote than a few hours or a few days is too uncertain to justify striking first.

Some Just War theorists argue that, even if there is an imminent attack, states that are about to be attacked cannot strike first. Richard Falk argues that preventive war is at odds with Just War thinking and a denial of the norm of state sovereignty (2003: 125). Richard Betts argues that preventive war is never a good idea, regardless of the situation, because it makes conflict more likely and stops the potential belligerent from reversing its own cycle of violence (2003: 2). Neta Crawford argues that pre-emptive and preventive war have a tense relationship with the Just War principle of last resort, and that the appropriate evidentiary standards for measuring the threat would be almost impossible to determine (2003). Jeanne Woods and James Donovan link pre-emption to the dehumanization of the enemy through prisoner abuse and war crimes, arguing that the 'new' 'capacity pre-emption' leads members of militaries to understand a broader mandate of disabling not only the bodies but also the spirits of the enemy (2005: 487). They contend that there is a strong link between capacity pre-emption and the ideology of conquest (2005: 490).

Even given these critiques and the infrequent use of pre-emptive or preventive war in the twentieth century, a number of scholars contend that neither Just War theory nor international law entirely closed off the possibility for states. As Cook explains, 'in fits and starts, for over fifty years, states, non-governmental organizations, and ordinary

people have recognized the moral and political deficiencies of an international system focused exclusively on states and their sovereignty'
(2004: 805–6). Instead, 'time and time again, the international community has witnessed situations that cried out for intervention into
states' and witnessed 'the absence of real international commitment
to act with some consistency on these principles' (Cook 2004: 806).
In other words, in some situations where pre-emptive, preventive,
or even interventionist war would have been justified, states chose
to honor the sovereignty norm over the moral permission to take
the first strike.

While the sovereignty norm is not absolute in either Just War
theory or international law, the standard for starting a war based
on the threat of attack has always been high. Cook describes the
'test' that has been used by most Just War theorists to measure the
prudence of striking first:

(1) The adversary possesses, or is imminently about to come to possess, a
    capability to do great harm (the 'means' test);
(2) The adversary is known (by declaration, overt action, or reliable
    intelligence) to have the intent to use that means against one; and
(3) The attack is so imminent and the consequences foreseen to be so
    devastating that one cannot afford to wait to absorb the first blow.
    (Cook 2004: 809–10)

These criteria, a number of Just War theorists argue, are very restrictive concerning what counts as a just preventive war. They do not
privilege a certain group, nationality, or power status. They also
do not provide for what Woods and Donovan describe as capacity
pre-emption without a clear attack scenario. They are framed by
Just War theorists as rooted in the just war tradition's historical
understandings of the meaning of self-defense and the right to it
held by sovereign states.

The George W. Bush Discourse on Preventive War

Rather than referring to just war standards on preventive war, the
Bush administration discourse on preventive war distinguishes itself
from traditional just war thinking. Citing the NSS, Gaddis (2002)
points out that the United States discourse on pre-emptive warfare is
technically rooted in self-defense claims. For example, Bush explains

that 'nations need not suffer an attack before they can lawfully take action to defend themselves against an imminent danger of attack' (2002c). Still, to Gaddis, the link between Bush's idea of prevention and American superiority/hegemony is clear (2002: 52). According to Bush, 'we will not hesitate to act alone, if necessary, to exercise our right of self-defense by acting pre-emptively against such terrorists, to prevent them from doing harm against our people and out country' (2002). Some who have supported the Bush understanding of pre-emptive war trace it back to a Kantian categorical imperative for self-defense (e.g. Bradford 2004). Yet most argue that the Bush references to self-defense are really about a general sense of freedom from fear rather than a strict sense of defense from a material threat. As such, it is widely understood that the Bush NSS position on preventive war largely relies on the newness of the world of global terrorism to justify new standards for preventive war.

Among these new standards seem to be the uniqueness of American position and identity in the international system. The idea that the United States will not hesitate to act alone is linked clearly to America's desire to create 'a balance of power that favors human freedom' and to make sure that 'our forces will be strong enough to dissuade potential adversaries from pursuing a military build-up in hopes of surpassing, or equaling, the power of the United States' (Bush 2002). In fact, in his speech at West Point Military Academy, Bush explained that 'America has, and intends to keep, military strengths beyond challenge' (2002b). Gaddis notes that the Bush NSS was the first to advocate American hegemony as strategic doctrine (2002: 52).

The Bush rhetoric is not only about American military superiority but also about American moral ascendency. The 'axis of evil' or 'conflict between good and evil' language employed by Bush (2002b, 2002c) demonstrates an understanding that American preventive war is uniquely justified not only by the United States' military abilities but also by the United States' moral high ground. American hegemony is seen as desirable not only because the United States holds the preponderance of power, but because it is the 'good guys' in the fight against the 'bad guys.' As Gaddis reports:

> U.S. hegemony is also acceptable because it's linked with certain values that all states and cultures – if not all terrorists and tyrants – share. As the NSS puts it: 'No people on earth yearn to be oppressed, aspire to

servitude, or eagerly await the midnight knock of secret police.' It's this
association of power with principles, Bush argues, that will cause other
great powers to go along with whatever the United States has to do to pre-
empt terrorists and tyrants, even if it does so alone. (Gaddis 2002: 52)

This moral ascendancy is threatened, according to the Bush Doctrine,
by a broader range of threats than at any time in the past. The Bush
NSS argued that

> Enemies in the past needed great armies and great industrial capabilities
> to endanger the American people and our nation. The attacks of Septem-
> ber the 11th required a few hundred thousand dollars in the hands of a few
> dozen evil and deluded men. All of the chaos and suffering they caused
> came at much less than the cost of a single tank. (Bush 2002b)

This combination of a unique good – preserving American military
and moral superiority – coupled with a unique threat – evil terrorist
groups capable of pursuing their purposes even without considerable
material capabilities – justifies, in the argument of the Bush Doctrine,
the abandonment of the traditional treatment of preventive war.

Principles (and not of warfare) certainly do feature prominently
in the Bush NSS justification of preventive war. Woods and Donovan
explore the Bush administration's characterizations of the United
States and its 'enemies' in the NSS. They find that the United States
is associated with good, hope, innocence, liberty, freedom, greatness,
civilization, right, justice, and nobility (Woods and Donovan 2005:
499). Its enemies are associated with moral questionability (evil,
deluded, radical, guilty, mad, brutal, cruel, and lawless) as well as
power deficit (weak, small) (Woods and Donovan 2005: 499).

It is at least in part the rhetoric of the 'newness' of the problem of
the need for preventive warfare that allows the United States to use
a discourse of American power and moral supremacy to justify pre-
emptive and preventive action rather than seriously evaluate preventive opportunities within the framework of age-old debates about the
moral and legal legitimacy of preventive warfare. Hoping to rescue
preventive warfare from this discourse of new security, the remainder
of this chapter evaluates the Bush NSS position on pre-emption and
prevention by the standards proposed by Sun Tzu, Augustine, and
Vattel. Unlike many Just War theorists, all three argued that preventive war in some form is not only morally permissible but encouraged

in certain situations. Still, as these analyses will show, each of these theorists proposed standards for preventive warfare with which the 'new world' preventive wars proposed by the Bush government would stand in tension.

A Crew of Preventive War Standards:
Sun Tzu, Augustine, and Vattel

As mentioned above, the Just War tradition has a steady if uneasy relationship with preventive warfare, where there is very little consensus on if, or when, preventive war is acceptable. If there is a consensus, it is around the three standards listed above by Cook: means, intent, and imminence combined with dire consequences. The Bush NSS perspective on prevention does not attempt to justify the imminence of the attacks it claims to prevent; it is, therefore, in conflict with the third traditionally understood criterion for preventive war as defensive. In this section, then, we look at three theorists who had a more permissive approach to preventive warfare than that which Cook (2004) has identified as the Just War orthodoxy. Those theorists – Sun Tzu, Augustine, and Vattel – have little in common in terms of the time, place, and context of their work. Each, however, proposes a detailed framework for understanding preventive warfare. Sun Tzu advocates eliminating threats before they are fully developed by first attack in almost all situations where a conflict is warranted. Still, his approach, which I will call an ethical one, requires that the party starting the preventive war be benevolent, just, and righteous. Augustine, like Sun Tzu, argues that, when possible, a criminal should be attacked 'before the crime has even been committed,' and a belligerent has a right to attack an enemy 'lying in ambush.' Yet, in Augustine's approach, which I will call a transcendental one, it is not just to attack preventively to seek freedom from fear or vulnerability. Finally, Vattel characterizes preventive warfare as always in the strategic interests of states, and looks to explore the moral implications of this strategically beneficial approach to making war. Vattel's approach, which I will call calculative, argues that while preventive war is *always* strategically beneficial, it is only morally appropriate when the level of risk the potential victim is exposed to is reasonably certain and unacceptably high.

Sun Tzu: an ethical approach to striking first

Many readings of the work of Sun Tzu have seen preventive war as a key feature of his strategic planning. Mao's reading of Sun Tzu is that 'Attack may be changed into defense and defense into attack' (1938: 102–103). In other words, a party reasonably certain that it will be defending the attack of another party may strike first. As Samuel Griffith explains in his introduction to the *Art of War*, to Sun Tzu 'deception and surprise are two key principles' (1963: 53). In Sun Tzu's own text,

17. All warfare is based on deception
18. Therefore, when capable, feign incapacity; when active, inactivity
19. When near, make it appear that you are far away
20. Offer the enemy a bait to lure him; feign disorder and strike him. (Sun Tzu 1963: 66)

This passage advocates that a belligerent 'feign disorder' and then strike the enemy, so it is clear that first strikes are not only ethically acceptable to but strategically preferred by Sun Tzu. Yet the link between his advocacy of deception and his position on preventive war is not clear until later in the text. In Chapter 3, on offensive strategy, Tzu explains:

Tu Mu: ... The Grand Duke said: 'He who excels at resolving difficulties does so before they arise. He who excels in conquering his enemies triumphs before threats materialize.

Li Ch'uan: Attack plans at their inception. (Sun Tzu 1963: 77)

Sun Tzu justifies attacking first when a potential belligerent knows it will be attacked, because 'generally, he who occupies the field of battle first and awaits his enemy is at ease; he who comes later to the scene and rushes into the fight is weary' (1963: 96). Sun Tzu addressed questions of *jus in bello* in addition to these *jus ad bellum* considerations. Not only should a belligerent be first to the battlefield, he should attack with speed. He explains that 'speed is the essence of war. Take advantage of the enemy's unpreparedness; travel by unexpected routes and strike him where he has taken no precautions' (1963: 134).

This analysis makes it look like Sun Tzu advocates preventive or pre-emptive war at every opportunity. But moving back from his strategic text to his text about making decisions to go to war gives a different impression. Though Sun Tzu advocates preventive war *when war should be made*, he has a number of requirements for the decision to go to war. Tzu explains that 'war is a matter of vital importance to the state; the province of life or death; the road to survival or ruin' (1963: 63). As such, 'war is a grave matter; one is apprehensive lest men embark upon it without due reflection' (Sun Tzu 1963: 63). As Sun Tzu explains, 'with many calculations, one can win; with few calculations, one cannot' (1963: 68). Mark McNeilly, applying Sun Tzu's principles to modern warfare, argues that 'the United States definitely employed many of Sun Tzu's principles in achieving success in that theater [Afghanistan],' but points to calculative failures to critique the part of the 'war on terror' that involved Iraq (2001: 209, 219).

In fact, it is not only calculation that Sun Tzu requires. The reflection that he imagines being necessary to make war is detailed in the next paragraph of his text. He explains that a potential belligerent must 'appraise it in terms of five fundamental factors,' which include moral influence, weather, terrain, command, and doctrine (Sun Tzu 1963: 63). While weather and terrain are factors that influence the likelihood of strategic success, controlling for other factors, moral influence, command, and doctrine is a question of human action and interaction. Sun Tzu explains that, by command, he means 'the general's qualities of wisdom, sincerity, humanity, courage, and strictness,' and that, by doctrine, he means 'organization, control, assignment of appropriate ranks to officers, regulation of supply routes and the provision of principle items used by the army' (1963: 65). These requirements of military competence and readiness, however important, are subordinate in Sun Tzu to the requirement of moral influence. He details:

> By moral influence I mean that which causes people to be in harmony with their leaders, so that they will accompany them in life and unto death without fear of mortal peril.
>
> *Chang Yu*: When one treats people with benevolence, justice, and righteousness, and reposes confidence in them, the army will be united in mind and all will be happy to serve their leaders. The Book of Changes says: 'In happiness at overcoming difficulties, people forget the danger of death.' (Sun Tzu 1963: 64)

Some read this as an argument for, and only for, military efficiency, arguing that Sun Tzu is concerned with the disorder caused by political dissent. Certainly, it is obvious that at least part of Sun Tzu's concern with harmony is strategic. Yet some hints in the text suggest that there is more going on than a concern for the poor soldiering brought about by political disharmony. In his qualifications for a good general, Sun Tzu lists humanity, but does not associate it with any strategic advantage. In his description of moral influence, he does not include traits like manipulation and propaganda, which could produce the result of troop cooperation without the need for 'benevolence, justice, and righteousness' (Sun Tzu 1963: 4).

These inclusions, I argue, show that while Sun Tzu does argue for prevention or pre-emption by first strike when war is prudent, he has strong standards for judging the question of the prudence of war. Sun Tzu's approach, which I identify as ethical, has requirements that a potential belligerent must meet in order to be justified in fighting a preventive war. Among his requirements are humanity, restraint, and 'moral influence,' or domestic consent, obtained by benevolence, justice, and righteousness.

These requirements can be compared to the justifications for the Bush NSS stand on preventive war. The question of 'moral influence' and the 'war on terror' is an important one in this context. While the conflicts in Iraq and Afghanistan were favored by a majority of the population of the United States when they were started in 2001 and 2003 respectively, both conflicts lost the favor of public opinion in late 2004. Certainly, as the conflicts continued years later, the American people could not be described as 'in harmony with their leaders, so that they will accompany them in life and death without fear of mortal peril' (Sun Tzu 1963: 64). Instead, both the American population and the American military are deeply divided on the question of the warrants for the 'war on terror' and the proper methods for fighting (and/or ending) it. As Sun Tzu was concerned, this division has hindered American military effectiveness, strategically, operationally, and logistically.

However, Sun Tzu's concern for moral influence is more than just an interest in cohesion that can be leveraged into victory. He is interested in a belligerent behaving with 'benevolence, justice, and righteousness' both in trying to avoid conflict and in prosecuting it. These standards have been at the heart of many of the very public controversies surrounding the United States' *in bello* (war-fighting) behavior. Domestic and international reactions to the imprisonment of 'enemy combatants' in Guantánamo Bay, the Abu Ghraib prison abuse scandal, and the behavioral aberrations committed by soldiers and members of private military corporations employed by the United States in Afghanistan and Iraq have demonstrated that there is, at the very least, a vigorous debate about whether the United States meets the standards of justice and righteousness in fighting the (preventive) 'war on terror.' Growing domestic disapproval of the war in Iraq, particularly, suggested a broader questioning of the decision to go to war.

If the presence of justice and righteousness in the United States' prosecution of the 'war on terror' is in question, the absence of benevolence is frequently clear. As discussed above, some of the Bush NSS rhetoric expresses a concern for others' welfare, as Bush desires to 'create a balance of power in favor of human freedom' and expresses concern that 'no people on earth yearn to be oppressed' (2002a). Nevertheless, the strategic statements in the NSS make it clear that the intended benefit of the 'war on terror' for those outside the United States was, if anything, trickle-down. It is, in the Bush rhetoric, America that will keep the preponderance of military power in the world and therefore America that will defend herself from *any* outside threats. The NSS, then, does not express the altruistic spirit that benevolence implies. Also, the idea of benevolence in Sun Tzu seems to be extended to how the enemy ought to be treated, as he contends that a key characteristic of a good general is humanity. The 'good and evil' rhetoric in the Bush NSS and 2002 State of the Union addresses, combined with the differential treatment standards for 'real POWs' and 'enemy combatants,' as well as rumors of abuses of the laws of war, suggest that the 'enemy' in the 'war on terror' is not treated with the benevolence that Sun Tzu asserts is necessary in war generally and preventive war specifically.

Augustine: a transcendental approach to preventive warfare

Part of the argument that Gaddis makes about the uniqueness of the Bush NSS doctrine is that it is necessary to articulate a theory and policy of pre-emptive and/or preventive war outside of the system of sovereign states, given the increasing influence of non-state actors in the current age of global terror. Sun Tzu's approach to defining actors outside of the Westphalian understanding of sovereignty is to see states, as they were in the warring states period, as constantly fighting for their existence and subject to the continual shifting of borders with the shift of military advantage. While this world has some parallels to the post 9/11 world, Cook (2004) suggests that an analogy to the time and work of Augustine might be more fruitful.

Cook argues that, 'like the shift that occurred at Westphalia, the international system is undergoing a real and fundamental realignment,' which suggests that Bush is correct that analysis coming from the Westphalian era is of limited utility (Cook 2004: 813). He explains: 'that shift, rather than starting with state sovereignty as the bedrock, would instead start with the shared values and concerns of (for lack of a better word) the "civilized" world' (Cook 2004: 813). This starting point might lead theorists of the making and fighting of wars to see sovereignty as 'a provisional and contingent value – contingent on a state's willingness and ability to preserve and protect the lives and rights of its citizens and to participate meaningfully in the struggle for the maintenance of global order' (Cook 2004: 813).

It is here where Cook finds an analogy to the times and writings of Augustine. Cook explains that Augustine's 'ethical challenge was hardly the defense of the sovereign state'; instead, in the attacks by barbarians on Rome, 'he (correctly) saw an assault on the underpinnings of civilization itself' (Cook 2004: 813). As such,

> The destruction of Rome, even though it was not the destruction of the Kingdom of God, was indeed a prospect of incalculable human costs. Christians (and, to generalize the argument, all right thinking people) would recognize the defense of Roman civilization as an imperative – not because it is not deeply flawed, but because it provides the political and moral space in which human flourishing is possible. Whatever its many flaws and injustices, Augustine clearly saw that the Empire provided a 'tranquility of order' (to use his phrase) within which civilized life was possible. A victory by the barbarians, in contrast, did not. (Cook 2004: 813–14)

Cook contends that the Bush administration could see the 'war on terror' in much the same way – as a war where the civilized defend civilization from barbarians. Given this account, Cook argues, 'if one measures the contemporary situation by Al Qaeda's aspirations, the contemporary Global War against Terrorism bears much more striking resemblance to Augustine's circumstance' (Cook 2004: 814).

Indeed, a civilizational story is told of the 'war on terror' fairly frequently. Moreover, a number of scholars contend that this sort of oppositional understanding of the civilized world and those barbarians from whom it must be protected recurs throughout history. For example, Woods and Donovan link the Bush NSS American supremacy discourse to the terms used to describe native Americans in the 17th century. The terms most frequent in the Bush discourse about tyrants and terrorists include: 'brutal,' 'terrorists,' 'ruthless,' 'violent,' 'cruel,' 'dark,' 'deluded,' 'evil,' 'lawless,' and 'radical' (Woods and Donovan 2005: 504). These can be paralleled with the terms used to describe Native Americans around the time of King Philip's war: brutish, savages, merciless, destructive, cruel, dark, immoral, pagan, perfidious, and profane (Woods and Donovan 2005: 504). Woods and Donovan note that 'although Bush and Mather tell the story in different contexts separated by almost four centuries ... their method is characterized by generating fear of opponents that necessitates control over them' (2005: 505).

Even if we are to understand the 'war on terror' as a fight to save the civilized from the barbarians, however, Augustine's standards are not fully permissive. Though, according to Augustine, God is clearly not against all wars (1956: Letter 138), killing for glory is not acceptable. Instead, killing out of obedience to God is both acceptable and expected (1998: 1.21, 19.7). Thus intent matters, in the justice of even a war which defends the civilized from the barbarian (Augustine 1998: 4.15). Not only does intent matter to Augustine, 'it is integral; even proper behavior with improper intent will not pass his test of Just War' (Ramsey 1992: 10).

As such, in Augustine, resistance to a love of violence separates the people of God from infidels. As Ramsey explains:

> Social justice arises from a common agreement as to the objects of their love (will); and, since the agreement would break down and the people become a mere multitude without minimum or greater degrees of participation in the life of the nation, accepted schemes of justice serve to strengthen that common will or love which constitutes *res publica*. (Ramsey 1992: 17)

Augustine divides the love that motivates wars into love for transitory goods (things which can be taken away against your will) and transcendent goods (those which transcend material life).[2] Even in a war against the infidels, it is important that a belligerent's motive comes from love of transcendent goods rather than transitory goods. In other words, Augustine asks, 'does the soldier's motive for drawing blood arise from the love of transitory goods (which can be taken against our will) rather than the proper love of transcendent goods, which are invulnerable to attack?' (Smith 2007: 144–5). While this standard does not justify defense of one's goods (or even, always, oneself), Augustine does suggest that it can justify certain preventive attacks, using the example of killing a would-be rapist 'even before the crime has been committed' (Smith 2007: 145). Augustine also suggests that it is as appropriate to attack an enemy lying in ambush as it is to attack one who has already begun to fight. In this understanding, according to Smith, 'pre-emption is merely an active, rather than passive, form of self-defense based on one's reading of the circumstances' (2007: 145).

The apparent tension between the Augustine who argues that attacks cannot be made for the love of transitory goods and the one who argues that preventive attacks are acceptable in some circumstances can be read in a number of ways. First, as Smith notes, sometimes Augustine the character in dialogue disagrees with Augustine the thinker (2007: 145). Second, while Augustine does not always justify defense of self for transitory goods, he has a strong understanding that it is acceptable to defend against others' loss of transcendental goods. When transcendental goods are at stake, Augustine prioritizes the committing of lesser evil over an absolute rule concerning who attacks first. Therefore, a preventive attack can be justified when it would prevent a greater loss of transcendent goods. He explains:

> It is, however, evident that this law is well-prepared against such an accusation, for in the state where it is in force it allows lesser evil deeds to prevent worse being committed. It is much more suitable that the man who attacks the life of another should be slain than he who defends his own life; and it is much more cruel that a man should suffer violation than that the violator be slain by his intended victim. (Augustine 1955: 1.12)

In other words, the justification for preventive war is the question of a just result for the conflict. The reason that the Romans were justified in fighting the barbarians was because the consequence (the loss of civilization) was so dire that it justified not only fighting but fighting by striking first. With this standard, Smith reports, Augustine is not concerned with the problem of proportionality of preventive warfare, but instead with 'protecting the innocent from suffering unjustly and more importantly preventing the would-be aggressor's carrying out his unjust will' (2007: 147). The justice of normal warfare is measured by the proportionality of the response to the *actual* offense, but the justice of preventive warfare is measured by its effectiveness in preventing the would-be aggressor's action rather than on proportionality with a (potential) forthcoming offense.

However, Augustine draws a line where certain preventive wars would be unjust even when they prevented a would-be evildoer from doing evil. While it is paramount to stop a would-be aggressor from carrying out his unjust will, Augustine condemns the choice of Rome to start its third and final war with Carthage. He emphasizes that there has to be some specificity to that unjust will, rather than just a nebulous and general threat to security. Augustine objects to the search for 'freedom from fear through complete security' as 'neither an attainable or desirable goal of national policy' (Smith 2007: 149). This is in part because it is difficult to distinguish from the desire for conquest, and partly because, as Smith explains, 'peace and security untempered by fear allow the citizens to abandon caution and self-restraint' (2007: 149). Instead, 'geopolitical vulnerability is not the same as an imminent threat of attack' (Smith 2007: 151) because

> The larger the city, the more is its forum filled with civil lawsuits and criminal trials, even if the city be at peace, free from the alarms or – what is more frequent – the bloodshed, of sedition and civil war. It is true that cities are at times exempt from these occurrences; they are never free from the danger of them. (1950: 24.5)

In other words, defending a transcendent good from an actual threat justifies preventive warfare, but trying to shore up the security of that good from any possible threat ever does not. The potential belligerent must be able to qualify and quantify the nature of the threat. With this distinction, 'Augustine draws to our mind the complexities of seeking and preserving a relatively just order in a fallen and frequently violent earthly city' (Smith 2007: 157). Smith explains that Augustine contributes an important reminder that

'Freedom from fear' cannot for Augustine be the goal of foreign policy. Instead, he reminds us that in this age we must live with the uneasy knowledge of the fragile and transitory nature of our existence. For only by living in the fearful reality of our vulnerability and our ultimate impotence can we be free from the self-complacency or will to power that themselves are the very cause of our mortality and fear. (Smith 2007: 158)

Three main questions, then, come from the Augustinian transcendental approach to preventive warfare for the Bush NSS strategy. The first is whether what is really at stake in the 'war on terror' is a transcendent good or a transitory one. The second is whether, if there is a transcendent good at stake, the United States is fighting for love of that transcendent good or for love of a transitory good. The third is, assuming that there is a transcendent good the United States is fighting for, whether the threat to that good is definable and measurable, or a general vulnerability with no specific threat. In other words, is the United States fighting against a specific threat to its security or generally trying to decrease its geopolitical vulnerability?

The transcendent goods that the 'war on terror' could be about include Western civilization generally and American society specifically, as well as some sense of universal justice or human rights. Certainly, the Bush NSS rhetoric frames the 'war on terror' as about these transcendental goods – human freedom, the American way of life, Western civilization, and human rights have all been cited by the United States government as motivations for prosecuting the 'war on terror.' If the Roman empire qualified as a transcendent good, it is possible to see the American society/empire as a similar transcendent good. Yet others have argued that what is really at stake in the 'war on terror' is relative power, money, oil, or competition between governments – goods that Augustine would classify as transitory. Even if the 'war on terror' is actually about the 'American way of life' or something to that effect, the question of whether Americanness is actually a transcendent good is anything but clear.

Even if Americanness is a transcendent good, Augustine would then ask if the United States' true goal in the 'war on terror' is the transcendent good of American-ness or some transitory good being fought for instead of the claimed transcendent good. In other words, is the United States claiming pure motivation while really following lust for earthly goods? While true intent is hard to determine,

Augustine finds it crucial to discover, if there are mixed motives, the love for *which one* motivates the Bush NSS? Is it the love of a transcendent good? Or are Americans using the transcendent good as a cover for the love of some earthly or transitory good like power or economic gain?

Assuming that Americanness is a transcendent good *and* that the United States is really motivated by that transcendent good, Augustine has a third question: whether the threat to the transcendent good of Americanness is measurable and real, or whether it is more an existential threat to security or a general geographical or philosophical vulnerability. Those who argue that it is a measurable and real threat to the United States argue that both the government of Afghanistan and the government of Iraq were real and consequential threats to the security of the United States. Others argue that, if they constituted any real threat at all, Afghanistan and Iraq constituted general threats, with no clear timeline, plan, or operation to attack the United States – that they fell within Augustine's second category of general vulnerabilities (and, therefore, not just causes) rather than the first category of real and measurable threats.

In either case, even though the Bush NSS invokes Augustine with its civilizational rhetoric, it avoids a serious engagement with his complicated standards for permitting preventive war by declaring the newness of the world of global terrorism. A serious engagement with Augustine's questions about what is at stake, what motivates belligerents, and whether the threat is material would make the Bush NSS standard for preventive warfare look substantially more questionable. The 'new world' rhetoric avoids that, as well as other serious questions, like those invoked by Vattel's calculative approach to judging preventive war.

Vattel: a calculative approach to preventive war

Eighteenth-century legal theorist Emmerich de Vattel viewed preemption as 'an integral part of the most fundamental legal right, the right to self-preservation, held by individuals and states alike' (Rivkin et al. 2005: 468). Writing in support of armed action against Louis XIV's France following the Bourbon family's inheritance of the Spanish Crown and Empire in 1701, Vattel explained:

On Occasion, where it is impossible, or too dangerous to wait for an absolute certainty, we may justly act on a reasonable presumption. If a stranger presents his piece at me in a wood, I am not yet certain he intends to kill me; but shall I, in order to be convinced of his design, allow him to fire? What reasonable casuist will deny me the right of preventing him? But presumption becomes nearly equal to certainty, if the prince, who is on the point of rising to an enormous power, has already manifested an unlimited pride and insatiable ambition. (Vattel 1883: 309)

While previous theorists, like Hugo Grotius (1952: 173), had argued that a state may act in anticipation of a deed by an enemy known to have the means and intent, Vattel went further. Though he cautioned against the tendency to 'act upon vague and doubtful intentions,' Vattel made clear that states 'may even anticipate the other's [aggressive] design' (Rivkin et al. 2005: 470).

However, in Vattel's classification, questions of pre-emption and prevention are subcategories of offensive war. Vattel sees pre-emption and prevention *not* as extensions of defense as a just cause, but for the purposes of the pursuit and enforcement of rights and/or state security (1883: 3.1.5).[3] While many Just War theorists think about pre-emption as a way to protect from imminent harm, Vattel assumes that states have moral license to engage in such activities and is interested more in prevention as a moral problem. The key questions, according to Vattel, are:

Whether the aggrandizement of a neighboring state, in consequences of which a Nation fears that it will one day be oppressed, is a sufficient ground for making war upon it; whether a Nation can with justice take up arms to resist the growing power of that State, or to weaken the State, with the sole object of protecting itself from dangers which weak States are almost always threatened from an overpowerful one. (Vattel 1883: 3.3.42)

As Vattel sees it, this question 'presents no difficulties to the majority of statesmen' but 'is more perplexing for those who seek at all times to unite justice with prudence' (1883: 3.3.42). In other words, Vattel sees that, from the standpoint of state interests, preventive war is not only permissible but desirable.[4] It is only when one wonders about moral rightness that the question of prevention is an interesting one. In terms of morality, Vattel tells us that, strategically, states should not use 'illegitimate means in order to obtain a just and praiseworthy end' (1883: 3.3.43). Therefore, he argues, 'the aggrandizement of a neighboring state cannot alone and of itself give anyone the right to take up arms to resist it' (Vattel 1883: 3.3.43).

Instead, 'one is justified in forestalling a danger in direct ration to the degree of probability attending it, and to the seriousness of the evil with which one is threatened' (Vattel 1883: 3.3.44). This is measured by the capacity of the potential enemy, its intent, the signs it has shown, and the level of risk that the potential victim would be exposed to (Vattel 1883: 3.3.44). In other words, the key distinction between Vattel and traditional Just War thinking on prevention is that he is *not* relying on the imminence of harm to justify pre-emption or prevention. A state, in Vattel's view, might be justified in acting preventively to counteract a state whose threat may still be months, years, or even decades away. As he explains, if a 'prince'

> betrays his plans by preparations or other advances, other nations have the right to check him; and if the fortune of war be favorable to them, they may profit by the favorable opportunity to weaken and reduce his strength, which upsets the balance of power and constitutes a menace to the common liberty of all. (Vattel 1883: 3.3.49)

Vattel 'first obliged rulers to distinguish between an increase of power which a ruler undertook with the determination to do harm to someone else and an increase of power which a ruler promoted in service to the population under his control' (Kleinschmidt 2000: 131). Also, Vattel argued that 'suspicious acts should be on record' and those acts had to be by people 'well known and easily recognizable from past experience as untrustworthy' (Kleinschmidt 2000: 131).

Compared to Augustine, Vattel argues that a remote threat is not necessarily an unjust cause for preventive war. Unlike Sun Tzu, Vattel requires no benevolence or justice on the part of the party responding to the threat. Vattel is certainly the most permissive of the three theorists in terms of the standards for fighting a preventive war. Several theorists (e.g. Rivkin et al. 2005) have invoked Vattel in defending the United States' right to start a preventive war against Iraq in 2003. For example, it is not a stretch to say that suspicious acts of the Saddam Hussein regime were on record, and the Saddam Hussein government was easily recognizable from past experience as untrustworthy. While we do not know whether Iraq's attempts to amass power were really for the good of the Iraqi people or for the good of Iraq's competition with other nations, there is a strong inference to be taken from Iraq's attacks on Iran and Kuwait. Certainly, at the very least, a strong case could be made for the Saddam Hussein government's untrustworthiness and development of military power for aggressive reasons.

The other question Vattel asks, though, concerns the proportionality of the threat both to the potential belligerent and to the common liberty of all. Perhaps this question is not as easily answered. Previous to its 2003 invasion of Iraq, the United States expressed its confidence that Iraq possessed weapons of mass destruction (WMD), and would at some point use those weapons. The scenarios described ranged from selling them to terrorists to using them against Israel. Iraq had, a few times during the 1990s, used conventional military force to quell internal rebellions. It had not engaged in military aggression past its borders since the end of the Gulf War. Repeated UN inspections showed no WMD in Iraq, but the UN was afraid that it had not uncovered all possible hiding places. Iraq had ejected UN weapons inspectors in 1998, and did not allow them back in until after September 11th, under the threat of military attack by the United States. International consensus at the time understood Iraq to be rebuilding its weapons arsenal.

Yet, there is not certain evidence that Iraq had rebuilt its weapons: weapons inspections in 2002 found only the (objectionable?) weapons that Iraq had admitted to possessing. Iraq agreed to destroy those weapons. Iraq had allowed the weapons inspectors back into Iraq because it feared an American attack in 2002; this fear caused the government to show a renewed interest in compliance with UN Security Council resolutions (Richter et al. 2003). Iraq's interest in compliance may have been born of fear, but nonetheless should be considered as mitigating the legitimacy of a claim to the need for a preventative war against the government of Iraq.

Still, the Bush NSS claimed that Iraq (not mentioned specifically, but inferred as a part of the 'tyrants and terrorists' Bush classified as meriting preventive action) was a threat important enough to go to war against, not only because of its possible possession of weapons of mass destruction, but also because of its aggressive past, its cooperation with terrorists, and its general hostility to Western civilization.

Vattel argues that if a state is going to be attacked there is no reason for it to lose the strategic advantage of striking first, *especially* when the threat is substantial. The Bush administration could have answered Vattel's standard by arguing that the Saddam Hussein government did pose a substantial threat not only to the United States, but to the region and the world. Its opponents could then have pointed out the flaws and exaggerations in such an argument.

Judging 'New' Preventive War

While the Bush NSS doctrine of preventive war appears to fall well short of the traditional Just War consensus on the justice of pre-emption, the three theorists presented in this chapter take more permissive positions on the question of whether preventive war can ever be just without an immediate scenario for the threat to play out. Sun Tzu argues that preventive warfare is always strategically preferable, so long as it is carried out by a belligerent with 'moral influence' – justice, benevolence, and righteousness. Augustine argues that preventive war is acceptable as well, but requires it to be motivated by a love for a transcendent good rather than a transitory one. Vattel holds the least restrictive understanding of preventive war – requiring only a consequential threat with reasonable probability. In this chapter, I have expressed doubts about the viability of the Bush NSS doctrine when held up to the standards of Sun Tzu and Augustine. While there are hurdles to be cleared, however, it appears that the Bush administration might have had a plausible argument that the NSS doctrine, at least in its manifestation in the war on Iraq, represented a just theory of preventive war. That point remains open for further investigation.

The important point this chapter makes, however, is not about whether the Bush NSS doctrine of preventive war measures up to any of these standards or not; it is that the Bush administration successfully avoided serious dialogue with the standards proposed by philosophers, strategists, and political theorists of the past – even those who might be friendlier to their political perspective – by relying on and continually proclaiming the newness of the world of global terror, the newness of the security threats within that world, and therefore the need for new strategies to combat those security threats. With the rhetoric of newness, the Bush NSS broke with centuries and even millennia of thought on the prudence of preventive war, legitimating only 'post-9/11' discourse rather than seriously engaging ethical approaches to the question – be they Sun Tzu's ethical approach, Augustine's transcendental approach, Vattel's calculative approach, or the more restrictive approaches characteristic of most Just War theorists. In doing so, the Bush NSS decontextualized its political and moral claims, ignoring the history of political thought and practice that could serve as a guiding and restraining force in this 'new' age.

Yet the actual newness of this age is also called into question by the application of these theorists to the problem of preventive war. Each of these theorists lived during a time when non-state actors like al-Qaeda were prevalent, meaning that security threats emanated from a similarly broad category of actors, yet they would still not justify the expansive approach to preventive war advocated by the Bush NSS.

4

Genocide:

An Obligation to Fight?

Rebecca Glazier

Since the end of the Cold War, there has been a marked increase in ethnic conflict and genocide in the international arena, including conflicts in the former Yugoslavia, the Democratic Republic of Congo, Rwanda, Somalia, and Darfur (Power 2002). While genocide is not a new phenomenon, it has increasingly appeared on the international security and international human rights agenda in the past two decades (Harff 2003; Staub 1993).

While there is no universally accepted definition of the term, William Rubenstein suggests that 'genocide might be defined as the deliberate killing of most or all members of a collective group for the mere fact of being members of that group' (2004: 2). In the 1953 Convention on the Prevention and Punishment of the Crime of Genocide, genocide was defined as attacks, murder, torture, or abuse 'committed with intent to destroy, in whole or in part, a national, ethnic, racial, or religious group.' This definition has been reaffirmed by the United Nations Commission on Human Rights several times, most recently in 2003.[1]

Particularly in the post-Cold War world, there has been substantial debate between those who would characterize genocide as a supreme emergency obligating intervention (e.g. Power 2002) and those who would argue that states should limit interference in genocide in accordance with national interest or other criteria (e.g. Kuperman 2001). These debates have not been contextualized in terms of traditional thought about the ethics of war, at least in part because Just War theory has been seen as permitting, rather than obligating, potential belligerents to engage in conflict. Few doubt that intervention in genocide would be *just*; still fewer have read Just War theory as making that intervention *obligatory*. Because intervention is not seen as obligatory, many genocides continue without intervention from the international community.

This chapter attempts to determine if the principles of Just War theory might be extended beyond their current focus on limiting or permitting war to requiring it in certain situations. Is there a time when states or other actors are morally obligated to fight a war? If so, can the framework of Just War tell us when that is? How might the classic Just War principles be reconceptualized for a theory of just *and* obligatory war?

In genocide, surely, might the obligation to use force apply? From genocide, then, it may be possible to extrapolate the principles of a theory of obligatory war. By applying this concept of obligatory war to the 1994 Rwandan genocide it is possible to understand more fully the circumstances which might merit obligation. This is useful because the apparent simplicity of this theory may belie the moral complexity involved in making the decision to intervene. Thus, the brief examination of a historical case of genocide where the obligation to intervene described in this theory was present, but no intervention took place, underscores the complexities involved in answering the call of obligation.[2]

Just War Theory in the 21st Century

The history of Just War doctrine is a long and rich one. Although questions of justice in war and the appropriate nature of conflict have been asked and addressed by many cultures and traditions,[3] the principles that are most commonly referred to when Just War theory is discussed were canonized by St Augustine and Thomas Aquinas and are still salient today.

The most prominent concern of Just War theory since its inception has been to limit the resort to war. This purpose is reflected in the writings of the classic Just War authors. It was St Thomas Aquinas, drawing heavily on the work of St Augustine before him, who systematically laid out the early principles that make a Just War. Aquinas (as interpreted in d'Entreves 1959) argued that for a war to be just three conditions are necessary: 'first, the authority of the sovereign by whose command the war is to be waged'; this is the principle that came to be known as just or right authority. The purpose of this principle of the Just War tradition was to make it more difficult to resort to violence, specifically by limiting private warfare (Coates 1997). Second, Aquinas says that the sword is only to be used against those 'who deserve it on account of some fault.'[4] This is the principle of just cause. And finally, Aquinas said that force should be used for 'the advancement of good, or the avoidance of evil,' which is the principle of right intention (2006: 133).

These are the three most important aspects of Just War theory and the ones that are most seriously considered when the decision about whether or not to go to war is made. But these are not the only principles. Proportionality is another main point of traditional Just War theory and in modern literature the probability of success serves as subset of this principle. Finally, war should only be undertaken as a last resort. This is another principle that is more modern in genesis, but is often included in this traditional list (Lackey 1988).

These principles comprise *jus ad bellum*, the first component of Just War theory and the principles that relate to the decision to go to war. The principles of *jus in bello* govern actions on the battlefield and make up the second half of the Just War tradition. Some authors have also suggested we utilize principles of *jus post bellum*, principles which would govern the conduct of the parties after war, ensuring that justice persists (Walzer 2004). Because this chapter focuses specifically on the decision to engage in conflict, and in particular on the decision to intervene in genocide, its appropriate realm is *jus ad bellum*.

An Obligation to Fight?

One major question is raised in this chapter is whether the principles of Just War theory, under the right circumstances, may be used to necessitate a resort to force. In this modern era of pre-emptive engagement, can Just War theory take us beyond reaction to proactive action? The principles of Just War theory are meant as guidance for moral decision-making. States contemplating whether or not to use force turn to these principles in order to determine if it is justified. Because states make moral evaluations when contemplating the presence of Just War principles in particular conflicts, we can consider states moral actors. Additionally, because states can be morally constrained when using force is not just, they can also be morally obligated when using force is just. Thus, Just War theory represents a moral standard that requires both positive and negative action. This standard requires that states refrain from conflict when it is not just *and* that they engage in conflict in certain circumstances.

Whereas some moral standards[5] require only negative action – 'thou shalt not kill' requires simply that one refrain from killing; other moral standards require only positive action: 'impart of your substance to the poor' requires that one give of one's possessions to someone who has less. However, there is a third category of moral standards that requires both positive and negative action. Although they have not traditionally been understood as such, the principles of Just War theory fall into this category. The moral standards of this category are more abstract than the direct commandments of the previous two categories. For instance, 'love thy neighbor as thyself' requires both that one show kindness to one's neighbor, a positive action, and that one refrain from harming one's neighbor, a negative action. Because Just War theory is the type of moral standard from which both positive and negative duties flow, states are morally obligated to refrain from unjust wars and to engage in very just wars. Of course, moral obligation is not something to be taken lightly. This obligation would only apply in the most severe of circumstances – the cases in which war is not only just but also meets stricter requirements of moral obligation.

The most basic idea behind the theory of obligatory war is that human suffering is bad and, as human beings, we have a prima facie duty to relieve suffering. This line of thinking follows that of theorists like Mayerfeld (1999) who argue that we have a powerful duty to stop suffering. But there are additional reasons why the suffering caused by genocide is particularly horrible and the obligation to relieve suffering, or intervene, in this case is more powerful than others.

First is the fact that genocide by definition includes murder on a mass scale, not just suffering. The cessation of human life is not something that can be reversed, and the suffering imposed by such action is not only great for the person that is killed but also affects the family, the community, and the world (Rummel 2000; Hirsch 1995). Genocide also often includes death on a particularly cruel and systematic scale, making it more evil than other kinds of suffering (Staub 1989; Storr 1991). One need only hear testimony from a concentration camp survivor or victim of systematic rape in the Balkans to be assured of this fact (Hansen 2000).

Second, genocide includes a national, ethnic, racial, and/or religious factor in its violence. It is more terrible to say that an entire race or an entire religious group deserves not to exist because of that identity than it is to commit random atrocities. It is not just the demise of individuals, even great numbers of individuals, that should concern us (Barnett 2002). The collective whole of any ethnic or religious group is greater than the sum of its individual members. Genocidal acts are aimed at destroying the identity of that group in addition to the individuals that constitute it. The third reason why the obligation to intervene in genocide is greater than other obligations to relieve suffering is because not intervening in genocide legitimates the practice and may precipitate further crimes. When President Clinton visited Rwanda for the first time in 1998, he argued that the lesson of Rwanda was that 'each bloodletting hastens the next, and as the value of human life is degraded and violence becomes tolerated, the unimaginable becomes more conceivable' (quoted in Gourevitch 1998: 351). Allowing genocide to go unpunished sends a powerful negative message to the world that such atrocities will be tolerated.

Finally, with the acceptance of the Genocide Convention, genocide has been recognized as a historic evil. Holocaust museums scattered all over the world are a testament to the desires of individuals and states 'never again' to let such horror occur. These terrible deeds, which 'shock the conscience of mankind,' have been recognized as the worst that human beings are capable of. Gelb (1995: 6) said: 'If democratic leaders turn away from genocide, or merely pretend to combat it, their citizens will drink the hypocrisy and sink into cynicism.' The historical reminder of previous genocides should cause the world community to respond more quickly to their occurrence. In fact, it is one of the reasons why I argue the international community is obligated to respond.

The next section will address each of the principles of traditional Just War theory in turn and enumerate their role in a theory of obligatory war.

Right authority

The principle of right authority was originally meant to restrict the countries or institutions that could justly initiate action. It is a principle that has been central to Just War theory and has also played an important role in recent attempts develop a standard for 'just interventionism' (Ramsbotham and Woodson 1996). As discussed earlier, there are certain conditions, like genocide, which necessitate action. States have a moral imperative to intervene in these situations. It is this imperative that gives them the right authority to act.

The obligation to intervene in genocide arises from another source as well: the Genocide Convention. The Genocide Convention of 1948 provides a clear basis for holding its signatories responsible for reacting to and intervening in genocide. Article 1 of the Convention provides that the parties will 'undertake to prevent and punish' the crime of genocide, and Article 8 provides that 'any Contracting Party may call upon the competent organs of the United Nations to take such action under the Charter of the United Nations as they consider appropriate for the prevention and suppression of the act of genocide.' Quite frankly, this document gives right authority to any of its signatories, and along with that authority the obligation to act.

However, the problem with interventions in genocide is usually not that the intervener fails to demonstrate why they have the right authority, but that no country wants to assume authority and the responsibility for action that goes with it. This problem is clearly illustrated by the fact that very few signatories of the Genocide Convention are willing to claim right authority, and have instead allowed genocide to occur. Thus, the concept of right authority in cases of obligatory intervention is qualitatively different from that of traditional Just War theory. When it comes to the principle of right authority, the original standard of Just War theory may not be directly applicable to interventions in genocide. In this situation, states have the right authority because they have an ethical responsibility both as members of the international community and as signatories to the Genocide Convention.

In order to ensure that an intervening state has right authority, and that it is not exploiting the obligatory principle, it is important that the state be held accountable to the international community. Additionally, some authors have suggested that the intervening state act with impartiality (Ramsbotham and Woodhouse 1996). This is unnecessary for two reasons. First, intervening impartially may not be the most effective tactic. Recent literature suggests that impartiality is not necessary, and may even be detrimental to the success of an intervention (Kaufmann 2004; Walter 2004; Rauchhaus 2006). Forestalling impartiality is actually a much more ethical approach in the case of genocide because the situation is often such that there is a clear perpetrator and a clearly oppressed victim. A possible exception could be a protracted conflict like that in the Balkans in the 1990s, where 'ethnic cleansing' was committed by many sides of the conflict. However, even this situation does not require that the intervener be impartial, but only that they not commit to defending only one side. Should the tide of genocide turn, the interveners need to be prepared to turn with it and confront the new perpetrators.

Second, requiring impartiality may prevent a state from intervening in genocide. The key point to remember is that when a state is obligated to use force, it is because of an extreme international emergency. These extraordinary acts of brutality are in a class all of their own; they are crimes against humanity which require intervention (Wheeler 2000). The moral imperative associated with stopping the suffering and death inherent in such emergencies is enough to override concerns over impartiality voiced by the just intervention literature. It is enough that the interveners be accountable to the international community; such accountability will hopefully prevent any biases from becoming malicious.

Right intention

Traditional Just War theorists included the principle of right intention so that any country embarking on war would only be allowed to do so in order to advance a good cause or thwart an evil one. Thus, wars of conquest and similarly unjust causes were not allowed under

Just War theory. For obligatory wars this principle holds a slightly different meaning: the obligation referred to in this theory of obligatory war is a moral one. Because of this, we can usually assume that those responding to the obligation have right intention. While this may be the case most of the time, one can imagine a situation where the intervening country supports the genocide and does not try to stop it and may even facilitate it. Or, less terrible and more likely, a country could have alternative motives for intervening because of their desire to access natural resources or a hunger for power, and could use intervention as a guise to achieve these ends. Thus we are faced with a dilemma: are purely humanitarian motives the only acceptable 'intentions' behind intervention? Many members of the international community were disturbed by the French intervention in Rwanda because it was seen as stemming from a desire to continue to play the great power game in the area (Fixdal and Smith 1998). But would preventing the French from intervening have been a better solution?

What if right intention in the traditional sense is not present? An additional complicating problem is the fact that it is difficult to ascertain ulterior motives before the fact. When it comes to stopping atrocities, it may not be requisite for interveners to have *only* right intentions; they may have some right intentions and some national security concerns. So long as the other Just War requirements are met, those intentions are relatively benign. 'The requirement of an intent to right a wrong does *not* preclude the existence of *other* motives' (Brown 2003: 46; emphasis in original). Humanitarian actions are rarely based solely on humanitarian motivations. Lucas (2003) recommends that intentions be publicly proclaimed before a humanitarian mission so the international community can ensure that the mission is progressing according to international standards.

Another way to ensure that the mixed intentions of a single country do not corrupt the justness of the mission is to strive to undertake action in a multilateral manner. This is not a perfect solution of course, but it is more likely to result in the principle of right intention functioning as intended.

In cases of obligatory intervention, right intention is met if intentions are publicly proclaimed and humanitarian motives are among them, even if all the intentions aren't completely pure. For instance, the desire to live in a world without gross violations of human rights is a motive that is technically about self-interest, but it is one that the revised theory is willing to allow if it means that genocide is stopped (Brown 2003: 46). In this principle, as with all of them, this is the clear overriding motivation. The fact that intervening is obligatory means that the intervention is the overriding goal. Stopping genocide is such a just cause that the minimal unjustness of multiple motivations for intervention is relatively unimportant. At the risk of being accused of justifying any means to achieve the just end of a stop to genocide, I assert that considerations of intention are of secondary or even tertiary importance when it comes to an overriding moral imperative. This is why states are required to act, even under imperfect conditions.

When we argue that the intentions of a state disqualify it from intervening in genocide, we are making that state the center of our analysis, rather than focusing on the victims who would be saved by the intervention. I agree with the perspective of Wheeler (2000) that we should place the victims of human rights abuses at the center of our theoretical reasoning. In developing a theory of obligation, we should focus on those who are suffering more so than those who have the potential to relieve the suffering. By making the victims the theoretical referent, we take the emphasis away from the intentions of the intervening state and place it on the outcome of their intervention.

Just cause

Historically, the most just reason for resorting to war has been self-defense. But limiting the just use of force to only defensive wars creates two problems. The first is that self-defense is too narrowly construed in most instances. But some authors, like Regan, interpret the writings of the ancient Just War theorists as justifying the resort to war 'in order to defend the community and all its members, not to defend themselves as individuals' (1996: 6). This reflects the Just War theorists' Christian perspective and their belief in the importance of helping one's neighbor (Regan 1996). Ambrose, the bishop of Milan and a major influence on Augustine and his philosophies, considered actions 'on behalf of the common good, to be instances of "courage" and "wholly just"' (cited in Cahill 1999: 59). Thus, the Just War tradition supports the defense of others, not just self-defense, and it sees this motivation as more just than that of defending oneself.

The second reason why self-defense should not be considered the only just cause is that there are other, equally valid, reasons to resort to force. Punishment for a transgression and righting a wrong are also considered just causes by the traditional Just War theorists, particularly to the extent that innocents are protected and defended (Fixdal and Smith 1998). Indeed, there is a long tradition of moral goodness being on the side of those who are willing to sacrifice themselves to save others. Occasionally, stopping genocide may require this kind of ultimate sacrifice, but usually the sacrifice is a minimal one of money spent or troops deployed. Stopping genocide is on a higher moral plane than intervening for reasons of economic instability or a refugee crisis, although there are times when intervention in these situations may be warranted.

Defense of the innocent, which is the case when a country intervenes in order to prevent the loss of innocent lives through ethnic cleansing, can actually be considered more just than self-defense. In genocide intervention, it is not the intervening country that has been attacked; they are not fighting to save their country or their liberty, but they are fighting for a higher cause – to save another. Frankly put, 'in Just War terminology, genocide is just cause for intervention' (Donnelly 1995: 297).

A theory of obligatory war takes this reasoning a step further. Building on the work of Destexhe (1994/5) and Plant (1993) on human rights abuses, this theory argues that genocide and similarly extreme cases of human suffering not only provide moral permission to intervene, but also require a moral responsibility. This is a major departure from the classic Just War theory. Traditionally, fulfilling the requirements for a just war meant that you were now justified in your actions should you *choose* to go to war, but doing so was by no means required. However, this chapter takes the position that Regan advocated: 'Justice will be wanting not only if rulers resort to war when right reason indicates that they should not, but also if they do not wage war when right reason indicates that they should' (1996: 11). If genocide is indeed happening and all of the criteria laid out here are fulfilled, then there is a just cause for stopping the genocide and any nation or body with the right authority is morally obligated to do so. Thus, the just cause principle in this framework does not stop with simply allowing intervention; it requires it. Intervening in genocide is a just cause, but not to do so when the other requirements of just action are met is morally unjust.

Proportionality

The burden of responsibility grows heavier yet with the adaptation of the principle of proportionality. Traditionally this principle has meant that the evil caused by going to war is less than the evil prevented by fighting it. The application is similar for obligatory war, but a better phrasing would be that the evil caused by *not* intervening is greater than if one intervened. The meaning is virtually the same, but the weight of responsibility rests on the shoulders of the non-intervener. The decision to allow great evil to continue to happen when one could have done something to stop it is morally unjust and not in accordance with the spirit of the Just War principles.

When a state is responding to an obligation to use force, for instance intervening in genocide, it is important that force be 'sufficient,' but it should not be overwhelming. The problem with using a cannon to kill a fly is that there is likely to be a lot of collateral damage. In a region where genocide is happening the oppressor and the oppressed are likely to live in close quarters and an overwhelming amount of force may be uncalled for according to the rule of proportionality.

In Lucas's (2003: 90) theory of *jus ad pacem*, he 'demands that a reasonable evaluation of the likely overall outcomes ... be undertaken before deciding whether to undertake the mission.' This is an excellent starting place for decision-making. What is unique about the theory of obligatory war is that once these considerations are complete, and if the results are that not intervening will result in more harm than intervening, the decision-making body has a moral obligation to intervene.

In talking about proportionality, Walzer says:

> Certainly we want political and military leaders to worry about costs and benefits. But they have to *worry*; they can't calculate, for the values at stake are not commensurate – at least they can't be expressed or compared mathematically, as the idea of proportion suggests. (Walzer 2004: 89–90)

This brings us to the second component of proportionality as it applies to obligatory intervention. There may be cases when states are unsure whether or not the obligation to intervene is applicable. In these cases, the countries considering intervention should err on the side of intervening. This decision-making hierarchy is usually reversed in decisions about initiating a war or engaging in humanitarian intervention, but the theory of obligatory war posits that in cases of extreme human suffering, like genocide, it is not just the lives of the oppressed that are at stake. As argued earlier, genocide is particularly terrible because refusing to intervene not only leads to death and suffering for so many, but also encourages others to commit similar crimes. Intervening in genocide sets a precedent with effects that cannot be measured by seemingly proportional body-counts on a balance sheet. One reason that failing to follow the obligation to intervene has such detrimental consequences is because it sets an example to rogue nations that genocide will be accepted by the international community (Sharp 1994). The 'moral price of silence' may have material costs as well, in the form of violence and lawlessness inching ever closer to our own backyards (Walzer 2004).

A similar point is made by the medieval Just War theorists, and quite powerfully: 'Always, Augustine's central point is the same – war is evil and dreadful, and yet, like the work of the jailer and the hangman in any society, it is sometimes necessary if wrongdoing and rank injustice are not to be permitted to flourish' (Deane 1963: 161). Deane goes on to emphasize that wars are just when they restrain this rank injustice, not so much when they advance the cause of justice.

Deane's interpretation of Augustine implies that just war can serve as a punishment against the aggressive or avaricious state and that 'other states then have not merely the right but the duty to punish these crimes' (1963: 156). This punishment by the intervening state is seen as parallel to the roles of judge, police officer, and executioner within the state. The just war is necessary as a punishment to the offending state and as a deterrent to other states that might consider similarly offensive actions. Additionally, 'the punishment of criminal men or nations is justified not only because it protects the innocent but also because it prevents the offender from continuing to misuse his liberty and from adding further crimes to his previous offenses' (Deane 1963: 165). Just as the judge, police officer, and executioner have an obligation to carry out their duties within a state, so do states have an obligation to ensure the horrors of genocide no longer torment humanity.

But what if stopping genocide requires the use of resources that are also needed elsewhere? This was precisely the dilemma facing the Allies in World War II. During the war, the United States was flooded with pleas to stop the Nazi killing machine. At the time, the US War Department rejected pleas to bomb Auschwitz and the railroads leading to the concentration camp, arguing that it needed the resources elsewhere (Wyman 1984). This situation clearly presented a dilemma of proportionality. Would bombing the camp have led to greater death and suffering elsewhere by diverting needed resources? A careful consideration of the various potential outcomes was certainly warranted, but history has shown that in the very months that the US War Department turned down requests to bomb Auschwitz it conducted raids within 50 miles of the camp. Noted historian David Wyman (1984: xv), who has researched the plight of the Jews during World War II extensively, concluded that 'twice during that time large fleets of American heavy bombers struck industrial targets in the Auschwitz complex itself, not five miles from the gas chambers.' There surely could not have been much doubt about the probability of a successful bombing raid on the gas chambers. The principle of proportionality was clearly on the side of action, and the subsequent inaction by the Allies was an immoral decision.

The principle of proportionality requires that, even when the use of force is obligatory, consideration should be taken to ensure that the appropriate amount of force is employed, decisions based on proportionality should err on the side of intervention, and the great and lasting evil that is perpetuated by genocide should always be at the front of decision-makers' minds, reminding them of their obligation.

Probability of success

The principle of probability of success goes hand in hand with proportionality in Just War doctrine. Simple logic tells us not to engage in a war we have little or no chance of winning. When considering any type of intervention, this logic must be considered. The intervener

must have a reasonable hope of success. It can be much more dangerous to intervene, 'but to do so with such restraint and caution that we
merely add damage to an already bad situation, with no reasonable
hope of success in solving the underlying cause of the intervention'
(Cook 2003: 153). However, the applicability of this principle in the
context of obligatory war is less evident. Of course, intervention in
a case where one has very little chance of success is unwise, but in
situations where obligation is present this is not often the case. For
instance, the combined power of the responsible signatories of the
Geneva Convention is surely sufficient to intervene in a collapsed or
collapsing state that is likely lacking a legitimate government. The
chance of a less successful intervention is not an adequate offset for
the chance of stopping genocide. The horrors of genocide require
action, and a lowered probability of success is not reason enough to
stand by and watch.

One reason for the lack of intervention in the case of Rwanda
was that the perceived chance of success was too low (Regan 1996).
This indicates that there needs to be a fundamental rethinking of
what success is. History has shown that the United States and/or
the United Nations could have sent in just a few thousand troops to
deter the people with machetes and hundreds of thousands of lives
could have been saved (Power 2001). This clearly would have been
a success. In cases of extreme suffering when obligation applies, the
principle of probability of success should be given some consideration,
but only after the other principles. It is not reason enough to prevent
an intervention. If the chances for success are not high enough, a
larger coalition might be needed, but intervention should not be
abandoned. While the obligation to intervene is not something that
should be taken lightly, uncertainty about the probability of success
is not powerful enough to outweigh the obligation.

Last resort

In traditional Just War theory, 'the criterion of last resort underlines
the primacy of peace over war' (Coates 1997: 189). This principle means
that all other options have to be exhausted before the decision is
made to go to war. Resorting to war is not just so long as there is a
reasonable hope that means short of war resolve the problem (Regan

1996). Hoffmann (2003) argues that last resort can be a tricky concept because opponents of force will never believe that absolutely every option has been exhausted and proponents of intervention will argue for an early entry in order to save more lives. Thus, the principle of last resort may create a bias against using military force until all other options have been exhausted (Haass 1999). Because of this bias, last resort as it is currently understood is inappropriate for the case of obligatory intervention.

The theory of obligatory war recognizes that sometimes the evil being committed is so great that military intervention is the first *and* last resort. For instance, this may likely be the case when it comes to genocide. Unfortunately, it is rarely or never the case that genocide can be stopped by means short of forceful intervention. There may be cases where genocide has been prevented without the use of force, but once the mass killing has started any means short of intervention are not likely to be effective. The Just War principles as they are adapted for this case of obligatory war do not necessitate diplomacy or sanctions; what they do necessitate is the use of force.

The original formulation of Just War theory allows the decision-maker a choice between war or inaction; the fulfillment of the Just War principles simply permit an act of war – they do not require it. This is a fundamental difference between original Just War theory and the theory of obligatory war. When it comes to significant crises, like genocide, that require intervention, it is unlikely that rogue governments, militias, or even ordinary and unorganized people, as was the case in Rwanda, are going to be willing or even able to negotiate with the international community. Traditional bargaining tools like economic sanctions and international shaming are not likely to be effective when genocide is taking place. Sanctions and diplomacy will not work with these actors. It is the onset of genocide itself that signals the need for the last resort. The obligation is an obligation to use force.

Case Study: Rwanda

One of the major questions that have been raised about efforts to put together a theory of obligation to intervene in humanitarian crises asks whether it is necessary to have such a theory when a moral obligation to intervene exists independent of the application of Just War principles. Genocide is an area where many scholars have posited a moral obligation to intervene outside of a theory of obligatory warfare, arguing that 'the absence of forceful response is moral failure' (Power 2002; Ansah 2005). Even given this supposition, however, states often fail to respond to genocide with forceful intervention. When faced with the difficult decision of whether or not to intervene in genocide, many states shirk their obligation and allow it to continue. No case in recent history is more compelling evidence of the failure of states and intergovernmental organizations to intervene in genocide than the case of Rwanda in the summer of 1994.

In the early 1990s, Rwanda was an unstable country, wracked by civil war, and precariously held together by the peace agreement of the Arusha Accords. The conflict between the Hutus and the Tutsis in Rwanda has been described as resembling a caste division. Rubenstein observes:

> As is well-known, Rwanda's population consists of two distinct groups, the Hutu and the Tutsi, who between them comprise 99 per cent of the population. They are not precisely distinctive 'ethnic groups' in the normal sense of the term, as they speak the same language and are not separate tribes ... In some respects, they correspond more to separate castes, with, traditionally, the Tutsis being dominant. (Rubinstein 2004: 287)

On April 6, 1994, President Juvenal Habyarimana's plane was shot down and the presidential guard began slaughtering the Tutsi. Most investigators hypothesized that the Hutu president was assassinated by extremist Hutu groups within Rwanda, interested in exterminating the Tutsi population, with most fingers pointing towards the president's wife, Agathe, and her political group, the Akazu (Prunier 1995; Sjoberg and Gentry 2007). After the assassination of the President, the conflict 'erupted into a full-scale genocide' (Power 2002: 331). As Sjoberg and Gentry describe, 'Before the genocide ... there were between 900,000 and 1 million Tutsis in the population. At the end of the summer of 1994, only 130,000 Tutsis survived; between 70 and 80 percent of the Tutsi population had been killed' (2007: 159). This genocide was of unprecedented speed and brutality, the 'fastest, most efficient killing spree of the 20th century' (Power 2002, 334). As Sperling has documented: 'nearly all the victims were killed in the first ninety days of the Rwandan genocide, making the rate of genocide five times as swift as the Nazis' extermination of the Jews during the Holocaust' (2006: 639).

Just three days after the genocide began, the *New York Times* ran a story reporting that tens of thousands of Rwandans had been murdered already (Schmidt 1994b). In fact, information concerning the swiftness and brutality of the killing was being transmitted from peacekeeping forces on the ground to world leaders all over the globe in real time (Power 2001; Wheeler 2000). As Samantha Power later explained, 'lists of victims were prepared ahead of time ... many early Tutsi victims found themselves specifically, not generally, targeted,' and the international community watched as they were killed (2002: 333). Hutu leaders made public statements like 'without the Tutsi, all Rwanda's problems would be over' (Melvern 2004: 229) and instructed soldiers 'not to spare anyone, not even the fetus or the old' (Sperling 2006: 649). The international community was aware of *this* genocide almost from its outset, and as it was occurring. It was clear from very early on that intervening in the mass killings would have saved tens of thousands, even hundreds of thousands, of innocent lives and would have been a just cause.

The conditions in the Rwandan genocide were close to the best possible for intervention. Not only was the international community aware of the genocide from the beginning and morally obligated to intervene; the United Nations already had troops in Rwanda to ensure that the peace of the Arusha Accords was kept. The multilateral nature of the United Nations makes it a clear right authority to intervene in such a case, although France, the United States, and Belgium, all potential candidates for intervention, also had a moral obligation to act. Somewhat disturbingly, it appears as though the international community knew of its obligation and, instead of responding to it, avoided it. When Belgium decided to withdraw its peacekeeping forces, it did not want to be the only country doing so, implicitly acknowledging the moral cowardice of withdrawing at such a time of crisis, and so requested that the United States withdraw in tandem (Ronayne 2001).

The United States was perhaps the most cognizant, and the most evasive, of its obligation to intervene in the genocide. Interestingly enough, the Clinton administration was very careful to avoid using the word 'genocide,' seemingly acknowledging that recognizing the slaughter as a genocide would obligate them to action. Even those in the administration who were trying to stop the genocide, like Prudence Bushnell, were reined in by the administration and forbidden from using the politically loaded term 'genocide' (Department of State 1994). In fact, it is noted in the relevant State Department memo that although there are no legal consequences of using the term, doing so would increase pressure on the United States to act (Department of State 1994). The very act of strategizing to avoid obligation supports the notion that there is a moral responsibility to intervene in genocide.

Clearly, neither the United States nor any other state or governing body had right intention at the time of the genocide; if they had, their intention would have led them to make attempts to stop it. However, even lacking right intent, if these states had intervened, this principle of obligatory war would have been fulfilled. In the case of obligatory war, it is the action that is most important, not the intention. While right intention is desirable, even a self-interested intention would have brought the desired result. The ends are able to trump the means in this case because of the justness of the cause.

Perhaps the most controversial requirements of obligatory war in the case of the Rwandan genocide are the principle of proportionality and the related principle of probability of success. How many people might die and what greater destruction might be caused in the process of attempting to stop the genocide? UN force commanders believed that between 5,000 and 8,000 troops would be able to stop the slaughter (cited in Wheeler 2000), a number that the collective signatories of the Genocide Convention could easily muster. In his assessment of the conflict three years after the fact, Scott Feil (1998) concluded that Rwandan civilians could have been protected with little or no risk to US soldiers. Instead, when the ten Belgian peacekeepers who were protecting the moderate Hutu prime minister in Rwanda were murdered, the Belgian government withdrew its forces from the country. The UN similarly withdrew its forces and no obligated nation deployed the needed resources in a timely manner.

It appears that in this situation proportionality was calculated according to classic standards of self-interest. Just weeks after the genocide began, President Clinton emphasized that intervening was not in America's self-interest, stating: 'whether we get involved in any of the world's ethnic conflicts in the end must depend on the cumulative weight of the American interests at stake' (1994). Such an approach ignores the moral obligation of intervening in genocide and neglects to acknowledge the international impacts of such a tragedy. In 1994 the world ignored Rwanda, and has had trouble dealing with other occurrences of genocide that followed, particularly the most recent situation in Sudan.

Although some have argued that the probability of success in Rwanda was low, it should not have been a question of deploying troops quickly enough. Within days, the French sent paratroopers to rescue French citizens and other foreign nationals in Rwanda (Wheeler 2000). Other UN forces were already in place, but their mandate prevented them from intervening in the violence. The fact that information about the genocide was able to get out to the international community so quickly means that the last resort of forceful intervention was a viable option and should have been utilized.

The decision to use force is never one that should be made lightly. However, as the theory of obligatory war argues, there are circumstances under which using force is not only allowed but ought to be required. The Rwandan genocide represents just such a case. Bureaucrats may argue that deploying more peacekeepers, and the fatalities that would surely accompany such a deployment, would ultimately mean more criticism and fewer resources for the UN (Barnett 1993), but such arguments fail to justify inaction in the case of an obligation to stop genocide. The world had an obligation to act in the Rwandan genocide and now it bears the moral responsibility for what happened. Intervention in the 1994 genocide in Rwanda was obligatory, and it would have been a Just War.

The 'value added' of a theory of obligatory war, then, is that it puts the moral obligation to intervene in genocide in concrete terms within a tradition (Just War theory) that states often use to analyze and/or justify their war-making decisions. It not only articulates the circumstances in which a moral obligation to intervene turns into a concrete obligation to intervene, but does so in a language that is the common currency of war decision-making. In the case of Rwanda, the moral obligation to intervene that the existence of genocide brought about failed to inspire states to use force in order to stop the violence.

This chapter suggests that the use of the 'old theory' of Just War could be used to deduce a theory of obligatory war that translates that moral obligation into concrete terms and makes states more likely to intervene when obligated. The existence of a theory of obligatory war may encourage states to intervene in the next genocide.

Conclusion

In some ways, we can consider genocide a 'new' problem – certainly, ethnic conflicts have been on the rise since the end of the Cold War. It is also a new problem in terms of expressed concern by the international community, both in terms of governmental condemnation and the activism of transnational advocacy networks. But the mere recognition of its novelty as a serious problem in modern international relations does not mean that all previous knowledge of international political morality need be discarded. In fact, I have argued just the opposite. Just War theory can still inform international responses to genocide, but innovation is required to apply the solutions of the past to the problems of today. What is missing from our current understanding of the 'new' problem of genocide is a set of clear moral principles that inform the decision of whether and how to respond to genocide. The Just War tradition is able to provide these principles, and in doing so it both compels and requires action when it comes to these types of crises.

I have focused on the case of genocide, but this is not the inherent endpoint of a theory of obligatory intervention. By utilizing this arguably easy case, I have attempted to show how Just War theory can be adopted to modern problems like genocide and humanitarian intervention. We can consider states moral actors, and we can consider them morally obligated to act under certain conditions – the principles of Just War theory tell us as much.

5

Justifying Changes in International Norms of Sovereignty

Jennifer M. Ramos

Challenges to international peace and security in the twenty-first century offer us a chance to reflect on how we might understand the changing dynamics of state interactions within the international system. One of the 'new' developments concerns the evolution of the norm of sovereignty. As norms direct states in matters of appropriateness, this is essentially a matter of changing understandings of what constitutes 'right' or 'wrong' state behavior, internally and externally. This chapter focuses on this 'new' development, within the context of the United States' military intervention in Afghanistan. I draw on a classic social psychological approach, cognitive dissonance, to understand how state sovereignty partially depends on compliance with counterterrorism norms.[1] In the current environment, states are required to comply with counterterrorism norms or risk external interference by other states. I suggest that this new understanding of sovereignty has evolved, in part, as a consequence (often unintended) of state actions directed towards fighting terrorism.

Clearly, states with a preponderance of power have a disproportionate say in which norms get propagated within the international community because they have the capability to act on behalf of a norm, if they wish. However, what I will suggest here is that even when a major power state acts primarily out of its own self-interest, with the normative argument being secondary, the action may have the *unintended* consequence of modifying the normative environment within which other (minor power) states act.

Actions of the most powerful states transform the context within which states operate. That is, military interventions contribute to the evolution of the normative environment. However, the theory I propose to explain these changes is counterintuitive. One would generally expect an arduous military intervention to exhibit *less* commitment to the norms that it embodies. But the opposite may be true. Insights from social psychology, and cognitive dissonance in particular, lead us to expect that such a situation would actually yield *more* commitment to the norms that were used to justify the intervention. Leading states are able to pursue their material agenda, but with norm evolution as the by-product of military intervention.

State sovereignty is a norm at the very core of international relations. Thus far, state sovereignty has referred to the idea that a state has ultimate authority over its policies, which are legally protected under international law. For over 350 years, state sovereignty has arguably served as the guiding principle for state behavior.[2] It is central to the normative structure of the international system; one can imagine a web of interconnected norms, with state sovereignty at the center. Challenges to state sovereignty imply tensions with other competing norms. For example, a state cannot hold human rights norms and absolute sovereignty in equal esteem since human rights norms now compel states to act in cases of gross human rights abuses, which implies a sovereignty contingent upon certain standards of government performance. While many point to the human rights arena as the classic example of where legitimate infringement of state sovereignty is possible, we are also seeing parallels in other policy domains. In this chapter, I take up the emerging norm of counter-terrorism, in which states are bound by international law to comply with international counterterrorism conventions. In this context, sovereignty is contingent upon a state meeting these requirements. If not, a state risks interference by the international community.

This chapter is structured as follows. First, I offer a definition of sovereignty. Next, I highlight the significance of changes to state sovereignty by providing an overview of the current political and academic debates. I then propose cognitive dissonance as the mechanism by which changes in understandings of sovereignty occur, and set forth my expectations within the context of the global war on terrorism. I then demonstrate how this 'old' theory can explain changes in what is considered legitimate state behavior, as dictated by sovereignty norms, by examining the case of the United States' military intervention in Afghanistan.

Absolute and Contingent Sovereignty

It is generally agreed that absolute sovereignty can be broadly defined as 'supreme authority within a territory' (Philpott 2001: 16). Absolute sovereignty assumes that a government's policies are legally protected by international law and that external actors cannot seek to modify those policies. For many years, since its codification in the Peace of Westphalia, absolute sovereignty has served as the dominant norm in the international system. Yet, sovereign authority can be less than absolute, and so I conceive of sovereignty in the political sense as a continuum (Rosenau 1995: 195), from absolute sovereignty in the Westphalian sense to world government, in which states exercise little independent authority over their internal affairs.[3] More conservatively, world government does not necessarily mean a global *Leviathan*, but a 'federation, a union of separate states that allocate certain powers to a central government while retaining many others for themselves' (Talbot 2001; Etzioni 2004). Between these two poles, one may locate 'contingent sovereignty.'[4] With contingent sovereignty, a state is required to maintain certain standards of political performance, wherein external intervention is allowed when these standards are egregiously violated (ICISS 2001; Jackson 1990; Keren and Sylvan 2002). The closer we move in the direction of contingencies, the more numerous and stringent they become.

Sovereignty Continuum

Absolute ——————— *Contingent* ——— *World government*

Any conception of sovereignty reflects a process, rather than a constant state. Sovereignty has no inherent meaning in and of itself. Rather, it is an intersubjective process involving the existing rules of the international system (structure) and state actors (agents). A change in one affects the other, producing a dynamic relationship. For example, the action (military intervention) of the agent can influence the rules of the international system and in turn the subsequent behavior of states. It is at the interstate level, relations between states, where sovereignty resides. A state cannot be sovereign unless it is recognized as such by other states (Ashley 1984; Jackson 1990). Moreover, 'an independent political community which merely claims a right to sovereignty ... but cannot assert this right in practice, is not a state properly so-called' (Bull 1977: 9).

Sovereignty refers to a set of rights and obligations concerning a legally constituted state, which are opposite sides of the same coin. States have rights that dictate which of their actions are legitimate in the eyes of the international community. At the same time, they have obligations to uphold, and upon which their sovereign rights rest. Rights and obligations vary over time, according to the international context, making sovereignty an evolving norm. Rights and obligations may be positive or negative, in the sense that positive rights and obligations encompass what a state is allowed to do, whereas negative rights and obligations dictate what a state cannot be obliged to do. For example, a state has a right to file a complaint with the World Trade Organization (positive right), but a state also has the right not to grant citizenship to foreign nationals (negative right). A state is obliged to comply with international treaties (positive obligation), but a state has no obligation to become a signatory (negative obligation).

Sovereignty also can be viewed through the lens of a state (self) and the international community (other). As illustrated by current challenges to sovereignty, such as human rights norms, there is an emerging shift in sovereignty along these dimensions. Formerly, a state had the *right* to conduct its affairs as it saw fit, behind by the shield of sovereignty. Other states had the *obligation* to respect the sovereignty of that state, thereby reinforcing their own state sovereignty, which could not exist without a common understanding of that norm.

As the Cold War faded and new issues appeared on the global scene, such as genocide and a rise in civil wars, a change in conceptions of sovereignty emerged among major members of the international community. There is an incipient trend, in which a new 'division of responsibility' imposes revised 'rules of the game' for individual states and the international community. States now have *obligations* to fulfill in order to be sovereign, and the international community has a *right* to intervene in the internal affairs of states under certain conditions.

Current Political and Academic Debates on Sovereignty

The debate on sovereignty is not one easily resolved or dispassionately argued. At its core is the question about the 'division of responsibility' between the state and the international community: what falls to the international community, and what is reserved for the state? This is extremely important to the future of international relations, with implications for what is deemed legitimate behavior. States require an agreed allocation of rights and obligations between themselves and the international community, thus facilitating peaceful international interactions and minimizing uncertainty in an anarchic world.

Much of the political debate about these rights and obligations has taken place among the permanent members of the UN Security Council because of the UNSC's power to intervene in the internal affairs of other states, as well as the members' individual capability to act. Each member has a stake in how sovereignty is understood. The arguments on both sides are compelling. Those on the side of absolute sovereignty in all circumstances argue that anything less would be opening a Pandora's box of hegemonic interventions, justified under the cover of restoring international peace and security. In this view, violating sovereignty cannot be objectively justified, and thereby an intervention could not be legitimated.[5] On the other side, states argue that the international community cannot stand by while states fail to protect their citizens, as well as the international community (in some cases), from genocide or terrorism. Especially in the realm of human rights, with particular reference to the horrors of the Holocaust and the Rwandan genocide, the argument for contingent sovereignty is quite persuasive.

As norm-setters, powerful states are especially interested in how the debate plays out. China and Russia are often cited as the leading powers committed to the absolute notion of national sovereignty. In their view, regardless of repressive regimes or gross human rights abuses, a state's sovereignty should be respected. Chinese President Jiang Zemin is strongly opposed to the argument that 'human rights rank higher than sovereignty.'[6] In fact, when the international community sought to remedy the grave situation in Kosovo, Zemin, referring to the absolute sovereignty norm, stated: 'I hereby solemnly reiterate that the military actions against Kosovo and other parts of Yugoslavia violate the norms governing international relations.'[7] In his view, and thereby that of China, 'History and reality tell us that sovereignty is the only premise and guarantee of human rights within each nation.'[8] In other words, if the international community respects the sovereignty of each state, then human rights will follow. China's position is not that human rights abuses by a government are acceptable, but rather that they are an internal matter beyond the scope of the international community's reach. Sovereignty supersedes all other considerations.

These views are mirrored by Russia and, not surprisingly, the two countries often support one another when it comes to the issue of sovereignty. Russia recognized China's sovereignty over Taiwan, supporting the one-China policy, while China supported Russia's sovereignty with regard to Chechnya. Like Zemin, Putin questions the motives of the West in suggesting intervention in the internal affairs of another country. Russia's foreign policy statement in 2000 declared that 'Attempts to belittle the role of a sovereign state as the fundamental element of international relations generates a threat of arbitrary interference in internal affairs.'[9] Moreover, 'Attempts to introduce into the international parlance such concepts as 'humanitarian intervention' and 'limited sovereignty' in order to justify unilateral power actions bypassing the U.N. Security Council are not acceptable.'[10]

There have been instances, however, when states traditionally opposed to infringements on sovereignty have supported 'legitimate' interventions. For example, China supported the international intervention in East Timor and Cambodia. Moreover, it contributed to peacekeeping missions in several countries, such as Mozambique, the Western Sahara, and Iraq/Kuwait. Although China did believe that a legitimate claim for intervention could be made, it would argue that these are exceptions to the rule.

On the other side of the debate, major powers leaning towards a contingent norm of sovereignty include the US and Britain. As US Secretary of State Condoleezza Rice pointed out in April 2007,

The international system is experiencing a dramatic shift, one that we can trace through a series of humanitarian and political crises arising within nations, not necessarily between them; the failure of states from Somalia to Haiti, Bosnia to Afghanistan; and culminating in the events of September the 11th. As a result, we have been compelled to revise our old standard of sovereignty from mere state control to civil and global responsibility.[11]

This reflects the emerging consensus in the US among policymakers that sovereignty need not be the bottom line in international relations. Indeed, this movement began with the end of the Cold War and the US involvement in Somalia, Haiti, Kosovo, and most recently Afghanistan and Iraq. While positioned against significant opposition by China and Russia, the US has a strong ally in this debate, the United Kingdom. The UK argues that

> The UN needs new rules on when it can intervene to keep the peace within a state rather than between states. This is a real dilemma for an organization created to protect national sovereignty against threat. But it cannot be acceptable for oppressive regimes to claim the protection of sovereignty to carry out major violations of international law, such as genocide in Rwanda or ethnic cleansing in Kosovo.[12]

This brief overview of leading powers' perspectives reveals the emerging 'sovereignty divide.' Because sovereignty is at the very core of statehood, changes to it have significant implications for all players in the international system. Being recognized by other states as a sovereign member of the international system means that a state can participate in the community of states, empowered with the privileges and obligations that sovereignty brings. Yet, what it means to be a sovereign state is not only debated in the empirical world of politics, but also among scholars of international relations. Having discussed the political debates on sovereignty, I now turn to the theoretical debates in the academic literature.

During the Cold War, much of the literature in international relations rested on the parsimonious explanations of realism (Morgenthau 1948), later refined by neorealism (Waltz 1979). Realism and its variants have traditionally been used to explain state military actions. This school makes two primary assumptions: (1) anarchy dominates the international system; and (2) states are self-interested, unitary actors (Waltz 1979). States, as rational actors, seek power and security in order to survive in the international system (Jervis 1976; Oye 1985; Walt 1987; Waltz 1979). Geostrategic interests and economic concerns are the primary motivations for state behavior and, in particular, the use of force.

Regardless of the motives they assign to states, whether it be to enhance power or security, both realism and neorealism assume absolute state sovereignty; it is the ability of a state to 'decide for itself how it will cope with its internal and external problems' (Waltz 1979: 96). In addition, sovereignty is 'one [principle] that will not be dislodged easily, regardless of changed circumstances in the material environment' (Krasner 1988: 90).[13] However, the theory implies that sovereignty is contingent on the power of a state. In a world in which 'the strong do what they can, the weak do what they must' (Thucidydes 1910), some states are more sovereign than others. While realism and neorealism are useful to our understanding of the causes of conflict, they do not allow for any mechanism by which change can occur in international relations and thus offer little insight into how the rights and obligations of states vary across contexts.

The other major strand of literature, neoliberalism (including neoliberal institutionalism, liberal interdependence), while sharing some assumptions with realism/neorealism, acknowledges the possibility of change, if only indirectly (Keohane and Nye 1977). Scholars of this school are primarily interested in explaining cooperation among self-interested states, which has led to a plethora of analyses focused on international regimes and organizations. Cooperative developments in the international system, like the evolution of the European Union, pose important questions concerning the nature of sovereignty, since they challenge mechanistic, power-based, models of state interaction. International phenomena such as globalization contribute to the debate as well. Is sovereignty being 'eroded' by technological advances (Rosecrance 1986) or rising global trade? While research from this perspective recognizes the potential for change in the nature of sovereignty, it remains difficult to disentangle what potentially is an endogenous relationship (Thomson 1995). It could be that changes in sovereignty have enabled these phenomena to happen, or it may be that these occurrences led to renewed understandings of sovereignty. In these explanations, it is possible for sovereignty to be both a cause and a consequence. Further, the interaction of notions of sovereignty with other issues like rising trade may imply a mutually constitutive relationship, constructed by the practices of individuals.

The idea that humans contribute to the maintenance and creation of social reality, or social facts, is one of the core tenets of the constructivist school. In this perspective, concepts like sovereignty are variables, not constants. Constructivism takes seriously the logic of appropriateness, which refers to what states ought to do, given social conventions or rules, procedures, and principles for members within a particular group context (Finnemore 1998; March and Olson 1998). While not *dis*regarding material interests, constructivists offer a compelling explanation for state actions by emphasizing the role of identity, norms, and ideas (Black 1999; Hopf 2002; Legro 1997; Risse et al. 1999).

In explaining varying conceptions of sovereignty, these scholars rely on the ability of actors to shape intersubjective understandings of sovereignty (Biersteker and Weber 1996). For example, some argue that the definition of sovereignty fluctuates according to dominant ideas in the international system (Barkin and Cronin 1994; Philpott 2001). Barkin and Cronin argue that the post-World War II era stressed *state* sovereignty, rather than the nation-based definition, in reaction to the extreme nationalism of Nazim. This could be one reason why during this period sovereignty trumped individual rights. Similarly, others assert identity as the engine of change, in that changes in collective identities drive changes in the constitutive rules of sovereignty (Hall 1999). If the most salient identity of citizens is that regarding the state (e.g. patriotism), then sovereignty will be defined in terms of the state. In contrast, if group identity becomes the most important, it will be reflected in a sovereignty that focuses on the rights of the group.

These contributions and other constructivist research offer important insights for understanding state sovereignty and its evolution. They illuminate an important part of the story by demonstrating the influence of ideas and identities on conceptions of sovereignty. However, there is one missing link: action. Without this, we cannot know what sovereignty really means at any given point in time (Dewey 1929). Leaders in the international community can argue that states have certain obligations to fulfill, as in the area of protecting human rights, but without actions to bolster these claims this discourse remains empty rhetoric or 'cheap talk.' In other words, the concept of sovereignty (as with any concept) is necessarily grounded in action; the meaning of sovereignty is dependent upon the actions taken upon its behalf. Political actions have the ability to shape ideas about sovereignty. We know that changes to sovereignty have occurred when we see changes in both related actions and its corresponding discourse.

Explaining 'New' Norms through an 'Old' Lens

Whereas change may occur for some states through individual emulation (horizontal reproduction[14]) of successful states' behavior, I am interested in determining how the 'successful' states reinforce or modify existing norms. Emulation may reflect norm change in less prestigious positions, but whom do you emulate if you are one of the leading states?[15] Cognitive dissonance offers insight into how norm change occurs for such states, given the power realities.[16]

Within a complex and uncertain international environment, leading states may change their conception of certain norms only after knowing the outcome of a behavior based on that norm.[17] In this way, a norm may come into being without the explicit rational calculation of the leading states. This proposition rests on cognitive dissonance theory, which explains how our ideas may be influenced by our actions. Developed by Leon Festinger (1957), the theory begins with the observation that relevant cognitions, or pieces of knowledge, can be either consonant or dissonant. If consonant, they create no psychological tension because they are mutually implied. However, if the cognitions clash, or are not mutually implied, they create psychological discomfort for the person or social entity, which the latter will seek to lessen by avoiding information that accentuates it or by changing the cognition. One can exaggerate the benefits of the chosen decision and downplay the drawbacks, while applying the reverse to the alternatives not chosen (Shultz and Lepper 1996). For instance, US legislators who initially supported the Iraq War and now are faced with evidence that the United States has lost the war have either withdrawn support or have intensified their efforts towards justifications for the war. Both responses demonstrate the tendency of individuals to seek cognitive consistency, when confronted with conflicting information.

Cognitive dissonance has a long tradition in psychology, and has sparked a number of research paradigms. This is mainly because Festinger's original theory was set out in 'very general, highly abstract terms' (Harmon-Jones and Mills 1999: 5). One line of research has focused on the condition of forced compliance and cognitive dissonance. It further refines and specifies the mechanisms by which people bring their previously dissonant cognitions into line with one another. When someone behaves in contrast to their beliefs or attitudes, dissonance is aroused. However, promises of reward or threat of punishment help someone to alleviate psychological tension caused by dissonance (Harmon-Jones and Mills 1999: 8). These new cognitions aid in justifying the given action. The original study, by Festinger and Carlsmith (1959), found that the smaller the reward for saying what one does not believe, the greater the opinion changes to agree with what was said. In this experiment, researchers had subjects perform an extremely dull task. After some time, those subjects were asked to aid in the same study by telling new subjects (confederates) that the task was really exciting. In exchange for their help, some received $20 and others received only $1. Surprisingly, when the subjects were asked to rate the boring task, those receiving $1 were more likely to rate the task positively than those who were paid $20.

Several other research paradigms in cognitive dissonance research also exist. These include the free-choice paradigm (Brehm 1956; Shultz and Lepper 1996), the belief–disconfirmation paradigm (Burris et al. 1997; Festinger et al. 1956), and the effort-justification paradigm (Beauvois and Joule 1996; Aronson and Mills 1959). Each of these explores how cognition interacts with motivation and emotion within a cognitive dissonance framework.

Cognitive dissonance theory is especially applicable to interventions to halt terrorist activities within states because of the tension between sovereignty norms of non-intervention, on the one hand, and enforcing international peace and security as they relate to counterterrorism, on the other hand. Because of this tension and a host of other domestic and international concerns, the decision to intervene is not automatic. Most states are reluctant to use force abroad; when they do decide to intervene, there will be greater dissonant cognitions present than in easier decisions (Brehm 1956), particularly as the intervention persists. This dissonance has important implications for how states reconcile competing cognitions. For example, a state may take military action against another state that violates the norm of sovereignty. In the context of humanitarian military intervention, state sovereignty as a concept that includes obligations to protect human rights cannot exist merely as an idea in a vacuum; it becomes meaningful through action. Depending on the outcomes of the military interventions, this action may contribute to the idea that human rights norms trump absolute sovereignty norms since the two ideas cannot coexist in cases of humanitarian intervention because they are competing cognitions (Festinger 1957; Brehm 1956). Thus, sovereignty could become conditional on protecting human rights (contingent sovereignty).

Determining Dissonance

In order to apply cognitive dissonance to understanding how norms of sovereignty change (within the domain of counterterrorism), I focus on two important pieces of information (cognitions) about the intervention: its costs and success. This information is necessary in order to assess whether a situation of cognitive dissonance has occurred. By costs, I mean both the intervention's casualties and the political liabilities created at home. I regard success in terms of the degree to which the objective for the intervention has been achieved. Taken together, the costs and success of an intervention, via cognitive dissonance, aid in forming specific expectations about the conditions under which contingent sovereignty will be reinforced or challenged.

Why costs and success? Within the rational choice paradigm, scholars regularly employ models that incorporate the likely costs and the probability of success to predict the policy choices of decision-makers (Bueno de Mesquita 1981, 2000; Allison and Zelikow 1999; McDermott 1992). In these models, 'the decision maker uses a maximizing strategy in calculating how best to achieve his goals' (Bueno de Mesquita 1981: 31). The decision-maker evaluates different options and then selects the 'alternative that offers the best combination of a high probability of success and low cost' (Ray 1998: 123). In general, a rationalist would expect that a policy yielding minimal results would be shelved, while a student of cognitive dissonance would predict that the decision-maker might reinforce her commitment to the policy in the same situation, because doing so relieves the psychological tension posed by the dissonant cognitions. Rationalist approaches overlook the fact that, in addition to weighing pieces of information, decision-makers also typically work in a complex political environment that may alter the internal decision-making processes of individuals. Decisions are not simply a result of a mechanical process but are rather the results of an individual's cognitive interaction with information. In short, though both approaches use the same criteria, costs, and success, to form expectations for changes in sovereignty conceptions, there is a sharp divergence between rational choice and cognitive dissonance expectations.

Cognitive Dissonance and Norm Change

Because the act of intervention implies a contingent sovereignty norm, cognitions about the intervention will either be consonant or dissonant with that decision. The most dissonant situation, in terms of intervention outcomes, is one in which there are high costs and low success for the intervener. Here I would expect that contingent sovereignty would be strongly reinforced because it would require *more effortful* justification. By 'strongly' reinforced, I mean not only that the intervener's discourse focuses on the *obligations* of states to fight for a particular cause, but also that states have an implicit *right* to intervene if states fail in their obligations. Because of the mission's cost and lack of success, there will be a heightened need for justification of the action, grounded, at least in part, in the norm it reflects.[18] What follows will be greater efforts to articulate that justification(s), in order to mobilize those who believe in the justification or the norm. In other words, once the action is taken, there is a need to justify it and mobilize the leader's domestic and international constituencies through reiteration.

To examine this proposition, I analyze the content of speeches given by one of the main interveners in Afghanistan, the United States, to assess changes in the understanding of sovereignty, since political actions and discourse go hand in hand.[19] I look at the discussions of sovereignty as they relate to the global 'war on terror' prior to and during the intervention. I employ content analysis because 'language is essentially constitutive of institutional reality' (Searle

1995: 59). Content analysis focuses on the significance of communication in constructing social reality. In short, it examines what is said along with who is speaking and who is being spoken to. While some deny that every discourse has a corresponding practice (Fischer 1992), others demonstrate that the reverse may be true – that every practice has a corresponding discourse (Banerjee 1997). Within the context of this chapter, this means that military intervention has an associated discourse that can reveal meanings of the concept of sovereignty at particular points in time. Furthermore, as Searle rightly argues, 'One general principle is this: To the extent that the new institutional status is of major importance, we are more inclined to require that it be created by explicit speech acts performed according to strict rules. And these speech acts are themselves institutional facts' (Searle 1995: 116).

In order to collect the speech data, I used the search term 'terrorism' as a topic in the UN's database of speeches, UNBISnet.[20] In addition, I searched the database for specific events that were associated with terrorism, such as the Pan Am airliner bombing over Lockerbie, Scotland. The database contains all UNSC meetings for the time period under investigation, the post-Cold War era.[21] I use the universe of speeches, rather than a sample. For the United States, there are twenty-four speeches that meet the above criteria after the war in Afghanistan began, and nine speeches prior to its onset.[22]

The United States and the War on Terror

The war in Afghanistan constitutes the first time a global coalition has intervened in a state on behalf of counterterrorism. In reaction to the devastating terrorist attacks on the World Trade Center and the Pentagon in 2001, the UN Security Council unanimously adopted resolution 1373, which 'obliges all States to criminalize assistance for terrorist activities, deny financial support and safe haven to terrorists and share information about groups planning terrorist attack.' In other words, in the interest of international peace and security, states have the responsibility to the international community to uphold certain standards of internal behavior in the realm of counterterrorism. As demonstrated by the military intervention in Afghanistan shortly after the resolution, states that fail to comply risk the possibility of external interference and, at its most extreme, foreign military intervention.

Driven by the 9/11 attacks, the United States intervened in Afghanistan with two objectives: to remove the Taliban regime from power and to eliminate al-Qaeda and the Taliban as a terrorist threat (including capturing Osama bin Laden) (Bush 2001a). The first task was successfully accomplished, though the Taliban continues to challenge this. On October 7, 2001, the United States and the United Kingdom began aerial bombing, as troops from the Afghan Northern Alliance and NATO engaged their targets on the ground. Operation Enduring Freedom destroyed communications, electricity supplies, and terrorist training camps in and around Afghanistan's major cities. By November, the Taliban had left Kabul, the capital city, and an interim Afghan government began to form, headed by Hamid Karzai in 2002. However, with subsequent resurgence in Taliban activity, this can only be assessed as a partial success.

The second objective remains elusive. In December 2001, the hunt for Osama bin Laden continued in the mountainous region of Tora Bora, though he never was found. Many believed he slipped over the border into Pakistan under cover of night. Redoubling their efforts, the international coalition took on the Taliban and al-Qaeda in the Shah-i-Kot valley and Arma mountains in Operation Anaconda. This operation lasted a total of sixteen days, from March 2 to March 18, 2002, though the success of its mission to destroy Taliban and al-Qaeda forces remains unclear. These forces appear to have retreated into remote caves and border areas, but only for a short while. After recruiting and reorganizing, the Taliban and al-Qaeda came back strong in 2003, and continue to challenge the international coalition, according to statistics on the number of Taliban attacks.[23]

Accordingly, the costs to the United States have been increasing. In terms of public opinion, the percentage of Americans that believed the war in Afghanistan was a mistake has increased by a factor of four, from 9 percent in November 2001 to 25 percent in 2004 (Carroll 2007). At the same time, the number of American casualties has increased. Throughout the war, the United States has had between 10,000 and 21,000 troops in Afghanistan.[24] According to icasualties.org, the number of casualties per year remained consistent through the early years, averaging 50 deaths, but then spiked in 2005 and 2006 to 98 and 99 deaths, respectively.[25] This resulted in cumulative losses through 2006 of 357 soldiers, which represents 69 percent of the coalition's total losses (516 deaths).

Given the high-cost, low-success intervention in Afghanistan, it is clear that the military intervention presents a situation of cognitive dissonance for the United States. In order to relieve the dissonance, I expect that the justifications for the war in Afghanistan, in terms of sovereignty, will reinforce a contingent sovereignty norm, compared to the pre-9/11 discourse. Contingent sovereignty implies that sovereignty is dependent on a state's fulfillment of its counterterrorism obligations. As the war continues, there should not be any reference to the right of Afghanistan to conduct its affairs as it sees fit, but more focus on the responsibility of a state to its own citizens and citizens around the world for the sake of international peace and security. This should be complemented by discourse bearing on the international community's obligation and increasing responsibility to deal with this problem, if Afghanistan is unable or unwilling to do so. I expect this to contrast with American views on sovereignty and counterterrorism before the war, which would express greater recognition of the rights of states to conduct their affairs without outside interference, though limited, perhaps, by the need for states to comply with international law.

Stated US Views on Sovereignty before the War in Afghanistan

Prior to 9/11, and in the post-Cold War period, the United States described terrorism as an important concern of all states, and stressed the need for international condemnation of states that sponsor terrorism. In this period, the United States emphasized state compliance with international obligations as well as the international community's obligation to maintain international peace and security. To help illuminate the views of the United States on sovereignty in the policy domain of counterterrorism, the following are summaries of discourse with examples of statements that characterize views at this time. This will be followed by a review of the content analysis conducted on these speeches.

One of the most memorable terrorist attacks in recent history occurred just as the Cold War was ending. In 1988, terrorist bombs brought down Pan Am flight 103 over Lockerbie, Scotland. As the investigation progressed, mounting evidence pointed to the involvement of the Libyan government. The immediate perpetrators were alleged to be two Libyan nationals, which raised the question of how and where they would be tried. From the perspective of the United States, Libya had an international obligation to uphold, and the international community had a responsibility to see that Libya complied with its obligation to turn over the suspects to international authorities.[26] At no point did the United States mention Libya's prerogative as a sovereign state.

Similarly, after an assassination attempt by terrorists on Egyptian president Hosni Mubarak in 1995, the United States Ambassador to the UN, Madeleine Albright, argued that 'The Government of the Sudan, which must bear responsibility for the acts it allows its guests to perform, also has the responsibility to extradite those guests to face justice.'[27] Thus, Ambassador Albright acknowledged a state's obligation to enforce counterterrorism measures within the state, and to comply with international conventions against terrorism. In the same speech, she also mentioned that the international community condemns such behavior of a state (Sudan) for not having even met one of the 'minimum' obligations (extradite criminals) of a state that wants to live in 'peace with their neighbors.' For not meeting this obligation, Sudan faced international condemnation and isolation. Furthermore, the international community 'is prepared to apply measured, incremental pressure on the Government of Sudan until it meets fully its obligations.'[28] By 'pressure,' Albright implies the use of sanctions, which have been traditional measures of retaliation for 'bad' behavior of states, but do not directly challenge a state's sovereignty.

What is possible in the realm of punishment for infringements by a state of its international obligations is implicitly constrained by sovereignty norms. In US discourse, we find the United States encouraging cooperation in matters related to terrorism, while refraining from discussing the obligations of the international community to step in. For example, in the context of the US embassy bombings in Kenya and Tanzania, the United States declared that: 'We call upon Member States to support the ongoing investigations.'[29] This reflects a

Figure 5.1   US conceptions of sovereignty before military intervention

State rights ▯ 4%
State obligations 89%
International community's rights 11%
International community's obligations 77%

strategy of encouraging cooperation, without compelling it. This kind of discourse continues after sanctions were set in place against the Taliban regime in 1999. The United States implored: 'It is incumbent upon all of us in the community of nations to stand together and to stand strong. We must be relentless in our pursuit, using all means necessary to combat terrorists and their supporters, and we must continue to work together here and elsewhere to this end.'[30]

Along with this focus on cooperation, the United States also emphasized the use of sanctions against states that harbor terrorists, and urged other states to sign the numerous counterterrorism conventions.[31] The United States asserted somewhat vaguely: 'all of us have the responsibility to act accordingly.'[32]

The statements and their associated beliefs for the pre-9/11 period can perhaps most easily be illustrated through content analysis. As Figure 5.1 illustrates, the United States believed strongly that states had certain obligations to the international community to fulfill, as reflected in 89 percent of its speeches. With regard to the international community, the United States placed great value on the obligation of all states to fight terrorism together (in 77 percent of speeches). As a threat to international peace and security, counterterrorism presented an appropriate policy pursuit for the international community, with the possibility of a *right* to supersede states' prerogatives (in 11 percent of speeches), though the United States does continue to defend states' rights in some of its speeches (4 percent). Taken together, these indicators present a baseline for comparing post-9/11 beliefs to assess change, to which I now turn.

Stated US Views on Sovereignty
after the War in Afghanistan Began

Do US views on sovereignty continue unchanged, or move towards a firmer belief in contingent sovereignty? In the following, I first describe statements made as the war carries on, and then consider the results of the content analysis.

The day after 9/11, the United States asserted that it would make no distinction between terrorists and those who harbor them.[33] In this sense, host states are considered to be as culpable as the terrorists they harbor, and therefore subject to the same punishment. In the beginning, however, the United States was reluctant to let go of the traditional sovereignty norm: 'the War on Terrorism starts within each of our respective, sovereign borders.'[34] At the same time, however, the United States argued that 'all states now have the legal, as well as political and moral, obligation to act against it.'[35] This implies that in the pursuit of terrorism, nothing is off limits – not even violations of sovereignty. Taken together, statements by the United States form a conflicting picture of the rights and obligations of states and the international community. This is not surprising, given the changes affecting the sovereignty norm at the time. We should not expect an overnight change, but a gradual move towards a contingent norm, especially as the war in Afghanistan rages on.

The obligation for states to act looks more like a favor to the United States than like an international obligation: 'And so, in defense of shared values and out of a sense of shared vulnerability, the world answered President Bush's call for a great global coalition against terrorism.'[36] Yet, as the military intervention in Afghanistan continued, the discourse began to change to one of responsibility of states at home *and* abroad. There was much discussion about how states are obligated to 'weave counterterrorism' into national law, as well as international institutions.[37] We begin to see statements concerning external obligations, for states to work with other states. Furthermore, the Counter Terrorism Committee (and later with the CTED) was introduced as an independent monitoring body to check to see if states are actually implementing the international conventions against terrorism, a body that the United States continues to emphasize its support for in its discourse.[38]

In fighting terrorism, the United States maintained that the international community is 'charged with a heavy responsibility' and that Resolution 1373 'is generating a worldwide juridical transformation'[39] in the rights and obligations of states. The United States repeatedly emphasized the obligations of states to implement domestic legislation regarding counterterrorism and suggested that states will be pressured to comply if the CTC review finds them lacking. In fact, the United States asserted that the Security Council can be instrumental in overseeing sanctions implementation.[40] This was not an insignificant change in the meaning of sovereignty. In the context of fighting terrorism, the United States supported obligations to implement national laws in accordance with international laws. In addition, the United States approved of the monitoring of states to check their implementation of counterterrorism measures. Within these, states are obliged to freeze assets of suspected terrorists, share intelligence information, and tighten airport security, among other things.[41] These developments reach into realms of traditional state authority, such that even a state's laws become subject to international scrutiny. This clearly goes beyond the bounds of the traditional concept of sovereignty.

Content analysis offers more tangible evidence (see Figure 5.2). While the United States rarely defended absolute sovereignty in the period following the Cold War up to the war in Afghanistan, it *never* mentioned states' rights during its military campaign (from 4 percent to 0 percent). Moreover, the United States held more strongly to its belief in the obligations of the international community to lead the 'war on terror.' In terms of total speeches, such statements increased from 77 percent to 83 percent. However, it is more interesting that speeches discussing the obligations of states declined from 89 percent to 79 percent. One explanation could be that the number of states that are parties to international counterterrorism conventions has increased, so that there is less need to emphasize this. In that case, the United States has turned to an increased emphasis on the international community's efforts in fighting terrorism, especially since global terrorism is a threat that states alone cannot deal with. Thus, the only solution is to work together, even if it means that the international community takes on rights formerly accorded to the state. The United States mentions the *rights* of the international

Figure 5.2   US conceptions of sovereignty before and during military intervention

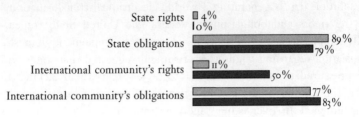

community with regards to states' affairs in half of its speeches, up from 11 percent in the pre-9/11 period.

In sum, the evidence supports my expectations. As the United States continued in an increasingly expensive and unsuccessful war in Afghanistan, the more it reinforced its commitment to contingent sovereignty in order to relieve cognitive dissonance. Stronger beliefs in both international obligations and rights pervade the United States' speeches given in the post-9/11 period, as compared to the previous years.

Conclusion

The case of the United States points to movement away from absolute conceptions of sovereignty, towards contingent sovereignty. As a participant in the military intervention in Afghanistan, the United States experienced shifts in its understandings of the rights and responsibilities of states and the international community in combating terrorism. Although counterintuitive, this change is consistent with the predictions of cognitive dissonance, which aids in explaining how attitudes change after a decision has been made. In the case of the United States, the increasingly costly and unsuccessful war in Afghanistan compelled the United States to reinforce more strongly the contingent sovereignty norm, in which sovereignty is contingent upon compliance with international counterterrorism conventions. In this situation, increasing its commitment to contingent sovereignty lessens the dissonance created by the outcome of the military intervention and absolute sovereignty. More broadly, this indicates that one way in which political norms change is via the effects of policy actions. These actions require that states justify their actions with a corresponding discourse, which either reinforces or modifies what the international community considers legitimate state behavior. The justifications for the intervention implicitly set a precedent for state interventions about acceptable means of norm enforcement, and reveal standards by which states are judged 'good' or 'bad.'

Previously states were shielded by absolute sovereignty, which has served as a guiding principle of international relations since the seventeenth century. However, as was also argued in Chapter 4, it is currently being challenged by priorities of an apparently higher order, such as the global war on terrorism, which require states to act for the common good. As we have seen in Afghanistan and Somalia, weak, or failed, states are all too often a valuable base for terrorists. Those states may put the lives of millions around the world in danger, a danger which the international community is forced to weigh against the costs of violating sovereignty.

The implications of these challenges to absolute state sovereignty are that the range of legitimate activities within the purview of the international community is expanding, while those of the states are declining. Because the concept of state sovereignty is so central to the conduct of international relations, changes in understandings of it have profound implications for the workings of the international system and the context within which states operate. Moreover, how states and the international community understand their rights and obligations to one another is directly related to the possibility of international conflict and cooperation. As states pursue policies to deal with pressing international issues, their actions have the ability to influence the evolution of the norms that govern the conduct of international relations.

6

Honorable Soldiers,
Questionable Wars?

Frances V. Harbour

The 'war on terror' has reinvigorated the debate in the public and policy worlds about who is responsible for making and fighting unjust wars. Specifically, commentators have drawn attention to the 'new' problem of volunteer soldiers who object to the war that they are sent to fight. There has been increasing attention to the question of whether volunteer soldiers must fight in a war they believe to be illegal and unjust (Lynd 2006). Also, if those soldiers do fight in such a war in fulfillment of their commitment to their state's military, the question shifts to whether or not they have moral responsibility for that fighting, given that it was in some sense against their will.

The question of the voluntariness of individual soldiers' participation in the fighting of unjust wars is in fact not new, either in the policy world or in the theoretical literature. Issues of voluntariness were at the center of the debate about the use of the draft in the United States for the Vietnam War, for example. There is also a long history of scholarship dealing with this question in the Just War tradition.

This chapter argues that those who focus on the 'newness' of the 'just soldier's dilemma' have missed the interesting puzzle. The interesting puzzle is embedded in the Just War tradition that reveals the 'old' nature of the problem. It is the resolution that the Just War tradition comes to after examining the question of soldier responsibility. Curiously, it comes to a negative conclusion about a military person's responsibility to examine the moral status of the war as a whole. Evaluation of the justice of the war, *jus ad bellum*, and of the justice in conducting the fighting, *jus in bello*, are kept rigorously separate. In this paradigm a soldier could fight honorably in a war whose original premises were unacceptable under the principles of *jus ad bellum,* or fight even a just war unjustly. Modern Just War scholar Michael Walzer (1992) argues that the soldier should not be held morally responsible for *participating* in war because fighting a war is seldom a fully voluntary choice. Recently analyst Reuben Brigety (2006) went even further, arguing that soldiers give up their right or duty to make individual choices about the war in which they find themselves by virtue of their military oaths.

The claimed 'newness' of this problem gives us an opportunity to employ *and* reevaluate traditional Just War thought on individual responsibility. By looking at the roles of hypothetical participants in World War II, the Kosovo campaign, the civil war in Sudan, and Iraq, this chapter will argue for a resolution to the dilemma of finding oneself involved with a questionable war that does not discount the soldier's personal moral responsibilities or individual will, but still offers some individual moral distance from the decision to go to war at all. It will find a solution to the inadequacy of traditional Just War responses to the question of individual responsibility *within* Just War theory. It argues that an adaptation of the classic Just War principle of double effect can be used to justify some – but not all – participation when the war's overall justification is suspect. It cannot offer individuals a completely clean moral slate in such cases. It does, however, place fighting in certain questionable wars within the bounds of moral permissibility. It does so by focusing on individual intentions, on the one hand, and causal effects, on the other. To explore this argument let us start with the concept of double effect.

The Principle of Double Effect

In the Western Just War tradition, justice-in-war, *jus in bello*, has two main components: the principles of discrimination and of proportionality. Discrimination forbids military personnel deliberately targeting noncombatants. Proportionality requires that any harm that an act of war causes be kept in balance with the military good it is intended

Figure 6.1   The relationship between effect and side effect

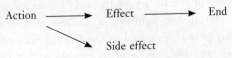

to produce. The ancillary principle of double effect explains how it possible to follow both rules. An act of war is permissible if it is not wrong in itself, does not *target* noncombatants, and also balances the *unintended* moral harm caused with the intended moral benefits. Thus the unintended harm is a side effect of the main action or intention and forms no part of the reason for choosing the main action. Michael Walzer adds a duty to make a good-faith effort to minimize or avoid the unintended harm, but more traditional Just War thinkers do not insist on this last condition.[1]

According to the principle of double effect, behavior can have two kinds of *causal* results: those we intentionally pursue and those that occur as a result of our actions, but are not in the service of our purposes and goals. We can undertake an activity in spite of the side effects, but not because of them. We psychologically *intend* our preferred end, but not the side effect.[2] Figure 6.1 illustrates this relationship. In this formulation one can intend to open a door to exit a house while not intending the subsequent entry of flies. The resulting foreseeable presence of the flies is likely to be inconvenient, but presumably not so harmful that it is wrong to open the door.

Sometimes the connection between intention and side effect is expressed as directly intending desired ends, but only indirectly intending side effects. Not all ethicists endorse such a moral distinction, but it is a key element in justifying the principle of double effect. The principle of double effect requires a metaethical account of morality that considers the will of the actor to be a necessary although not sufficient element in evaluating the morality of inhuman acts and will be explored below. In the meantime, we will treat the concept of double effect as if it were unproblematic in itself.

The principle of double effect is widely applied beyond the Just War tradition. Whenever our actions have complex results, especially harm we do not seek, the principle of double effect is potentially applicable. In everyday life we acknowledge a difference between accidentally harming someone and doing so on purpose, between killing someone and not saving a distant foreigner from starvation. In medicine there are numerous cases where helping patients in the long run involves hurting them in the short run. So, too, most legal traditions distinguish between intentionally committing a crime and various degrees of allowing harm to occur that could have been prevented (Benson 1999: 263–7; Boyle 1980: 527–38).

Consequences are not irrelevant, however, even in this deontological form of reasoning. Traditionally, in order to pass muster under the principle of double effect, the unintended harm that is caused as a side effect has to be proportionate to the good expected. Operations cannot occur without pain, but the pain is no part of what the surgeon wants for the patient, and is something to reduce or avoid if possible. The doctor's intention to heal is carried out by a means that is acceptable in itself, with unintended side effects that do not outweigh the good from the intended effects. The principle of double effect requires personal honesty and due diligence before, during, and after an action or event. It assesses moral responsibility by bringing together intention, act, and causal effects.

Intending to Go to War

Whenever one discusses moral responsibility for actions carried out in the name of a state, one of the first issues is deciding where the line between collective and individual responsibility lies. Scholars, including Toni Erskine, Chris Jones, Christian Barry, and others, argue that at least some groups can be considered collective moral agents and thus morally responsible as institutions for their actions (Erskine 2003b, 2004).

Because individual decisions are constrained by organizational culture, previous policies of the organization, and so on, the choices individuals make in a complex, hierarchical institution are seldom the result of fully 'voluntary' selection in the Aristotelian sense. According to W.H. Walsh, for example, the commitments, rules, and pressures of organizations on decision-makers virtually dictate their choices (Walsh 1970: 1). They are set in motion by their roles and allegiance to the collective. They act in ways they would not in a private capacity. Perhaps most important, the collective power of the institution adds logistical support and provides the possibility of actions that can only be successful if carried out with the resources and goals of a corporate actor.

As Dennis F. Thompson wrote of bureaucracies, 'Because many different officials contribute in different ways to ... decisions and outcomes it is difficult, even in principle, to decide who is morally responsible for policy outcomes' (1980: 905). Although, as Thomson argues, we can still tease out individual responsibility for aspects of policies, this problem of 'many hands' is a powerful argument for not losing sight of collective causation and responsibility.

Nevertheless, the individuals who act on behalf of their group or organization do not give up their own individual moral agency. Individuals retain their own personal responsibility in collective action. Overall policy is made by individuals at higher institutional echelons, and the decisions and choices that turn general directions into concrete behavior take place at all levels. In some tragic situations the only choices may be among doing wrong, observing wrong, and suffering wrong, but these remain choices. To claim otherwise is to make oneself into 'a mere means to the ends of another,' in Kant's famous phrase. Even in an institutional framework, individuals at least assent to acts they do themselves, and others they personally direct or are in charge of overseeing

Personal responsibility for effects of collective action thus differs by rank and function. The decisions of the commander-in-chief have more effects, in more areas, and over more people than a corporal, whatever their respective individual intentions. Nazi generals were generally more to blame than enlisted personnel; Saddam Hussein was more guilty for deaths by gas of Kurdish civilians during the Iran–Iraq War than a hapless draftee in another sector; Winston Churchill was at least as responsible for noncombatant deaths in air-raids as the pilots who actually dropped the bombs.

The traditional divorce of justice-in-war and justice-of-war captures an important aspect of this complex relationship between individuals and organizations in wartime. 'War' is inherently a collective action, carried out by organized groups, in the name of a broader group of organized collective actors. Thus, no single individual can be guilty of – or intend – a 'war' because no single individual has the scope to intend a collective social institution. People can act violently as individuals, of course, even for collective political purposes. Such violence is not 'war,' however, but something more personal.

People in military service intend the results of the *part* of the war to which they direct their own actions and desires, but, by definition, only the collective state actor can intend the collective social institution. To be sure, *all* citizens bear some oversight responsibility for the actions of the state that represents them, but that is a calculation distinct from the problem of identifying the actor who intends a war. Negligence or diligence in overseeing the actions of a state as a citizen should be an element of the causal chain to be evaluated in an individual's contribution to the good or harm caused by the state's war, but it remains the case that only a collective actor can intend the institution 'war.'

It is also morally relevant that the individuals who urge a war, approve a war, plan a war, fight in a war, or are citizens who belong to a group fighting a war cannot *conduct* 'war,' alone. No single individual can carry out all the actions entailed by 'war,' so no single individual can *intend* the whole enterprise. Individuals remain morally responsible for their own *contributions* to the war effort, including any support for the aims of the war, but war-the-collective-enterprise is a responsibility of a collective that is more than the sum of its individual parts.

Military personnel, as well as other citizens as individuals, have the capability to intend their own actions to *contribute* to meeting the collective goals of a given war as defined by the collective actor. Alternately they may simply know that their actions can change some of the probabilities of good or ill that the war will cause. This distinction is important. It opens up the possibility that individuals might 'intend to contribute to the war effort' without 'intending to contribute to victory.' There are important cognitive and affective differences between these intentions even for combatants.

The contention of this chapter is that *in some cases* the principle of double effect could justify continued 'contribution to the war effort' even though the war as a whole fails one or more *jus ad bellum* criteria. The relation between individual intention and wars that violate the various *jus ad bellum* criteria is complex, and will be discussed below. For now, however, the point is that contribution to victory might be a side effect of other actions and intentions.

It is also important to remember that a desire to help win the war is far from the only reason for intending to perform one's military functions during wartime. Even volunteers join the military for many reasons. Idealistic motives for enlistment can involve patriotism, a sense of duty, the desire to protect and serve others, family tradition, and so on. These ends can motivate the desire for military *service* whether or not it is wartime. These motives may not disappear even when a country marches down an immoral path. Indeed, the continuing idealism can make the personal decision of whether or not to participate in the war especially painful. More personal goals for joining might include supporting one's family, learning a trade or profession, improving self-discipline, getting money for college, and so on. Once in the military, even more motives can be added. These can include protecting comrades, keeping one's military oath, honor, professionalism, not letting one's family down, staying alive, or even the desire to avoid the brig. Such reasons for joining and staying in the military are all at least morally permissible projects, and most are regarded as morally desirable. To the extent that these other possibilities for joining and remaining actually drive behavior, 'contribution to victory' and to the harm any war causes could be a side effect an individual might wish would be otherwise. The adaptation of the principle of double effect outlined here suggests that military personnel must continue to be concerned with the consequences of unintended side effects of participating in the war at all.

One of the problems with the traditional distinctions between *jus ad bellum* and *jus in bello* moral responsibilities is that they go so far in disconnecting individuals from the unintended impact of the actions they do will. Professionalism might, for example, be a person's driving intention, but military tasks still have consequences that affect the costs of conducting war and the chances of victory. These side effects are foreseeable whether or not they are desired. By serving, one at least *consents* to the possible or likely outcomes of service.

One benefit of applying the principle of double effect to the individual decision to contribute to war is that it keeps individual moral responsibility in the equation. The Just War tradition already uses the principle of double effect when weighing the permissibility of individual acts of war such as choosing bombing targets. The proposal here is to evaluate the decision to contribute to the war at all, using the same concept. Applying the principle of double effect to an individual decision to participate in a war effort involves asking whether the unintended but likely public outcomes outweigh the good the individual's idealistic and personal motives represent. The main conceptual difference from the traditional *jus in bello* use of double effect is that this account does not assume the moral value of winning the war. Individual evaluation hinges on two factors: the level of foreseeable but unintended harm national prosecution of the war will cause, and how much causal difference a person's own contribution will make.

In wartime, not all military personnel are themselves likely to be individually and directly dangerous to any persons or property. 'Tooth vs. tail' – combat versus support services – distinguishes military functions in a critical way. A military doctor may be a 'warrior,' one who contributes to a war effort, but she is also in the business of healing and would tend wounded persons she is faced with whether there was a war on or not. The war affects the 'who' and the 'where' but not the 'what' of her function. Similarly, cooks, mechanics, supply officers, and clerks are just a few of the others who act in generic capacities. They support other military personnel whether or not there is a war, and their functions do not derive directly from the military nature of their employers. Support personnel are certainly part of the pursuit of victory and vital to the overall war effort, but direct causal contribution to the harm war produces is relatively small.

Applying the principle of double effect to individual contributions to fighting a questionable war requires strict attention to both intentions and effects. Contribution would be permissible when the soldier's direct intention is morally acceptable – and the full unintended consequences of contributing to the war effort as a side effect fall within the bounds of proportionality. Weighing personal goals on the same scale as individual contribution to a war effort requires a dispassionate evaluation of one's actual ability to produce harm or good by further service. The higher up in the chain of command, the more important *jus ad bellum* becomes, because the ability to make wide-ranging decisions that affect many other people increases with rank.

Jus ad bellum criteria and individual military personnel

To explore the plausibility of using the principle of double effect to justify continuing in military service in a morally questionable war, let us analyze the position of four hypothetical individuals. Later we will place these figures on the German side in World War II, with the allies in the Kosovo campaign, as Janjaweed paramilitary in the Sudan, and as Americans in 2006 in the Iraq War. To make the analysis as telling as possible, our hypothetical combatants include the equivalent in their respective national services of a cook, an infantry private, an air force bombardier, and a general officer on the general staff.³ All have qualms about whether the conflict in which they are engaged could pass muster on *jus ad bellum* grounds but expect to conduct their own war within the bounds of discrimination and proportionality. Each is personally motivated by professionalism, a sense of honor, the wish to defend the country, and the desire to avoid sanctions for refusing to participate in the war but not a personal commitment to the state actor's goals for the war. The principle of double effect is potentially applicable to these individuals' decision to contribute to the war effort in the cases outlined here because the fictional combatants have morally acceptable direct intentions, and are engaged in otherwise permissible military functions. They each regard contribution to potential victory as a side effect of their idealistic and personal intentions. The question still open is whether the actual cost of an individual's *unintended* contribution to the war effort is impermissibly disproportionate to the personal good *intentionally* being pursued.

For the sake of the evaluation we will assume without argument that using the following list of justice-of-war criteria is unproblematic. Just War theorist Nicholas Fotion offers the following list: just cause, proportionality, right authority, right intention, last resort, and reasonable probability of success (Fotion 2000).

Not all violations of *jus ad bellum* criteria have the same bearing on the permissibility of our fictional soldiers' intention to continue to carry out military duties. Some violations of *jus ad bellum* criteria produce considerably more human costs than others. An otherwise acceptable war fought without right authority is less damaging to civilians than a war in clear violation of the principle of discrimination. Furthermore, once the national command decision to go to war has been made, the wrong has already been *completed* by the state. Below the national command level, the soldier's future contributions to the war effort do not have any causal connection to what is morally wrong with failing to meet these two criteria.[4] The national command authority is the only group that can commit these violations on behalf of the country. Once the war has begun, those particular wrongs cannot be altered.

Just cause, right intention, proportionality, and reasonable chance of success are especially significant for people deciding on future actions of their own, because they pertain to future consequences of the war. Since the consequences have not yet occurred, one is not yet implicated by the harm or good the state actor will accomplish, except as a citizen. Moreover, whether an individual serves in the military has some effect on what the state actor will be able to do.

Just cause is future-oriented because the harm or good that victory would bring will not occur unless there is victory. The soldier's (unintended) contribution to that victory is *causally* relevant to whether those goals are turned into reality. So, too, if a person believes that the true intention behind a war is not morally justifiable – whatever the public stance – this switches the analysis from right intention back to justice of the cause and raises the same difficulties.

Proportionality of the war as a whole, even with a just cause, is a question about whether more harm will be done in the course of the war than the foreseeable good brought in the case of victory. The degree of harm still to be perpetrated depends causally to some extent on the actions of the soldier. The greater the expected harm for the war as a whole, or from a victory, the more harmful the soldier's personal contribution is likely to be. Since the outcome of double-effect analysis hinges on the balance of harm to good of *unintended* consequences, it matters a great deal what those consequences will be. The general officer, bombardier, and private all must seriously consider the overall causal effect of their personal war effort. Even the cook knows that eating is part of what enables the army to fight. The greater the harm from a future victory or the still unconsummated fighting, the less possible it will be to balance with good expected from private motivations.

Reasonable chance of success is the most complicated of the six criteria to weigh, and the most position-sensitive. The moral problem, from the perspective of the state, with having only a small chance of success is that the criterion encompasses two different kinds of potential harm. One is the harm any war causes to noncombatants on both sides, ranging from the civilians who are put into harm's way, to the loved ones of people who die or are injured in the line of duty. This kind of harm should be a side effect of war from the perspective of the state, something which presumably would be avoided if it were possible. A state fighting with little chance of success is thus likely to be in the position of causing harm disproportionate to the good that can be expected from the war effort.

The second kind of harm from a war with little chance of success stems from the special duties a state owes its citizens. Such a war requires sacrifices by its citizens, but offers only the scantiest chance that the sacrifices will produce the good being sought. Any war requires tragic sacrifices, but the state's part of the bargain is keeping good faith with soldiers and other citizens. A war with no chance of military success has the potential to waste the sacrifices of all concerned.

In some cases, of course, the real intention or aim of a war – its just cause – does not require military victory. Sometimes a cause seems so urgent that at least some people feel they must pursue it, even if military defeat is certain. The Finns facing Germany at the start of World War II is an example of this kind of situation. Where the choice of war or peace is not fully voluntary, as with resisting aggression, then the aim of going to war rather than surrendering immediately might be to buy time for escape for some citizens, to improve the country's bargaining position, or even the less tangible good of resisting aggressors per se. Just because military victory is not the *precondition* for achieving a war's goal does not mean that this kind of cause cannot be weighed in its own *jus ad bellum* proportionality analysis by the state.

Not fighting the war at all may well offer the state the best chance to protect both civilian and military citizens and the country as a whole. On the other hand, there are times when even a slim chance of success would not be a waste of honorable lives because it is the only chance for a morally urgent end. Czechoslovakia at the beginning of World War II is arguably an example of the former, but, as Thomas Schelling pointed out more than forty years ago, most surrender decisions come down to some such calculus (Schelling 1967: 30–31).

From the perspective of a military person, little chance of success is an even more complicated criterion. Can the principle of double effect with idealistic and personal ends as an individual's motivation justify participating if the only *jus ad bellum* flaw lies with reasonable chance of success?

The answer depends at least in part on the individual's position. A general officer who knows that even personal goals are unlikely to be met may be failing in his own personal duty to those he leads, by knowingly wasting their sacrifices. This is particularly true if he is sitting in the relative safety of the national command structure rather than the zone of battle. Arguably, however, he can justify continuing for a while under the principle of double effect. Not least, the general officer cannot be certain that the situation is really hopeless. Moreover, in our defined conflict, the goal the country is striving for is morally permissible, and right authority, right intention, and last resort are met. Nevertheless, the general officer is in a position where his own orders and directives affect many lives. His personal contribution to the war effort is a key aspect of how harmful the hopeless policy will be. It seems difficult to argue that he is morally blameless if he proceeds as if nothing were wrong, especially since he is one of the designated national experts in using war as a means. At minimum, he needs to take every reasonable opportunity to minimize or change the damage caused by the national policy. There may well come a time when he ought to resign or urge surrender on behalf of the national good.

The bombardier, the infantry private, and the chef do not have the same kind of institutional responsibilities in the chain of command. From their perspective, the moral problem of a slim chance of overall success in the war is with their future ability to cause harm to innocents. For the bombardier this calculus is the most difficult, because he has a greater ability to cause unintended harm to noncombatants on both sides. Buttressing the permissibility of continuing, they have an even greater potential than the general to be incorrect in their assessment of hopelessness, because they are in a worse position to judge the war as a whole. Like the general officer, they still have just cause, right intent, right authority, and last resort, suggesting limits to the amount and degree of harm the war is causing. The value of their personal and idealistic motives weigh in on the positive side of the double-effect equation and suggest that continuing is permissible, even morally desirable, under these conditions. Indefinite service would not be morally mandatory, however, given a means of exit that does not conflict with their motives of professionalism, honor, desire to defend the country – and avoiding sanctions for refusing to contribute.

In history, of course, problems with *jus ad bellum* do not present themselves one at a time. This makes the decision-making of even fictional characters much more difficult.

Hypothetical People in Real Wars

The historical cases that I use to explore questions of individual responsibility are Germany in World War II, NATO in the Kosovo campaign, the Janjaweed in today's civil war in Sudan, and the United States in 2006 in Iraq. These cases present a range of issues for *jus ad bellum*. Each of the wars has been said to violate more than one Just War criterion and thus to raise the degree of harm for which an individual participant would be causally responsible. The more numerous and serious the violations of *jus ad bellum* the less likely that the military personnel could justify continued service with the principle of double effect.

Germany in World War II failed just cause, proportionality, right intention, and last resort requirements. The government-allied Janjaweed militia in the current civil war in the Sudan raise serious *jus ad bellum* proportionality issues, to say the least, even if one is prepared to accept a government's right to oppose secessionist rebels with military force. In both these wars genocide as an undeclared war aim not only requires wholesale violation of the *jus in bello* principle of discrimination by individuals, but contaminates any claim of just cause by strongly implying violation of the principle of right intention. In the case of the Janjaweed, as a paramilitary militia they do not have right legal authority to act on behalf of the government in prosecuting rebels anyway, particularly since the government in question denies the connection. Claiming last resort would be a cruel joke for either of these cases. Unfortunately for the world, for both Germany in World War II and for the current Janjaweed, only the criterion of reasonable probability of success is left on what would normally be considered the permissive side of *jus ad bellum*.

Critics argue that the Kosovo bombing campaign and the 2006 allied war in Iraq also raise questions about proportionality and right intent. I will not evaluate these controversial arguments here, but assume they form the basis of at least some qualms experienced by the four combatants. These are controversial enough, however, that it is fair to assume that combatants would not necessarily assume their qualms to have absolute moral weight even while they are troubled by them. Reasonable chance of success is, however, a violation of *jus ad bellum* for the war in Iraq. Even after the 2007 'surge' the misgivings reported by the bipartisan Baker–Hamilton Commission and in a separate report by the Joint Chiefs of Staff in December of 2006 suggest that once the additional American forces are removed or significantly reduced, the war aims of restoring political stability to the country, much less establishing the conditions for a fully functional Western-style democracy, are unlikely to be met.[5] It is this aspect of the Iraq war that will receive the most attention below in the decision-making of the fictional military personnel.

To reiterate, the hypothetical combatants include the equivalent in their respective services of a cook, an infantry private, an air-force bombardier, and a general officer on the general staff. All have qualms about whether the conflict in which they are engaged could pass muster on *jus ad bellum* grounds but expect to conduct their own war within the bounds of discrimination and proportionality. Each is personally motivated by professionalism, honor, the wish to defend his country, and the desire to avoid sanctions for refusing to participate in the war.

The chef and the private are once again the easiest of the four to evaluate. Their causal contributions to moral costs of the war are real, but remain relatively limited in scope by their rank and sphere of action. Moreover, the chef should be able to stay within *jus in bello* rules because of the noncombatant nature of his role. The private has a degree of personal discretion in the war he actually prosecutes, and so may be able to keep his vow of staying within the principles of discrimination and proportionality. For these two enlisted persons, their limited ability to producing future harm makes it possible to balance their personal and idealistic goals if they stay within the bounds of *jus in bello* discrimination and proportionality. Problems with right authority and last resort are not within their personal purview. Further service seems clearly permissible in Kosovo and Iraq for both.

The situation is more difficult for the bombardier and the general officer in all four wars, and for the private in the Sudan or Germany in World War II. Each has personal motives that are permissible, even laudable. The problem, however, is that their direct causal connection to major harmful effects of the war is considerably higher than for the chef. For World War II and the Sudan the objective costs to humanity of a victory for their side must be added to the potential moral costs of continuing service. In these two wars even aiming at otherwise acceptable strategic targets carries the risk of bringing the morally unacceptable victory closer, whatever their individual intentions in that regard. The amount of harm that the bombardier can personally produce is, as noted above, considerably greater than the private, and the general officer gives orders and directs the actions of many. Even if they do not themselves desire that their country win this particular war, these three contribute in different degrees to the harm intended by those who do want victory – and to the unintended harm inherent in all wars.

The German bombardier and infantryman in World War II and the Sudan are not only blameworthy but, arguably, beyond the point where duty should have stopped their cooperation. The fact that objecting would put them and their whole family into direct lethal threat from their government is of course a strongly mitigating factor. There are ways for bombs and bullets to go more or less harmlessly astray, however, even on strategic missions. If they do not look for such opportunities, these personnel have placed themselves in a tragic dilemma. Objections to continued service apply even more strongly to a general officer.

Even for the three war fighters the bar of continuing contribution to a potential victory is much lower in Kosovo and Iraq. Achieving the war aim of saving Kosovar lives via the bombing campaign would not add to their moral burden. If one accepts that the American (and British) goal in Iraq is achieving political stability or establishing a working democracy, these too, are morally permissible. Contributing to the success of either overarching goal does not obviously harm innocents, and so need not be added to any blame from participating in the war.

For the bombardier and general officer in Kosovo, the most severe moral problems with unintended but negative effects of continuing service lie with the strategic decision to prosecute the war from high-speed aircraft flying at 16,000 feet. This combination not only reduced military effectiveness against Serb strategic targets but also reduced the likelihood that any given sortie could actually help anyone on the ground. By the same token, the high-altitude campaign increased the chances of unintended harm to noncombatants on both sides. Taken together these raise the possibility of an overall *jus ad bellum* violation of proportionality. Questions about *jus ad bellum* proportionality have clear implications for the ability of individual military personnel to rely on the principle of double effect to justify continuing service. There is, however, evidence that high-level military personnel strongly urged a change in strategy, and that at least some pilots withheld bombs rather than violate what they regarded as their own personal proportionality equation.[6]

In 2006 Iraq the *jus ad bellum* issue with the most immediate bite for military personnel is probability of success. Compliance with Just War criteria should affect the considerations of every citizen as one of the supervisors of his or her own state, but probability of success is especially important for military personnel because it engages their professional judgment. As Augustine, Aquinas, and Grotius point out, however, not all personnel are in a position to be able to make this judgment with confidence. Moreover, in Iraq, the bombardier, like the infantryman and chef, is not in a position to be able to alleviate this particular violation of *jus ad bellum*, even if it is strongly suspected. And, finally, their participating neither adds to nor detracts from the most often voiced additional charges, problems with the original national intent, and the authority and timing of intervention in the first place. It seems plausible to conclude that an array of morally positive personal motives could justify their continued military service because negative effects of their decision are so limited. The longer the war goes on without reasonable chance of success, however, the more fragile the justification via the principle of double effect becomes. The general officer needs to be much more proactive in considering the issue of probability of success, because it has a direct bearing on the degree of unintended harm his own activities will cause to noncombatants and military personnel in his command. It is not surprising that a number of retired general officers have come out with strong public criticism of the Iraq War and the war effort.[7]

The dilemma explored here is that of military personnel who are and intend to be fighting within the bounds of *jus in bello*, or are simply carrying out support duties. Their question is what to do when they are imbedded in a conflict that violates *jus ad bellum* criteria. Questions about the political desirability of the war do not place military personnel on the horns of a tragic dilemma, a situation for which there is really no acceptable moral solution.

Moral Consequences of Applying the Principle of Double Effect

The question of whether the principle of double effect – rigorously followed – ever fully justifies action is a controversial one. Double effect maintains that an act can have more than one effect. It judges the moral character of an act by its intended good effect (the saving of one's life through self-defense, for example) rather than its unintended evil effect (the killing of an attacker), provided that the latter is not disproportional to the former. There are many who conclude that double effect does not provide a full justification (Holmes 1989: 192, 211). In some formulations, however, the actor is not considered guilty of a moral crime, essentially 'by reason of double effect' (Anscombe 1990). It is, however, very hard to argue with those who conclude that moral responsibility remains, even when the effect in question is indeed intended neither as a means nor an end in itself, and meets the principle of proportionality (Lee 2004; Bica 1997). After all, the actors in question are *causally* responsible for harm, whether or not there were mitigating factors.

One can, of course, simply assume by fiat that there is no wrong left. This certainly is a comfortable assumption for institutions and even for those who are caught in a tragic dilemma between two moral duties. Unfortunately, this solution leaves unaccounted for real-world damage to people who should not be considered morally liable to receive it.

Alternately, one can blame the enemy (Kellogg 2006). No matter what the *jus ad bellum* status of the war, adversaries may be morally responsible for harm because they are conducting warfare in such a way and in a place that requires that killing or wounding enemy innocents be part of one's own victory. This latter argument has the merit of a connection to the principle of discrimination: it should not be acceptable to use one's own noncombatants as shields to reduce the damage one's military or quasi-military installations will suffer. So-called 'lawfare' that is intended for just this purpose is an act of cynical manipulation by a group conducting warfare.

The actual harm to innocents in the physical world at the hands of real-world actors is not, however, removed by the complementary wrongdoing of the adversary. It makes moral sense to judge intended and unintended acts differently, but a vestige of wrong*doing* still remains whether we are discussing collateral damage to civilians or contributing to a war that violates principles of *jus ad bellum*.

One situation where double effect is called into service is a clear example of the so-called dilemma of 'dirty hands.' That is, one is in a situation where nothing can be done that will not entail some wrong-doing – and that includes doing nothing at all. Nevertheless, action is called for and the best that can be hoped for is the choice of lesser among evils. There are many analysts, including Michael Walzer, who argue that much of governing a state involves this dilemma. In any case, if innocents are in fact always negatively affected by large-scale violent conflicts, then warfare cannot be separated from the 'dirty hands' dilemma, whether or not *jus ad bellum* is suspect. Robert Holmes concludes in this context that pacifism, not getting involved in wars, is the only morally acceptable response when war inherently includes killing innocents (1989: 203). Just War theory – and, indeed, the world's five largest religious traditions – conclude to the contrary

In a secular vein, it is useful to look more closely at categories of judgments about moral matters in everyday life. According to deontologists such as Robert Fullinwider (1999), it makes sense to consider moral evaluation a continuum. Right and wrong should not be considered simple binary evaluations, like saying whether a light is turned on or off. Fullinwider describes a dividing line beyond which one cannot regard an action as morally permissible, but argues persuasively that line is not the only relevant distinction.

At one end of the continuum are actions and intentions that go beyond what is expected of human beings, those which are super-erogatory or saintly. Short of that point are required duties and those that are 'good' to do, but not morally required. Moral neutrality lies in the center. The remaining categories are a mirror image: acts and intentions that are morally undesirable but not forbidden; violations of moral absolutes; and utterly heinous acts and intentions. The middle categories – praiseworthy but not required, neutral, and undesirable but not forbidden – are all morally permissible. Adding this complexity allows for nuances in judgment, and argument about where the line between permissible and impermissible falls. Some acts can be morally undesirable (i.e. wrong), but not absolutely forbidden. An action that fulfills all the requirements of the principle of double effect fits in this category. The actor intends to meet a goal or undertake a goal that is at least permissible in and of itself. Accomplishing the goal will also lead to harm that would be forbidden if it were intentional. Causing the secondary harm is certainly not morally desirable, much less a duty.

The principle of double effect thus need not wipe the moral slate completely clean. It simply says that causing secondary harm is *permissible* provided the actor does not want it as an end, or intend it as a means to other ends, and the unintended harm is not out of proportion to the good accomplished by the main goal.

Defending the Principle of Double Effect

The argument that the distinctions involved with the principle of double effect make moral sense is central to the conclusions presented here. Laura Sjoberg (2006) is among the theorists who argue against the principle of double effect.[8] Others, including Elizabeth Anscombe (1970), disagree strongly. This debate probably can never be ultimately settled, because, as Norvin Richards points out, 'neither side is moved by the arguments of the other. Each considers the opposing view to rest on an erroneous general approach to moral questions, and to use as paradigms exactly the wrong examples' (1984: 381). Nevertheless, an argument in support of the principle of double effect follows below. The argument has several elements, ranging from a defense of its internal consistency to an explanation of plausible metaethical underpinnings.

Sjoberg argues that the principle of double effect is internally inconsistent because it requires doing evil that good may come. The argument that war is always an evil (i.e. morally impermissible) does not, however, distinguish the concepts of evil and harm. Likewise, this argument conflates 'good' and 'right.' According to Aristotle and others, moral goodness – that is, rightness – is just one subcategory of what contributes to human flourishing, the good in general. In this more complete sense of the good, the opposite of good is what is *harmful* to human flourishing. Just as not everything that is 'good' is morally righteous (e.g. love of learning), then not everything that is harmful belongs to the category 'evil' – that is, forbidden on moral grounds. Just war in general does not belong in the evil category, even though it accepts some harm that would *otherwise* be forbidden.

By the same token, if one accepts the idea that human will affects the degree to which a state of affairs belongs to the category right or wrong, then a side effect that would be rejected or avoided if possible does not have the same moral status as a means or end that a person embraces. Accepting such a side effect can, by the principle of double effect, be designated morally undesirable, but permissible.

Although a full-scale examination of intention is beyond the scope of this chapter, as John Boyle argues (with Aquinas) there are all sorts of causal relationships that stem from human behavior (1980: 535). Most of them are morally neutral, other things being equal, such as washing dishes. What distinguishes an act belonging to the category 'moral' or 'immoral' is that a person knowingly undertakes it with the understanding that doing so is good or evil. A dog, for example, can cause great harm, but we do not usually conclude that a dog is capable of evil. It is human understanding and will that push mere effects into the category of morality. To be sure, one gives a form of consent to foreseen side effects but one does not act *in order to* bring them about. As Boyle points out, if actions belong to the category moral/immoral because they involve an evaluation of intention and will, and a person has a very different intention towards a side effect, then intended acts and causal side effects are in two different categories, in formal terms at least. If one chooses not to act because of a side effect, this decision and consequent behavior belong in the category moral/immoral because they involve application of intention. But if the effects of behavior are *simply* a side effect, then one's will is not applied to them and the act that produces them is in itself neither moral nor immoral.

To put it another way, when we intend to pursue a goal or adopt a direct means to our goals, we make it part of ourselves as persons; we embrace it. The initiator of intended harm embraces the consequences of her acts because she wills them to lead causally to her goals. If those consequences are evil, then she is embracing evil. Yet, as Thomas Nagel argues, '[T]he essence of evil is that it should repel us' (1989: 40, 182). We do not embrace to ourselves as persons mere side effects in the same way. The character of those who actively embrace evil is thus more deeply harmed than the character of people who undertake the same activity reluctantly, especially if they attempt to reduce harm indirectly caused by their actions. On balance, the consequences are worse because of the effects on character. As Immanuel Kant concluded, one of the worst effects of war is the effect on the character of individual participants (Kant 1970: 112). More recently Norvin Richards argued that the bad character such an action displays is also a warning of a strong future potential for other deliberate acts of harm in different contexts (1984: 396).

It is also worth asking why it is morally desirable to go beyond a simple utility analysis. The short answer is that the Just War tradition is a deontological tradition. Intention and duty are at its heart. Effects alone do not justify or condemn in this tradition. Moreover, the Just War tradition already uses the principle of double effect when thinking through *jus in bello* and therefore its application of the principle to the personal decision to go to war is a logical extension of the tradition. The issue here is a very serious judgment about a matter that is notoriously difficult to judge objectively. Applying double-effect analysis has the strong moral benefit of raising the moral bar of justification and thus reduces some of the dangers of such subjectivity.

With double effect we do begin with a utility analysis. By definition, the moral benefits of participation have to be sufficient to balance the moral cost, including the side effect, or the main action would not be permissible in itself. Applying double effect adds two more limitations, however. First, under the Just War version of the principle of double effect, the main action, participation, cannot require violation of the principle of discrimination or *jus in bello* proportionality, or the main act is not permissible in itself. This completely eliminates proportionality as a potential, although far-fetched, justification for participation in genocide.

Second, even if there are positive effects from what is for the soldier a side effect of her personal intentions, these may not be counted in the decision to participate. Our just soldier is considering participating a war that violates *any* of the *jus ad bellum* criteria. Just cause might actually be met in such a war, for example, even though it violates the principle of proportionality. At most, a person who is personally intending to 'do her duty' while repudiating the war as a whole may expect that any positive consequences do not add to her personal moral burden. A double-effect evaluation of participating brings with it all of the moral costs of contribution to the war but does not weigh in any potential benefits either of the war effort itself or of winning. The standard of double effect is harder to meet than utility alone.

Conclusion

Not all *jus ad bellum* criteria have the same bearing on the permissibility of soldiers' intention to continue to carry out military duties in a war that fails to meet one or more of the criteria. Some violations of *jus ad bellum* criteria produce considerably higher human costs than others. An otherwise acceptable war fought without right authority is less damaging to civilians than a war in clear violation of the principle of discrimination. Just cause, right intention, proportionality, and reasonable probability of success are especially significant for people deciding on future actions of their own because they pertain to future consequences of the war.

The harm different wars cause differs in part because national war aims differ; success for the state may be morally positive or negative from the perspective of a neutral observer. Germany winning World War II would have had very different implications than Allied success in the Kosovo campaign. So, too, because military personnel are agents of the state, whether and how an individual decides to contribute is directly relevant to the amount of harm that the state has the ability to cause in the future. In particular, at the start of a war the individual's decision matters because much of the harm the war will cause is still in the future. The US Civil War with Robert E. Lee leading the Union forces instead of the Army of Northern Virginia would have been a very different war.

There are outer limits for the effects of an argument for applying the principle of double effect to a decision to remain in military service during a morally questionable war. Above all, the double-effect evaluation proposed in this article does not in any sense exonerate military personnel who are committing atrocities or war crimes. Soldiers are *personally* bound by the principles of discrimination and proportionality, whatever the justice of the overall war. The principle of double effect always requires that the main action, the intended action, be permissible in and of itself. War crimes, deliberately targeting civilians, and otherwise using their pain as a direct means to another end all fail the principle of discrimination and therefore cannot be mitigated by the principle of double effect. Even if an atrocity is carried out as a contributory means to another of the actor's ends, such as avoiding consequences of refusing service, the actor still intends to *utilize* the harm as a tool toward that other end.

The dilemma explored here is for military personnel who are and intend to be fighting within the bounds of the principles of discrimination and double effect, or are simply carrying out support duties. Their question is what to do when they are embedded in a conflict whose overall morality they doubt. There are some wars, however, that go so far beyond the point that reasonable people ought to be able accept that double effect cannot reasonably be applied. A war of extermination or genocide has such heinous effects that merely withholding intent to contribute to the so-called victory is not enough to balance the actual harm that will occur as a result of the war.

Short of this point the principle of double effect is applicable to the question of participation because it is possible to serve in the military even while withholding the direct intention of winning a questionable war. As discussed above, a soldier's direct intentions can be different from the government's or even the nation-state as an organized collective. He or she may simply intend to fulfill the promises made in joining the service, to protect the country, family, or fellow soldiers from the danger that now exists for whatever reason. Consequences still matter, however. Participation is only permissible if the *unintended* harm produced by contributing to the war does not overshadow the good produced by the individual's personal intentions.

Using the principle of double effect to evaluate participation in a war about which a soldier has moral qualms is not simply a metaphysical exercise but is related to the future in a very concrete way. Attitudes towards one's own service affect the difficulty of reintegrating military personnel into civilian life, the incidence of post-traumatic stress syndrome, even the chances of a nation accepting a long-term peace that is not, in Kant's words, 'the peace of the grave' (Kant 1970: 96).

The problem of individual soldiers' responsibility has assumed a significance that is 'new' and allows for the reappropriation and reevaluation of the Just War tradition's work on the issue. This chapter has argued that the 'old' Just War work on the question of individual responsibility is in itself inadequate to deal with the ethical complexities of the question, but that Just War theory provides another tool, previously not applied to individual responsibility, that can help substantially in dealing with this question. That tool is the principle of double effect. Analyzing individual responsibility though the lens of the principle of double effect helps us to see that soldiers are neither wholly responsible for nor wholly absolved from their actions in war-fighting. Instead, a complex matrix of intent and effect can assign responsibility in a more nuanced and more ethical manner.

7

Outsourcing War

Amy Eckert

A monopoly over the use of force lies at the heart of contemporary thinking about the state. Max Weber's definition of the state as the entity with a monopoly over the legitimate use of force is a leading example of this conception (Weber 1964), and has become influential within the discipline of International Relations. Many mainstream international relations theories also incorporate this assumption about the state (Waltz 1986). Despite the centrality of this idea, the view of the state as wielding centralized control over the use of force obscures the extent to which private actors are again becoming essential to the conduct of warfare. Such private actors were abundant during the Middle Ages and even for a time after the creation of the Westphalian state system, until they were eventually displaced with a system of national militaries. The eventual consolidation of force under the authority of the state relegated private actors like mercenaries to the margins of the international system. Transformations within the system are leading to a re-privatization of force in which non-state actors are again playing a central role in warfare. Private military companies (PMCs) have been hired by state and non-state actors, including corporations, international organizations, and NGOs, to perform a variety of tasks once performed by national militaries exclusively.[1]

International Relations as a discipline remains centered around the state. As Hall and Biersteker argue, the state enjoys a unique position:

> Not only have states been asserted to be the principal actors in the international arena, but they are also considered to be the only legitimate actors in international relations. The authority they exercise over their subjects in the domestic realm conveys to them a legitimacy and agency to interact with other states in the international society of states. (Hall and Biersteker 2002: 3)

The re-emergence of PMCs poses real problems for theorizing about war generally. It is especially troublesome for Just War theory, which assumes an international system in which states are the sole participants in warfare. Walzer's domestic analogy, in which states are citizens of international society in the same way that individuals are citizens of their states' societies (Walzer 2000: 58–9), leaves little room for private actors like PMCs. As such, the involvement of such non-state actors in warfare often remains unacknowledged. While Just War theory pre-dates the state system, its contemporary format is heavily invested in it. To the extent that Just War theory cannot see past the state, it cannot adequately account for the growing role of PMCs and other private actors. The statist assumptions on which contemporary Just War theory operates have become problematic because of the ever-increasing significance of these private actors in warfare. Because Just War theory seeks to evaluate the justice of particular wars, focusing only on the state without accounting for the role of PMCs provides only a partial picture of the war. Still, this is a problem that is not entirely without precedent. Private actors dominated the security landscape before Westphalia and, to a considerable extent, even after the emergence of the state system.

The tradition of theorizing about justice and war predates both the emergence of the state system and the state's subsequent consolidation of authority over force through the emergence of the national army. What has changed is that these private actors are now re-emerging within an international system that is dominated by the state. When private actors last played this extensive a role in warfare, there was no presumption in favor of the state as there is now. The real newness of this problem, then, lies in adapting norms of Just War theory that have become statist to the re-privatization of force. Utilizing PMCs carries a number of benefits for the states that employ them, in part because of the perception that they are outside the structure of the state as private actors. In reality, though, the 'old' solutions to preventing or mitigating the horrors of war are more than capable of being applied to the PMCs that have re-emerged in significant numbers over the past decade.

PMCs now perform a variety of functions once carried out by members of the military. These may include anything from logistical support, as in the case of DynCorp's recent contract to support peacekeepers in Darfur, to combat and combat support, as in the case of the now-defunct Executive Outcomes in Angola and Sierra Leone. While PMCs performing these latter types of functions are relatively rare, states are increasingly outsourcing the former logistical functions to private actors. This chapter considers the problems that this growing privatization poses for ethical reasoning about war. It begins by looking at the state's consolidation of authority over war and the wave of privatization that threatens to undo this process. After looking at the current market for private force, it then turns to the question of Just War theory and the complications that privatization poses for the theory's ability to restrict violence. Finally, it considers how these private actors might be integrated into thinking about justice and war. I will argue that the actions of PMCs and the states that hire them should be considered together for the purposes of assessing the justness of a privatized war.

The State and the Use of Force

The model of the national military under the control of the state has been the exception rather than the rule over the course of human history. Prior to the rise of the state system, wars were fought almost exclusively by those hired to fight them. The earliest records of warfare reflect this use of hired fighters (Singer 2003). The Roman Empire employed hired units as it expanded and encountered ever-greater difficulties in recruiting native Romans. By the Middle Ages, hired troops had virtually taken over the battlefield. This was due in part to the constraints of the feudal system. The feudal system meant that rulers could only rely on troops to the extent that their lieges were obliged to them. The limits of these obligations meant that these forces were only available for short periods of time and, further, that rulers had no troops to rely upon when the lieges themselves became the threat (Singer 2003: 22). Due to the political limitations of the feudal system, bellicose monarchs during the Middle Ages had no real alternative but to rely heavily on mercenaries for war-fighting (Thomson 1994: 27). Moreover, these hired troops filled a vital niche. Weapons like the crossbow were considered ungentlemanly, but were too complex to be operated by peasants (Singer 2003: 22).

The Peace of Westphalia in 1648 marked a point of transition as sovereign states began to displace empires and other actors that populated the pre-international system. With Westphalia, states began to consolidate political power. The presence of territorially defined sovereigns was in stark contrast to the largely personal relationships of the feudal system that preceded this rising state system. The political transformations were more sweeping than the military changes. The emergence of this state system did not immediately lead to the nationalization of force under the authority of the states that emerged post-Westphalia. New states continued to rely extensively on hired troops to fight their wars. As Thomson notes, certain types of reliance on private actors, such as privateering, actually increased (1994: 22). Mercenary forces retained a role in combat until the successes of the post-revolutionary French army, drawn from its citizenry, inspired a similar nationalization of militaries within other states. The influence of the French national army was both strategic and normative (Singer 2003: 30). The successes enjoyed by France after the Revolution inspired other states to imitate the French model of a citizen army. Likewise, the Enlightenment ideals of nationalism made fighting out of patriotism more noble than fighting for profit. These factors contributed to the eventual nationalization of military force. Eventually, national armies displaced hired military forces. Over time the national army became essential to the concept of the state, as evidenced by the Weberian definition of the state. The transition brought about by Westphalia and the French Revolution signaled that the widespread use of private military forces had come to an end, at least for the next two hundred years.

After the nationalization of militaries, mercenaries continued to operate on a small scale, even following the emergence of the

Westphalian state system. At the zenith of national militaries, the mercenaries who continued to participate in conflicts abroad were typically either individual soldiers of fortune or small numbers of individuals who participated in a conflict with the blessings of their own state, as in the American use of foreign troops in the Vietnam War. The mercenaries who persisted after the nationalization of force were both small in number and only 'marginally legitimate' (Thomson 1994: 97). These individual mercenaries, often drawn into African civil wars and wars of independence, cast an ugly shadow over today's PMCs. Muthien and Taylor recall

> British mercenary Tyrone Chadwick [who] was later imprisoned in South Africa after admitting to a London reporter his and other mercenaries' roles in several murders while serving on an apartheid hit squad firm. (Muthien and Taylor 2002: 190–91)

Some members of one of the best-known PMCs, Executive Outcomes, were implicated in similar abuses, doing little to dispel this legacy (Muthien and Taylor 2002: 191).

Nevertheless, comparisons between contemporary PMCs and these lone soldiers of fortune are somewhat facile. PMCs differ in nearly every respect from their Cold War predecessors. Contemporary PMCs often have a highly organized corporate structure. Many are part of larger corporate conglomerates. Within the category of PMCs, there are many different types of outfits providing different categories of services. Some firms limit their provision of services to a support capacity. Others offer military training, and still others engage in planning and actual combat. Some scholars of the PMC industry distinguish among these types of firms based on the type of services provided (Brayton 2002: 307–8; Mandel 2001: 171; Singer 2001; Avant 2005). In terms of understanding the role that PMCs play in contemporary warfare, these distinctions hold some value. For purposes of Just War theory, these distinctions are less relevant for two reasons. First, even support functions like transport or training play a significant role in the state's ability to wage war. To the extent that the state can 'outsource' these functions, waging war becomes less costly and difficult. The diminution of these costs discourages serious thought about the justice of the cause and can skew reasoning about factors like reasonable chance of success. Second, even PMC personnel engaged in non-combat functions can violate *jus in bello* norms like non-combatant immunity. The PMC personnel implicated in the Abu Ghraib prisoner abuse scandal were translators, linguists, and interrogators – functions that are removed from the scope of combat.

Unlike the shadowy mercenaries of the Cold War era, today's PMCs openly advertise their services and contract with states and other entities to provide them. With the end of the Cold War, several factors converged to create an environment in which PMCs could flourish. In many respects, the explosion of the private military industry is a story of supply and demand. The end of superpower rivalry, in addition to the end of apartheid in South Africa, led to the downsizing of military forces. The downsizing of these military forces created an oversupply of unemployed soldiers. These individuals had military training, but were no longer needed by their national militaries. At the same time, the end of the Cold War also allowed many conflicts that had been dormant to again become active. While US–Soviet rivalry persisted, each superpower was willing and able to support governments and suppress conflicts within its sphere of influence. Subsequently some of these client states failed and others became embroiled in civil conflict. States within the West, whether individually or collectively, demonstrated a limited will to intervene in these conflicts, prompting parties to the conflicts to turn elsewhere for military aid. While the immediate post-Cold War period brought a brief period of cooperation, exemplified by the first Gulf War and a flurry of humanitarian intervention through the UN Security Council, a combination of failed operations and overextension quickly brought this cooperation to and end. These developments facilitated an explosion in the number of PMCs and their employment by a panoply of actors (Singer 2005: 120).

One can imagine post-Cold War security needs being met in any number of ways other than recourse to the market. States, either individually or multilaterally, could have reversed the cuts they made to their militaries and stepped into the void to meet these security needs. The decision to turn to the market was, ultimately, a function of ideology. A number of conservative governments in the 1980s and 1990s pursued a path of privatization because of their ideological preference for the free market (Spearin 2004: 41). In the

American case, the belief that relying on private forces yields more 'bang for the buck' has created a preference for reliance on PMCs (Spearin 2003: 29). American political culture has long favored a small government coupled with a robust civil society and market (Lipset 1996). Globalization has diffused these particular values across the global political institutions. Since then, these ideological preferences have been institutionalized at the international level in the form of the free-trade regime. The neoliberal ideological underpinnings of globalization push the resolution of this particular supply-and-demand problem toward a particular outcome, which is the re-privatization of force (Singer 2005: 120). This has had the effect of promoting privatization both globally and within states. One hallmark of the globalization regime has been the 'outsourcing' of manufacturing or services from areas perceived as less efficient to those seen as more efficient. Manufacturing and service jobs have flowed from high-wage areas to low-wage areas. The privatization of war fighting is both the apparent logical extension of this pro-privatization ideology and a potential transformation of the state system, as the state outsources even its core security functions to private actors.

Technology is also a factor in this trend toward the re-privatization of force, reinforcing the ideological push toward the market. The role that technology now plays in the re-privatization of force echoes the need for trained forces with specialized skills during the Middle Ages, though the present needs surpass the ability to use a crossbow. The costs involved in training military personnel to use the technologically advanced weapons systems make purchasing this expertise on the private market an attractive option for states. Ironically, the high salaries paid by PMCs make the private market an attractive option for those leaving the military as well (Spearin 2003: 30). In a sense, then, these dynamics create a cyclical effect: military personnel are lured to the private sector by high salaries while the cost of training military personnel discourages the state from investing resources in training its own soldiers. The effect of this dynamic means that the states that are reliant on technologically advanced weapons will also continue to grow even more dependent on the private sector to manufacture and operate them. Over the short term, at least, hiring this expertise is more cost-effective than cultivating it, meaning that these technological demands also push states to outsource these functions.

This combination of supply, demand, ideology, and technology has revived the private market for force. The re-emergence of this private market for force has started to reverse the process by which the state consolidated the use of force under its auspices. Instead of the use of force being monopolized by states, a number of actors now legitimately use force. This reality mirrors the privatization taking place within a number of other arenas, in which the state now competes with other actors performing essentially the same functions. The rise of this new private market for force suggests that the same thing is now true of security as well.

Force and the Private Market

With the increased security needs and decreased interest from the West, many state and non-state actors began turning to the market-place to meet their security needs. The PMCs that meet these needs resemble their private counterparts from earlier times, but they are distinctive because of their highly corporate structures. The growth of the private sector's involvement in the military sector is unprecedented within the Westphalian state system in two respects: the number of personnel involved and the type of functions that these PMCs are performing. The first Gulf War, which followed Iraq's invasion of Kuwait, and the second Gulf War, the more recent US-led war in Iraq, provide us with a gauge for measuring the numerical growth of PMCs. In the first Gulf War, the ratio of contractors to active duty military personnel was 1:50; in the second Gulf War, this ratio had become 1:10 (*Military Balance* 2006: 411). The current level of participation by PMCs is 'unparalleled amongst the militaries of the world' (Spearin 2003: 28). The number of PMCs and their personnel is difficult to track because of their decentralized and unregulated nature. The extensive role that PMCs now play in war and security will likely only grow in future conflicts. In terms of revenue, PMCs earned an estimated $55.6 billion in 1990. Current estimates pinpoint the industry's earnings at $100 billion (Bures 2005: 535). By 2010, the industry's revenues are expected to rise to $202 billion (Avant 2004: 154).

The real distinction between this wave of privatization and the earlier wave is the present statist foundation of the international system. This presumption in favor of the state poses challenges to the incorporation of private actors like PMCs into statist theories like Just War theory in its present form. The fact that PMCs are non-state actors in a statist world, private and outside of the state structure, which makes them more difficult to track, also contributes to their appeal for client states. Estimates of the number of PMC personnel in Iraq number around 20,000, roughly the same as the number of troops provided by all members of the coalition aside from the US (Singer 2005: 122). In effect, the US created a 'coalition of the billing' that rivals the troops committed to Iraq by the coalition of the willing. This means that if all PMC personnel were united into a single force, their contingent in Iraq would be second in size only to the American force. In addition to Iraq, the US has utilized PMCs in its anti-drug efforts in Colombia (Shannon 2002). Exemplifying the many-faceted role that PMCs play in contemporary conflict, Colombian drug cartels and anti-government insurgents are also rumored to have hired different PMCs. This means that PMCs are participating on both sides of civil conflict in Colombia. The UK has long been in the business of privatizing its military for ideological and economic reasons (Edmonds 1999), and it has plans for further privatization, including key research and development functions (Singer 2003: 12).

PMCs have also participated in peacekeeping, stepping into the void created by state actors unwilling or unable to contribute their own troops. Military Professional Resources Incorporated (MPRI) performed some functions in connection with the Dayton Accords, including modernizing the Croatian army (Brayton 2002: 315–16). In Stephen Brayton's estimation, the use of MPRI in that case 'delivered a less expensive and less politically risky American foreign policy victory than would have been possible had US troops been used' (2002: 311). The US, UN, and Economic Community of West African States (also known as ECOWAS) contracted with International Charter Incorporated to provide services in connection with regional African peacekeeping operations (Bures 2005: 538). PMCs also provide services in connection with operations in East Timor (Bures 2005: 538). In addition to offering their services to states and international organizations, PMCs have also contracted with corporations and non-governmental organizations. Taken collectively, this clientele suggests that PMCs can perform state-like functions both for states of varying capabilities and for non-state actors. The effect of this widespread PMC activity is to bring warfare and security functions into the realm of privatization.

The re-emergence of PMCs, then, poses theoretical and practical problems today that the presence of non-state actors did not pose prior to Westphalia. During earlier periods in history, the operation of non-state actors alongside states posed no real problem. From a theoretical perspective, it is the claim of the state to have consolidated authority over legitimate violence that makes contemporary PMCs problematic.[2] Yet, actors using force with a license from the state can hardly be treated as illegitimate or criminal. In this respect they pose a challenge to the state system. Because this private use of force is licensed by states and therefore cannot be dismissed as criminal activity, then, the dominance of the state as the key actor in international relations has been somewhat diminished in the present global era. This diminished role for the state is at least partly relative to other private actors that have been assuming increased significance within the international system. Some see the emergence of PMCs as an unraveling of the consolidation of violence under state control. This consolidation forms part of the underpinnings of the state system in its present form (Strayer and Munro 1959). Christopher Coker connects the emergence of PMCs with the rise of a new, post-modern polity that differs from the modern polity along three lines: first, in the post-modern polity, the military has lost its dominance over society; second, the public–private divide, once drawn in favor of the public, is redrawn to favor the private; and, lastly, ideological debate has diminished (Johnson 1981). With the re-emergence of violence as a market commodity, provided largely by PMCs, non-state actors like corporations and NGOs can have at their disposal force comparable to a state. Within the population of states, a weak state can hire additional capability, perhaps allowing its government to postpone its demise artificially, as in the case of Sierra Leone. By selling force on the free market, PMCs are engaged in the decentralization of what the Westphalian state system has spent centuries centralizing. This development does not undermine the state system – the state remains the key actor in the international system even if it is relatively less dominant than it was – but it does fundamentally alter the context within which states operate and it affects the application of ethical norms, such as Just War theory principles, that were developed for state actors exclusively. The re-emergence of PMCs creates significant theoretical and policy challenges for the application of these norms. To the extent that Just War theory pre-dates both the centralization of force under the auspices of the state and the recent trend toward decentralization, the norms associated with this theoretical tradition are certainly capable of restraining even private actors.

Just War Theory and the Restraint of War

The tradition of recorded theorizing about the conditions for a Just War began with the ancient political philosophers, pre-dating the state by many centuries. Earlier civilizations, including the Greeks and Romans and a number of non-European civilizations, had well-developed ideas about the relationship between justice and war. Aristotle argued in *The Politics* that wars against those peoples who were intended to be governed but who would not willingly submit were 'by nature just' (1984). During the Middle Ages, the central questions of the Just War tradition reflected the political context of that time, a key aspect of which was the existence of competing political authorities, both ecclesiastical and secular. The fall of the Roman Empire had created a political vacuum in Europe that no single actor was able to fill. In the post-Roman era, several competing authorities strove to fill this void, including the Catholic Church and competing secular authorities within the feudal political system.[3]

In contrast to the state system, in which one political authority claims supreme authority within a piece of territory, the medieval political system was a tangled 'patchwork of overlapping and incomplete rights of government' (Strayer and Munro 1959: 115). Authority in the feudal system was heavily dependent on personal relationships. This system of social organization sometimes created absurd outcomes, as illustrated by the Hundred Years War:

> one belligerent, the king of England, was technically a vassal of the king of France because of the former's hereditary lordship of the French territory

of Guienne; at the same time the English king claimed the French throne for himself because of direct inheritance through the female line, which was allowed by English, but not by French, law. (Johnson 1981: 152)

Individuals derived power from the obligations that others owed to them, and in turn owed obligations to others who were higher in the hierarchy. Even in the case of manorial relationships, which were partially defined by one's residence within a particular lord's holdings, that lord's holdings were in turn ultimately determined by his location within this chain of personal obligation (Orend 2006). The decentralization within this system meant that individuals could be accountable to multiple religious and secular authorities simultaneously, with no one of these actors having a definitive claim to final authority over those individuals or the territory that they inhabited.

Even within this political complexity, Just War principles applied to conflicts. During the Middle Ages, the most significant constraints were *jus ad bellum* rules that applied to the initiation of conflict. A particularly pressing problem was, understandably, the problem of proper authority to declare war. The patchwork of overlapping secular and religious authorities provided no clear answer. Gratian's *Decretum*, a key effort at codifying Just War principles, suggested that kings, princes, barons and even vassals could potentially make a legitimate declaration of war, in addition to the Pope in his capacity as God's representative on earth (Bellamy 2006: 33).[4] This complex system of political organization did little to resolve the problem of right authority and also posed problems for thinking about just cause for war. Just cause in the Middle Ages was often treated as an all-or-nothing proposition, particularly within the holy war tradition, meaning that justice was on the side of one combatant alone. The rise of the state system and the evolution of territorially defined political actors would resolve many of these problematic aspects of Just War theory. The existence of territorially sovereign, juridically equal states suggested that both sides to a conflict could be at least partially just. These developments also conferred increased significance on *jus in bello* rules. With just cause more ambiguous than previously acknowledged, the manner in which war was prosecuted became more significant with respect to analyzing its justice.

In its contemporary form, Just War theory imposes limitations on states both in the decision to wage war and in the fighting of that war once it has been initiated. *Jus ad bellum* assumes that the war is waged by an actor with the authority to wage war, the capability of forming an intention, and the ability to assess costs and benefits – in other words, a state. *Jus ad bellum* rules are, in particular, 'thought to be the preserve and responsibility of political leaders' (Orend 2006: 31), placing them by definition within the public sphere both domestically and internationally. The decision to wage war belongs to the state's political leaders (Walzer 2000: 289–92). Johnson also overtly refers to Just War theory as being, in part, a guide for statecraft (1999: 26).

These statist assumptions are also present in *jus in bello* norms that govern the conduct of war. These norms were in their infancy during the pre-Westphalia period, and only became well developed within the era of the state and the national army. This context is reflected not only in the rules but in their application. *Jus in bello* norms are 'defined by two concerns: discrimination, or avoiding direct, intentional harm to noncombatants, and proportionality of means – that is, avoiding needless destruction to achieve justified ends' (Johnson 1999: 36). This system of rules assumes that the combatants on either side are under the control of a single entity, the state. It further assumes the existence of a disciplined national military with a chain of command in which soldiers obey the lawful orders that they are given. This assumption is built into the idea of command responsibility, by which a commanding officer can also bear some responsibility for the war crimes committed by subordinates.

The introduction of private actors outside of the state system and national militaries challenges the assumptions on which contemporary versions of Just War theory operate. The Abu Ghraib detainee abuse scandal is a dramatic illustration of the complexities that private actors can introduce into the context of warfare. The now infamous photographs of prisoner abuse at Abu Ghraib document the use of violence and humiliation against Iraqi civilian prisoners. The Taguba Report on the Abu Ghraib abuses found that military police and civilian contractors committed 'sadistic, blatant, and wanton criminal abuses' against detainees (Article 15–6 Investigation). These abuses were documented by photos and videos too graphic and disturbing to be included in the Taguba Report. Among other abuses, detainees were raped, sexually assaulted, photographed naked and in sexually explicit positions, threatened with (and in one instance injured by) dogs, beaten, and threatened with various sorts of weapons. In one instance, a prisoner under the control of the CIA suffered abuse so severe that he died. As with other aspects of the Iraq War, many of the positions in this prison had been outsourced to civilian contractors. All of the translators and as many as half of the interrogators at Abu Ghraib were PMC personnel from two companies: CACI and Titan Corp. The army had a policy against using non-military person-nel as interrogators, but this was ignored in part due to personnel shortfalls.

Investigation of the Abu Ghraib scandal revealed the extent to which PMC contractors were involved in the abuse of prisoners and the extent to which these contractors lacked formal military training in interrogation (Jehl and Zernike 2004). Some complaints about the personnel extended to their ability to perform their intended func-tions as translators (Washburn 2004). The Taguba Report singled out two PMC personnel in particular: Steven Stephanowicz, a civilian interrogator employed by CACI; and John Israel, a linguist supplied by Titan Corp. Despite their connection to the Abu Ghraib abuses, both remained on the job and in Iraq for months after the report was issued (Brinkley and Glanz 2004). A total of six PMC personnel were ultimately referred to the Department of Justice for prosecution, based on their involvement in Abu Ghraib (Merle and McCarthy 2004). To date no charges have been filed against them. CACI's own report into its employees' connection to Abu Ghraib found no wrongdoing on the part of its contractors, including Stephanowicz. While the report did acknowledge that 'a few' of its employees had been removed from Iraq at the army's request, CACI denied that these removals were punitive in nature or connected with the abuses at Abu Ghraib (Cushman 2004). The abuse of prisoners through the use of controversial 'interrogation' techniques created outrage in Iraq and scandal around the world, and PMC personnel were at the center of the conduct.

While Abu Ghraib is a particularly compelling example of PMC deviation from the standards imposed on states by the Geneva Con-ventions, it is far from being the only such case. Because PMCs operate outside the jurisdiction of any military system, information about their operations can be difficult to obtain, but scattered reports provide insights into the abuses that PMC personnel sometimes commit. For example, two former employees of Triple Canopy, an American PMC operating in Iraq, filed suit against their former employer, claiming that they were terminated after complaining about a supervisor shooting at civilians. The former Triple Canopy employees allege that their shift leader, after stating that he was 'going to kill someone today,' fired deliberately into a stopped white truck and later into a taxi, in both cases immediately leaving the area after the gunfire. After that shift leader left Iraq, the Triple Canopy employees reported his actions, leading to the termination of their employment with the company shortly thereafter (Chivers 2006). These allegations recall similar events in connection with PMC activities in Bosnia. Personnel belonging to the US-based PMC DynCorp, hired to train Bosnian police, were implicated in a sex-slavery operation in which young girls were bought and sold. One individual, a site supervisor, reportedly videotaped himself raping two women. None of the employees implicated in any of the misconduct were prosecuted, and the employees who were whistleblowers in this case likewise had their contracts terminated (Bures 2005: 541–2).

These types of incidents raise in a compelling fashion the challenges that PMCs pose for contemporary Just War theory standards, which assume a statist international system. The involvement of PMCs in war has created not just potential but actual harm, as the incidents above indicate. Moreover, these specific violations have gone unpunished, suggesting that Just War theory principles, rules of international law, and the mechanisms for enforcing them are inadequate in the case of PMC personnel. While the emergence of the state has undeniably influenced the shape of Just War principles today, their existence prior to the rise of the state system suggests that they can survive the transformations that the state system is currently experiencing. The current incarnation of Just War theory assumes a system in which states alone wage war, but the tradition has its origins in an earlier era when private actors also played a significant role in the waging of war. This suggests that Just War theory can again evolve to take account of the re-privatization of force that is presently occurring. If Just War theory is going to have continuing relevance to future conflicts, it must address the realities of privatization. The PMC industry has seen astounding growth over the past few years, and projections suggest that it will only continue. A Just War theory

that cannot speak to these realities will lose its power to speak as to
the justice of these future wars.

War in a Privatized World

The emphasis that Just War theory has placed on the state is not
unjustified. Since the rise of the state system, the state has been the
dominant political and moral entity in the global political system.
This reality is a key point of distinction between the current wave of
PMC activity and the private market for force that existed throughout
the Middle Ages. At that time, no presumption in favor of the state
existed; presently, such a presumption is strong. Although the state
continues to hold this position, the context in which it operates has
changed markedly because of the dynamic of privatization. To assess
the justice of a war in a meaningful sense, Just War theory needs to
apply its principles to both the actions of states and the increasingly
privatized context in which they operate. With the integration of
PMCs into warfare, state action alone is only a partial image of what
happens in any war. If it is to be an effective tool for assessing the
justice of a war, in its initiation and in its conduct, Just War theory
must find a way to make sense of this changing context.

With few exceptions, International Relations theory is focused
quite narrowly on the state, creating a public–private divide that
serves to obscure the private from view. In their discussion of emerging private authority, Cutler, Haufler, and Porter argue that 'the very
definition of the field as 'international relations' reflects a preoccupa-
tion with territorially specific and state-bounded notions of authority
that focus on the state as the essential actor and unit-of-analysis' (1999:
17). This focus on the state at the international level is not entirely
unjustified. There are valid reasons for the state to remain the focus
of the discipline, particularly with respect to international ethics.
Conceptions of justice derive their legitimacy from the public culture
of the international system, and this public culture is undeniably
statist. While non-state actors may be increasingly significant within
the international system, international norms still apply primarily to
the states that populate the international system. The public culture
of the international system is an important source of values within
the international system because of differences between states. The

content of this common political culture reflects the norms and values that are shared among the states within international society. The statism of this culture is, in this respect, important to theorizing about international relations and particularly important with respect to international ethics. The public–private divide does hold some utility in this respect, but it also obscures the incontrovertible fact that the context within which the state operates is changing, and that these changes bear on the manner in which ethical norms apply to the public sphere. But, increasingly, getting a complete picture of war, particularly for purposes of assessing things like the proportionality of a conflict or a state's reasonable chance of success when it initiates a conflict, looking across the public–private divide to take the role of PMCs into account becomes essential.

Because of their growing role in conflict, PMCs must be held responsible as well for their role in armed conflict. To make moral sense of the role that PMCs play in conflict, I propose a public–private intersection rather than a public–private divide. The rise of PMCs and their integration into warfare illustrates the extent to which this public–private divide is artificial and unhelpful. Both soldiers and PMCs are performing similar tasks on behalf of the state. In functional terms, these public and private actors are indistinguishable. While their differing relationships to the state mean that ethical norms and legal standards apply differently, this should not necessarily be the case. A greater transparency across the public–private divide would be more useful in applying ethical norms to moral problems. The extent of PMC involvement in contemporary conflicts makes assessing the justice of a particular war *without* reference to private actors impossible. When PMC personnel often constitute 10–20 percent of the individuals involved in a particular war, applying *jus ad bellum* principles like proportionality without taking into account the casualties among private actors renders these criteria all but useless. Likewise, turning a blind eye to the *jus in bello* violations of those individuals who fall outside the state structure makes a mockery of the protections in place for noncombatants, prisoners, and other vulnerable populations. Of course, this is exactly what has happened in the case of the Iraq War. Casualties among PMC personnel are disregarded, and the abuses that PMC employees commit – which would be war crimes if carried out by their military counterparts – go unpunished, as they did at Abu Ghraib.

This public–private intersection, in which the actions of states and PMCs are considered cumulatively, holds more promise as a strategy for meaningfully applying Just War theory to conflicts that are substantially privatized. It recognizes the moral primacy of the state, particularly with respect to *jus ad bellum* decisions, but it also acknowledges the influence of private actors even on those choices. In the conduct of war, where PMCs are acting with considerable autonomy, this public–private intersection allocates responsibility to both the PMC employees who commit the violations and, where appropriate, to the state that hired them. This public–private intersection recognizes that both states and private actors bear responsibility for the conduct of wars in which they are involved, and it seeks to allocate this responsibility in a meaningful way. It further acknowledges the goal of the Just War tradition, which is to limit the unnecessary use of force.

Conclusion

The Iraq war can provide us with great insight into the moral problems associated with the participation of PMCs in war. The large numbers of PMC personnel operate with little public notice. Even their casualties are not counted among the costs of war. These losses go largely unnoticed except for when they are carried out in a particularly visible or gruesome fashion, like the attacks on Blackwater employees in Fallujah. The only other time that the actions of PMC employees draw our attention is when they commit horrific violations like those that took place at the Abu Ghraib prison. Except for when they are victims of abusers in some horrifying manner, PMCs and their employees go unnoticed. This lack of attention belies the important role that these actors play in war, and Iraq is far from exceptional in this respect. PMCs have participated in conflicts on every continent. The private market for force is genuinely transnational both in supply and in demand. The companies and individuals that meet this demand are an integral part of contemporary warfare. As such, their participation is on a par with that of the individuals who make up the national militaries and should be incorporated into our thinking about warfare.

The reliance of states on PMCs, as reflected in that industry's revenue, has grown significantly since the end of the Cold War and will not be diminishing in the foreseeable future. More likely it will continue to be a feature of warfare indefinitely. The realities of privatization, which have only become more pronounced, mean that Just War theory must adapt to these new features of the international order or become irrelevant to the evaluation of war. Though Just War theory has persisted across a number of political orders, in its current form it is a statist theory in a world where non-state actors are playing an ever-growing role in conflict. For Just War theory to retain its relevance, it must acknowledge that states now operate in a very different type of international system, in which private actors influence the decision to go to war and, in large part, carry out the decision to go to war. While these actors are often disregarded private actors outside the purview of international relations, ignoring them would lead to an incomplete picture of war.

The public–private intersection offers a more promising approach to assessing the justice of wars that are waged, increasingly, by a coalition of public and private actors. Acknowledging this partnership and allocating responsibility between public and private actors more effectively takes account of the role that both play. While the choice to wage war is still the domain of the state and its leaders, these choices are influenced by the availability of PMCs to help fight the war. The potential of states to hire PMCs also bears on the more strategic elements of the decision, the reasonable chance of success. During war, these PMCs perform functions that were once performed by state militaries. They have the same potential to commit what are in substance war crimes. Under these circumstances, recognizing the potential of these actors to affect the justice of a war becomes imperative. If Just War theory fails to do so in some way, this tradition will cease to have any influence over our moral reasoning about war.

8

The Problem of Patriotism

Cheyney Ryan

I begin with some words of Rousseau's, from some fragmentary writings on war:

> I open the books on Right and on ethics; I listen to the professors and jurists; and, my mind full of their seductive doctrines, I admire the peace and justice established by the civil order; I bless the wisdom of our political institutions and, knowing myself a citizen, cease to lament I am a man. Thoroughly instructed as to my duties and my happiness, I close the book, step out of the lecture room, and look around me. I see wretched nations groaning beneath a yoke of iron. I see mankind ground down by a handful of oppressors. I see a famished mob, worn down by sufferings and famine, while the rich drink the blood and tears of their victims at their ease. I see on every side the strong armed with the terrible powers of the Law against the weak.... And that is the fruit of your peaceful institutions! Indignation and pity rise from the very bottom of my heart. Yes, heartless philosopher! come and read us your book on a field of battle! (Rousseau 1917)

Rousseau's words are of enduring cautionary value to the abstract speculations of philosophers. But they had a special resonance for me in the 1990s. These were the years of Francis Fukuyama's proclaiming the 'End of History' (1992). For him, the end of the Cold War meant that world peace was at hand. The form this took among progressive political theorists was a celebration of the cosmopolitan world order, assumed to be then emerging, aimed at establishing a global human rights regime. No one could quarrel with this in the abstract. As Rousseau says, such visions of peace, justice, and civil order can only be admired. Everyone wants a global order of peace, tolerance, and human rights. The question is: what does it mean in practice?

For many in the 1990s, it meant the importance of intervening in societies where rights were being abused. It meant, in other words, weakening, if not abandoning entirely, that aspect of state sovereignty associated with the principle of non-interference. Many wrestled with the implications of this, but some were not bothered by it at all. Quite the contrary. State sovereignty in their eyes was just an artifact of an outmoded order – or disorder, to be precise – in so far as the world of sovereign states had been one of almost constant warfare, culminating in the conflicts of the twentieth century. The bridge to the twenty-first century would take us from the outmoded world of nation-states to the cosmopolitan global order – now very much à la mode. At best, nation-states would have 'conditional sovereignty,' conditional on their respect for the human rights of their own citizens. Or this is how the thinking went.

'Humanitarian interventions,' in name if not in fact, were nothing new. People have always argued about their pros and cons, just as they continue to argue about the merits of the Kosovo action or the failures in Rwanda. Previously, though, no one thought that endorsing such actions meant a fundamental rethinking of state sovereignty and the principles of war – any more than the problems of civil war compelled such a rethinking. They were problems of the penumbra, in Hart's (1990: 3) phrase. The novelty of the 1990s was that humanitarian interventions moved from the penumbra to the center. They stood at the heart of a new paradigm, exemplifying fundamental changes in the logic of sovereignty and war-making.

Future historians of international relations theory may find this curious, to say the least. The Cold War was not ended by one side 'intervening' to defend the rights of those oppressed by the other side; quite the contrary. It was ended by popular actions of peoples to secure their own rights. The 'interventions' that the United States and Soviet Union did carry out all ended badly, for the people being 'saved' most of all, but also for the power in question. The first Gulf War – the principal source of the United States' troubles with al-Qaeda, remember – was an old-fashioned defense of Kuwaiti

sovereignty against Iraq. The most successful humanitarian intervention of our time, the Vietnamese invasion of Cambodia to stop
the genocide, received little mention; certainly no one drew larger
conclusions from it about the nature of politics and war.

No one could doubt in the 1990s that traditional notions of state
sovereignty were under siege. At the time, though, it struck me
that the most significant erosion of state sovereignty in matters of
war-making was overlooked; it is still overlooked, in my view. I am
thinking of the end of conscription. Since Hobbes, theorists of sovereignty had regarded the right to compel people to fight for it to be a
defining feature of sovereign power. This view of sovereignty was at
the center of the 1918 US Supreme Court decision upholding the draft
against the charge of slavery. Speaking for the court, Chief Justice
White invoked Blackstone and Vattel to assert 'the very conception
of a just government ... includes the duty of the citizen to render
military service ... and the right of the government to compel it.'[1]
Sovereignty meant nothing if it did not mean the right to conscript.
By the early 1970s this idea was already headed into the dustbin of
history, in fact if not theory. In the United States, this was a major
consequence of the Vietnam experience. It meant that a central aspect
of traditional state sovereignty was being eroded.

Theorists of the nation-state stress that conscription was more
than a mechanism for generating soldiers. It embodied an ideal of
citizenship that many found attractive, which is why many did not
experience its coercive dimensions as onerous. Believe it or not,
prior to the Vietnam War conscription was one of the most popular
institutions in the United States![2] Call it the 'citizen-soldier ethic.' In
essence, the blessings of citizenship brought with them the burdens of
soldiering, and vice versa. The core of the nation-state consisted of a
bargain: citizens received the protection of their persons and rights
plus welfare benefits from the state, in return for which they served
the state in wartime. This explains why the story of the twentieth-
century nation-state was one of both expanding social benefits and
expanding military burdens for the average citizen. In the simplest
terms, the one was the flip side of the other.

The model of the citizen-soldier emerged with the nationalization
of military force under the control of the state. Prior to the French
Revolution, the extensive use of mercenaries was widespread. A

158 RETHINKING THE 21ST CENTURY

normative consensus against the use of mercenaries began to emerge, resulting from the rise of nationalism. Rousseau criticized these mercenary troops as a source of suppression. He referred to the example of Rome, in which 'mercenaries, whose worth could be judged by the price at which they sold themselves ... believed it brought them more honor to be the henchmen of Caesar than the defenders of Rome' (Rousseau 1997, 29). Rousseau's solution to this dilemma was to employ citizen armies, and then only as needed, lest the republic become 'downtrodden and miserable' as other imperialist peoples had (1997, 28). The key, for Rousseau, was for the legitimate use of public power, which created in citizens a love for their state and obviated the use of means of suppression or coercion.

My name for the system, as it prevailed in the United States, is 'martial liberalism.' The broader import of conscription for the political culture generally makes it all the stranger that it has received such little attention from political theorists. When noted at all, it is as a positive thing. Martin Shaw, a prominent sociologist of war, wrote:

> [A] little noticed, accelerating feature of the last half-century is the disintegration of states' traditional ability to mobilize men for armed service, and the development of a 'post-military citizenship'. Continental Europe has begun to follow Britain, America and Japan in abandoning conscription. After Afghanistan and now Chechnya, many young Russians and their families question the oppressive and dangerous conditions in which they are forced to serve. In the West, professional soldiers' lives are now valued. The mothers of British 'friendly fire' victims fought a legal battle to bring to account the American pilots who had shot them down. President Clinton went to extraordinary lengths to ensure that no American soldiers died in Kosovo. (Shaw 1991)

One can look at the end of conscription in the US as another instance of human rights trumping state sovereignty – in this case, personal liberty and the value of human life trumping the state's right to dispose of people as it pleases. But here, as with humanitarian intervention, the question is whether this tells the full story.

Building a Bridge (Back) to the Twentieth Century: Another Great Illusion?

In the 1990s, humanitarian intervention and the end of conscription were closely linked, to my mind. Listening to discussions of humanitarian intervention and their importance, my first source of disquiet was the question of who will be fighting and dying in these interventions. In the United States, at least, the end of the draft all but guaranteed that it would *not* be the children or family members of those urging such actions – be it the public realm, or more academic circles. The talk was of how 'we' had the duty to intervene, because 'we' had the obligation to be equally sensitive to the plight of distant sufferers. But in matters of ultimate sacrifice, shouldn't the status of this 'we' be of first concern? Imagine a politician, or a professor, proclaiming that a distant country needed body parts, and that 'we' had a duty to provide them. Would it be narcissistic to ask, '*Whose* body parts do you have in mind?' During the Vietnam era, the question 'Who does the dying?' was pushed to the center of discussions of war and peace. It vanished just as quickly from the discussions of the 1990s.

Michael Walzer had the most to say about who will do the fighting and dying, which may explain why he remained one of the more skeptical of such ventures. He wrote, 'Should we put soldiers at risk in faraway places when our country is not under attack or threatened with attack ... and when national interests, narrowly understood, are not at stake?' (Walzer 1995). Walzer's response was tentative, and not entirely coherent. He explained, 'I am strongly inclined, sometimes, to give a positive answer to this question' (Walzer 1995). I take this to mean that we sometimes should send soldiers under certain circumstances. But his reasons for saying so turn the problem back to one of self-defense. Walzer argues, 'All states have an interest in global stability,' and 'grossly uncivilized behavior' tends to 'spread,' hence 'pay the moral price of silence and callousness and you will soon have to pay the political price of turmoil and lawlessness nearer home' (1995). This sounds like a repackaged appeal to national self-interest, conjoined with an appeal to moral urgency. 'In the face of human disaster, however, internationalism has a more urgent meaning. It's not possible to wait; anyone who can take the initiative should do so' (Walzer 1995). Exhortations that 'we' must 'take the initiative' are more compelling, though, from people who will take the initiative. But the initiative they have in mind is sending someone else to do it.

Mary Kaldor has expressed a similar concern. Writing in 2000, she argued for reconceiving humanitarian interventions as 'cosmopolitan law enforcement.' This is an admirable idea. But, as she noted, there was a 'lacuna' in the question of who were the people who would do the enforcing (Kaldor 2000). 'In the new wars,' she wrote, 'is it possible to find cosmopolitans who [will] risk their lives to save others' (Kaldor 2000). She explained that 'dying for hearth and home is quite different from risking life for something as abstract as humanity' (Kaldor 2000). Isn't the idea of individuals dying for humanity 'ridiculously utopian'? Kaldor never answered this objection, except to note that dying for one's nation was also a relatively recent notion. While this is true, if our individualist ethic has rendered dying for one's country archaic, it's hard to see how dying for the world will fare any better. After all, the citizen-soldier ethic presumed a kind of bargain between citizens and their country: citizens fought for their land in return for the protection, and benefits, it provided. It's hard to see what the cosmopolitan equivalent of this would be. It is unclear what blessings are promised in return for dying for 'the world.'

This reveals a second problem. In the United States, at least, the end of the draft meant the end of a significant constraint on military action. Indeed, this was a factor in why it was ended. The man who ended conscription, President Richard Nixon, told his advisers that, once the draft was ended, professionals and especially college professors would lose all interest in the question of who fought our wars – since *their* children would no longer be affected.[3] He was absolutely right about this. I can attest, from my own unpleasant experiences, that bringing up the question 'Who fights our wars?' among most academics generates blank stares, vague annoyance, and the demand to move on to more serious questions. My worry in the late 1990s was that ending the draft had removed a major check on reckless war-making – should the occasion arise.

And I worried that it would arise. As an amateur scholar of World War I, I was struck by how the cosmopolitan visions of the 1990s, with their confident tales of global commerce and other interconnections rendering major war outdated, were eerily like the ones that had preceded the First World War (Ryan 1996, 1999). Then too, remember, globalization had reached unprecedented heights, Europe and America were embracing international arbitration, pro-peace organizations spanned the business and labor communities, and, of the best-selling books of those years, Norman Angell's *The Great Illusion* (1913), argued for the obsolescence of all war. It all proved to be the calm before the storm. Were the 1990s another calm before the storm?

The major question posed by the twentieth century is why it worked out so badly, especially given the optimism at the start. The horrors of the twentieth century are not disputed by those who have approached them historically. Isaiah Berlin once remarked, 'I have lived through most of the 20th century without, I must add, suffering personal hardship. I remember it only as the most terrible century in Western history' (Hobsbawm 1994: 1). Rene Dumont states, 'I see it only as a century of massacres and wars' (Hobsbawm 1994: 1). It was, above all else, the century of warfare. Consider these figures, drawn from several mainstream sources.

From 1900 to 1990 the world saw 237 new wars whose battles killed about 1 million persons per year. By the century's end that number climbed to approximately 275 wars and 115 million deaths in battle. While averages can be misleading, since most of the deaths occurred in the two world wars, this equals about 3,150 deaths per day or about 130 deaths per hour, twenty-four hours a day, throughout the entire century (Tilly 1990: 67).[4] And this does not include civilian deaths, which are harder to estimate, though for the first time in history civilian deaths due to war outnumbered those of soldiers. Total deaths due to war in the twentieth century may have approached 250 million, or almost 7,000 people a day, 300 people per hour.

No other century in history approaches these totals in numbers of conflicts and numbers of people killed. The comparative figures are equally striking. If one looks at the percentage of people killed by war relative to total population, the eighteenth century saw 5 deaths per 1,000, the nineteenth century 6 deaths per 1,000, the twentieth century 46 deaths per 1,000 (almost eight times higher than the previous century). As Niall Ferguson writes of the two world wars, the defining events of the century:

> Even allowing for the accelerating growth in the world's population, the world wars were the most destructive in history. Somewhere in the region of 2.4 per cent of the world's entire population was killed in the Second World War … compared with roughly .4 per cent in the Thirty Years War and .2 per cent in the Napoleonic Wars and the War of the Spanish Succession. The total death toll in the First World War amounted to something like 1 percent of the pre-war population of all 14 combat

countries, 4 per cent of all males between 15 and 49 and 13 per cent of all those mobilized. ... In the Second World War roughly 3 per cent of the entire prewar population of all combatant countries died as a result of the war. (Ferguson 1995, 34)

Casualties have been lower since the Second World War but Ferguson attributes this to the fact that wars 'have generally been fought against far less well equipped opposition.' 'The world has not become that much more peaceful,' he writes, 'It is just that the overwhelming majority of the victims of war have been Asians or Africans' (Ferguson 1995: 36).

There was actually little discussion of this, among political theorists at least. Perhaps the century was so terrible that no one wanted to think about it anymore. But surely the greatest question confronting the century's survivors was how to escape the cycle of endless war that characterized the era just concluded. Instead of building a bridge to the twenty-first century, were the 1990s building one back to the start of the twentieth?

Building a Bridge to the Eighteenth Century: The End of Patriotism

Soon after 9/11, many neoconservatives in fact proclaimed the 'war on terror' as the start of 'World War IV' ('World War III' for them was the Cold War). I continued to worry that the new conflict could become World War I redux: a 'War to End Terror' sounded an awful lot like a 'War to End All War.'[5] It quickly became clear that there were dramatic changes in how the war would be fought. Various factors – especially, I think, the end of conscription – meant that war as enterprise of fighting and dying would be increasingly detached from the ordinary citizen, certainly privileged citizens. We seemed to be returning to the eighteenth-century world of professional armies, fighting in far-off lands while the rest of us went about our business.

Someone who recognized this right away, and applauded it, was Representative (later presidential candidate) Ron Paul. Not long after 9/11 he proposed the 'Marque and Reprisal Act of 2001,' which would have granted the president the authority to issue letters of marque and reprisal against bin Laden and his cohorts (Paul 2001). Representative

Paul noted, correctly, that letters of marque were intended for situations like these – where the enemy was vague, conventional military solutions were impractical, and there was no reason to provoke a major war. His proposal tapped into the suggestion from some quarters that today's terrorists were just yesterday's pirates recycled. Specifically, the perpetrators of 9/11 were heirs to the Mediterranean pirates of Ottoman North Africa, the 'Barbary Pirates' – who had also fought in the name of Islam. West Point historian Glenn Voelz went so far as to claim that Americans were 'still fighting the same war' 200 years later. *Wall Street Journal* columnist Max Boot adopted the analogy to claim that military action against Islamic terrorists was no different to previous small wars, like the much-sung actions of the Marines on 'the Shores of Tripoli.'

Representative Paul was ridiculed at the time. But while no letters of marque have been issued, America has increasingly turned to the methods of the eighteenth century. Consider the phenomenon of corporate war (firms like Blackwater) discussed in the previous chapter. Here is an excerpt from the *New York Times* commenting on the congressional testimony of Blackwater chairman Eric Prince:

> Blackwater officials hoped that the testimony to Congress of the young, clean-cut former member of the Navy Seals [Mr. Prince] would dispel the notion that, as one Blackwater insider put it, 'he would be some guy with a peg leg and a parrot on his shoulder and an eye patch.' (Broder and Risen 2007)

This is the wrong analogy, though. Mr Prince and his cohorts are more like the privateers for Ron Paul's letters of marque, except that they do not keep the 'prizes' that they can steal from the enemy but are paid a flat salary, more like mercenaries. If humanitarian interventions signified the new form of war in the 1990s, the next decade will be remembered for the robust emergence of privatized forms of violence – pirates fighting privateers and mercenaries, if you will.

To its great credit, the main institution in the United States that has resisted this turn to privatized violence has been the military itself. After Vietnam, military leaders, notably General Creighton Abrams, were distressed at the detachment of the military from the citizenry. To address it, they instituted the 'Total Force Policy' to bridge the military–civilian divide by requiring that future mobilization would involve substantial segments of the Reserves and National Guard. Hence the experience of Iraq so far has been contradictory: more and more private soldiers have been employed, but they have fought alongside men and women from the Reserves and the National Guard who have been wrenched away from their lives back home.

But proponents of the traditional citizen-soldier model are fighting a losing battle. Now, as in the eighteenth century, privatized forms of violence are functional for states, especially politically. In the past, privateers and mercenaries allowed for a certain blurring of responsibility and a certain degree of deniability in acts against other states or peoples. States could avoid blame for those they hired. Privatized war serves the same function today, though with mixed success. Corporate security firms have largely worked outside any framework of legal responsibility, though their periodic, often spectacular, misdeeds have brought them under periodic press scrutiny.

The greatest push towards a fully privatized, or at least professionalized, military of some sort comes from the fact that, judging from the post-9/11 era, the average American does not have the slightest interest in fighting in a war, much less dying in one. If 'patriotism' means the willingness to do those things, recent years have demonstrated the end of patriotism as a factor in American life. The United States abolished conscription in the 1970s and turned to a 'volunteer' military, meaning that the military became just another job, at best a job-training program, for many with otherwise limited options. After some initial bumpy experiences, this system proved to be successful one. In the 1980s and 1990s it attracted an increasingly educated pool of soldiers and was able to raise its standards on all levels.

It is now apparent that this 'volunteer' approach was successful just so long as no real wars were being fought. The moment soldiering involved shooting and dying there was a precipitous decline in new enlistments. African Americans have been key here. A major factor in the 'volunteer' military's success in the 1980s and 1990s was African Americans and other minorities seeing it as a good career opportunity. Though racial tensions in Vietnam left a bad legacy, the military came to be seen (correctly) as offering equal opportunity. At the end of the twentieth century minorities represented 42 percent of enlisted soldiers in the army. African Americans constituted 29 percent of army enlistees, despite constituting 13 percent of the population as

a whole. Latinos represented 9 percent of army enlistees. Puerto
Rico is the army's primary recruiting territory (American Friends
Service Committee 2008). Recruiting offices there have averaged four
times the rate in the United States (capitalizing on the island's high
unemployment rate).

African Americans especially have been wary of enlisting in the
'war on terror.' Major General Michael Rochelle, commander of army
recruiting, stated in August 2005, 'We saw a most precipitous drop
[of African Americans enlisting] immediately after September 11th'
(Whittle 2005).[6] Noting that the army had long enjoyed a 'special
relation' with blacks, he bemoaned the fact that the relation might
be over. In fiscal year 2001 African Americans constituted 23 percent
of all new army recruits, as they had in each the previous five years.
In fiscal year 2005 they constituted only 14 percent. That's a decline
of nearly 14 percent in the proportion of black recruits. DeTorrian
Rhone, 18, a recent high-school graduate, stated:

> A lot of black kids, they don't want to be in it. Most of the kids say they
> don't want to fight for a country that's pickin' on other countries. I don't
> want to fight because this [Iraq] war was stupid, it wasted money. Army
> people are getting killed for nothing, and we should have stayed in our
> own business. (Whittle 2005)

From 2000 to 2004 the number of black enlisted troops declined
significantly in all three military branches. During this four-year
period new recruits in all branches fell from 38,034 in 2000 to 26,170
in 2004, a decline of nearly a third. All commentators ascribe this
to the greater unpopularity of the Afghanistan and Iraq wars among
African Americans (Moniz 2005).

Another barrier to recruiting has been the attitudes of parents. A
Department of Defense survey in November of 2005 reported that
only 25 percent of parents would recommend military service to
their children, down from 42 percent in August 2003. The problem
is not just lack of encouragement but outright hostility. Said one
recruiter in Ohio, speaking anonymously, since the army ordered all
its recruiters to refrain from speaking from reporters, 'Parents are
the biggest hurdle we face.' General Rochelle stated that parental
resistance could put the all-volunteer force in jeopardy. When parents
and other influential adults dissuade young people from enlisting, he

said, 'It begs the question of what our national staying power might be for what certainly appears to be a long fight' (Cave 2005).

Part of the problem results from the law that was supposed to make recruiting easier. The No Child Left Behind Act, passed in 2001, required schools to turn over students' phone numbers and addresses unless parents opt out. This has been a spark that ignited parental resistance. Some recruiters have even been threatened with violence. 'I had one father say if he saw me on his doorstep I better have some protection on me,' said a recruiter in Ohio. 'We see a lot of hostility.'

We're Looking for a Few Good Grandmothers: Trials and Travails of the Volunteer Military

The official United States policy is to maintain sufficient military capacity to fight major wars on two fronts. Since the Carter administration, it has committed itself to whatever efforts are necessary to maintain stability in the Middle East. The massive military budget has reflected these priorities. Yet today the military has been brought to the breaking point by insurgencies in two small countries. The government's response to this has been multiple.

First, the military has begun offering bonuses up to $20,000 as it sends more and more recruiters into the field. There is talk of raising this to $40,000. The army has raised college scholarship offers from $50,000 to $70,000 and has offered up to $50,000 in 'mortgage assistance.' As a result, the cost of recruiting soldiers increased from $7,600 per soldier in 1996 to more than $14,000 in 2004. In 2003 the Pentagon spent almost $4 billion targeting high-achieving low-income youth, especially on enlistment bonuses, commercials, video games, personal visits, and slick brochures (Turse 2005).

Second, the military has always made special efforts to attract minorities, especially when the more privileged had little interest in fighting. During Vietnam, a program called Project 100,000 was created specifically to recruit Southern black youths to the war's front lines. Secretary of Defense McNamara had standards lowered to recruit and 'rehabilitate' 100,000 youths annually who had previously been rejected for failing mental or physical requirements. This resulted in several hundred thousand men being sent to Vietnam and several thousands to their deaths that otherwise would have been spared (MacPherson 2002: 9).[7] (In 1970 a Defense Department study found that 41 percent of the soldiers were black as compared to 12 percent of the army as a whole and 40 percent were trained for combat compared to 25 percent in the services generally.)

Accordingly, today's troop shortfall has led to increased efforts to target minorities, especially Latinos, who as a community are less relentlessly hostile to the administration's war policies than African Americans. In April 2005, *Los Angeles Times* reporter Erika Hayasaki described the approach of one recruiter, Carloss, who had spent seven weeks in recruiting classes to hone his marketing and communication skills. His techniques were those endorsed in the army's *School Recruiting Program Handbook* of 2004. Carloss made a point of delivering doughnuts and coffee to school staffs once a month, attending faculty and parent meetings, chaperoning at dances, participating in Hispanic Heritage monthly events, meeting with student governments, and even leading the football team in calisthenics – the overall aim being to make himself 'indispensable' on campus. The *Handbook* encourages recruiters like Carloss to ingratiate themselves with student leaders or, for example, the captain of the football team – not because they are likely to choose the military but because they will 'provide you with referrals who will enlist' (Hayasaki 2005).

Finally, in the summer of 2005 the Pentagon announced it was raising the age limit for recruits to 42. A military spokesperson explained by insisting that 'age should not be a basis for discrimination' (*New York Times* 2005). This led to a spate of human-interest stories describing the military's new middle-aged members, numbering in the thousands by some reports. Forty-one-year-old Lauri Ann Fouca, a mother of four from Arizona, followed her son into the military. 'My son was like, "You're crazy, moms don't join the military",' she said. Despite being a grandmother, Margie Black of West Columbia, Texas, also served alongside her 21-year-old daughter. A spokesman for the local recruiting office remarked, 'Lots of people (over thirty-five) are fit and are living longer, and they figure they can do this.' Pfc. Kimberly Brown 'couldn't resist' cupping her 18-year-old son Derek Noe's face in 'jubilation' after they were both successfully graduated from basic training. With five children to support at home, Ms Brown said that the work in the army was welcome.

The army continued to loosen its standards of who was morally fit to serve. As one commentator observed, the new slogan 'Army Strong' was accompanied by a weakening in its standards for enlistment.[8] It instituted a system of 'moral waivers' to bypass existing regulations. Recruits with serious criminal records, drug problems, histories of gang membership, and other questionable factors that would have excluded them were now accepted. From 2001 to 2006 the army's acceptance of moral waivers increased about 40 percent; from 2004 to 2005 the number of recruits brought in and with serious criminal misconduct waivers jumped 54 percent, drug and alcohol waivers increased 13 percent.

In the fall of 2007 the military was looking to further relax its standards, the Associated Press reported:

> Faced with higher recruiting goals, the Pentagon is quietly looking for ways to make it easier for people with minor criminal records to join the military. The review, in its early stages, comes as the number of Army recruits needing waivers for bad behavior – such as trying drugs, stealing, carrying weapons on school grounds and fighting – rose from 15 percent in 2006 to 18 percent this year. And it reflects the services' growing use of criminal, health and other waivers to build their ranks. Overall, about three in every 10 recruits must get a waiver, according to Pentagon statistics obtained by AP, and about two-thirds of those approved in recent years have been for criminal behavior. (Baldor 2007)

The article noted: 'According to the Pentagon data, the bulk of all conduct waivers are for recruits involved in either drug offenses or serious misdemeanors. Over the past five years, the overall percentage of recruits involved in serious misdemeanors has grown.' The relaxing of standards is necessary to meet Pentagon targets of increasing the army by about 65,000 soldiers to a total of 547,000, and the Marines by 27,000 to 202,000. But many are not enthusiastic about the prospect. Army officers complain that they already spend too much time dealing with discipline problems. '[I]n a meeting with Adm. Mike Mullen, chairman of the Joint Chiefs of Staff, a number of officers vigorously nodded their heads when he asked if that was a concern. One officer told Mullen that when he was in Iraq he would spend long hours into the night dealing with "problem children."'

Congressional voices responded sharply. After Congress voted to increase the size of the Army and Marine Corps, Representative

THE PROBLEM OF PATRIOTISM

Ellen Tauscher, a California Democrat and chairman of the House Armed Services subcommittee on strategic forces, charged that the wars in Iraq and Afghanistan had made the military so unattractive that 'moms and dads and spouses have voted with their feet,' urging soldiers to get out of uniform and discouraging young people from joining in the first place. She specifically cited problems raised by lowering moral standards. 'I'm all for rehab and giving people a second chance, but that's not why we're doing this. This is about the fact that we need people with pulses that are willing to come into the military,' she said. 'If you have – as the nuns used to say – comportment issues, if you can't sit quietly and listen, if you can't be trained and if you have a predilection to pilfering – or bigger things – you're going to be a decrement to your unit' (Matthews 2007).

No one knows what the upshot of such lowering of standards will be. Thus far, the most dramatic consequence has been the increase of groups like skinheads and neo-Nazis in the armed forces. Ten years ago the Pentagon toughened policies on admitting such elements after the Oklahoma City bombing by Timothy McVeigh, a decorated Gulf War veteran, and the murder of a black couple by a skinhead gang in the elite 82nd Airborne Division. Recruiters were given advice on how to identify such young men and exclude them. The Pentagon launched a massive investigation and crackdown within its own ranks. One general ordered all 19,000 soldiers at Fort Lewis, Washington to be strip-searched for extremist tattoos. But they are now looking the other way. 'Recruiters are knowingly allowing neo-Nazis and white supremacists to join the armed forces, and commanders don't remove them from the military even after we positively identify them as extremists or gang members,' said Department of Defense investigator Barfield (Kifner 2006).

One case in point was Forrest Fogarty, who, before he attended Military Police counterinsurgency training, attended Nazi skinhead festivals as leader of the hate rock band Attack. Before army engineer Jon Fain joined the invasion of Iraq, the neo-Nazi National Alliance member fantasized about fighting a war on Jews. 'Ever since my youth – when I watched World War II footage and saw how well-disciplined and sharply dressed the German forces were – I have wanted to be a soldier,' Fain said in a Winter 2004 interview with the National Alliance magazine *Resistance*. 'Joining the American military was as close as I could get.' Neo-Nazis 'stretch across all branches of service, they are linking up across the branches once they're inside, and they are hard-core,' Department of Defense gang detective Scott Barfield told the Intelligence Report. 'We've got Aryan Nations graffiti in Baghdad,' he added. 'That's a problem' (Holthouse 2006).

What we can say with some certainty is that the days of the traditional citizen-soldier military are over. No one wants to serve in the military, least of all the children of the politicians who call for war. I have spoken of the 'end of patriotism,' but the situation is more surreal than that. The rhetoric of patriotism lives on. Our leaders' discourse remains one of burdens 'we' must bear, in the defense of 'our' freedoms. But while the rhetoric of the nation-state endures, the substance of the ethic (the ethic of shared sacrifice) is ignored. The talk is that of community, the reality is one of privatization. The disparity is just most dramatic among the nation's leaders.

Well, not all its leaders. In a July 2005 *New York Times* article, describing how the United States was 'trolling' its Pacific territories for new recruits (these are the *Times*'s words), the article remarked on the devotion – to the United States – of Pacific island leaders, noting that the governor of American Samoa has a daughter serving in Iraq. The son of the president of the Federated States of Micronesia was a colonel in the Marine Corps. The governor of Samoa explained: 'The sacrifices of war should be shared by all, especially the leaders.'

I have looked for historical parallels to this disconnection between rhetoric and reality but have not found one. As a professor in a mid-sized state university, I cannot exaggerate the political cynicism it induces among my many students. But I cannot believe that such a contradiction can last forever. We are headed towards a post-nation-state privatized military. I do not know how this will be squared with America's nation-state political ideals.

Alienated War and Personal Responsibility

The situation we face is not unlike that which the great American anti-war critic Randolph Bourn, described almost a century ago in the waning days of World War I:

> We are learning that war doesn't need enthusiasm, doesn't need convic-
> tion, doesn't need hope, to sustain it. And that is why this war, with apathy

rampant, is probably going to act just as if every person in the country
were filled with patriotic ardor ... Our war is teaching us that patriotism
is really a superfluous quality in war. The government of a modern organized plutocracy does not have to ask whether the people want to fight or
understand what they are fighting for, but only whether they will tolerate
fighting. America does not co-operate with the President's designs. She
rather feebly acquiesces. (Bourne 1917)

My term for what Bourne is describing here is 'alienated war.' It is
both a set of institutions and a set of attitudes. The institutions aim to
minimize, or obscure, war's impact on the average citizen. The bodily
costs of war (i.e. who serves and dies) are shunted onto the poor, minorities, and non-citizens. The financial costs of war are passed on to
later generatation, through borrowing. The attitudes of alienated war
are principally ones of indifference, of the kind that Bourne describes.
Even those citizens who support a war have no intention of fighting
in it themselves, or have their children do so. Mainly people don't
think about it much at all. Not long ago my hometown newspaper ran
a guest editorial by a local high-school student, Michelle Spresser,
titled 'War Seems So Distant to Me and My Peers' (2007). 'Every time
the term 'Iraq War' comes up during conversations among my friends,
it's followed by heads shaking, eyeballs rolling, and laughter' (Spresser
2007). 'We observe war coverage with the same distant gaze that we
observe car commercials' (Spresser 2007). Bourne wrote long before
the age of post-modernism. But its hip, cynical detachment fits well
with the attitude of acquiescence that 'modern organized plutocracy'
needs to sustain its criminal wars (Bourne 1917).

One of the greatest challenges facing those of us distressed about
the prospects of future conflict is to comprehend and confront the
reality of alienated war. We are in a time of deep transition, and
contradiction, moving forward and backward in history at the same
time. Where we go next is a matter of political will and organization. My own view is that any credible future should focus on the
abolition of war entirely; for those who still believe in 'good' wars,
this chapter has stressed keeping in mind the question of who will
fight and die in them.

Some will respond to my concern with alienated war by claiming that I ignore the good side in it. Conscription did not render
countries more cautious, as nineteenth-century socialists like Jean

Jaurès believed it would. Quite the contrary: conscription and its citizen-soldier ethic provided the endless supply of soldiers that so contributed to the wastefulness of the century's mass wars. By contrast, eighteenth-century methods contributed to much more limited forms of war. Privateers were quite constrained compared to the twentieth century's nationalism-inflamed zealots. Letters of marque provided a more limited response to the aggressive actions of others than all-out war. If our driving concern is keeping war constrained, the eighteenth century's privatized forms of violence seem preferable to the more directly political forms of the twentieth century.

If we do not want to repeat the mass carnage of the twentieth century, these theorists tell us that we should celebrate the end of patriotism. There is a great deal of truth in this. As I said, we have yet to explore seriously why the twentieth century worked out so badly, but certainly the citizen-soldier ethic played a key role, conjoined with the powers of mass persuasion by large nation-states. At the same time, reality is complex. In keeping with Bourne, we must not ignore the profound moral challenges that the new face of war presents us. I can put these challenges in terms of a dilemma.

The nation-state, its citizen-soldier ethic, and conscription were massive engines of warfare. But implicit in the practice of conscription was a notion that I find quite attractive, as the foregoing discussion should suggest; and I worry about its demise. I am thinking of the notion that support for a war includes willingness to fight it yourself. The flip side of that coin, of course, is that one should not endorse a war one is unwilling to fight in. Indeed, unwillingness to fight should signal opposition. I find this ethic of personal responsibility to be an eminently plausible one. More generally, I think that the changing nature of war compels us to consider our personal responsibilities first and foremost. Alienated war severs the link of war and personal responsibility; indeed, it mocks moral questions generally. More than anything else, though, confronting alienated war requires a regenerated sense of personal responsibility and a clarity of moral purpose.

9

Sanctions as War

Laura Sjoberg

In fact, the siege was converted into a blockade, and the town, which
if the siege had continued must have very shortly fallen, held out for
six months. (Clausewitz 1989: 295)

In the 1990s, advocates of the use of economic sanctions and the
conditioning of humanitarian aid as political leverage argued that
economic sanctions were a new and peaceful solution to problems
which otherwise would have required military intervention. Citing
the successful use of economic coercion to end apartheid in South
Africa, advocates saw sanctions as a way to keep dangerous states
in check and to coerce reasonable states' interests into coincidence
with the interests of the international community more generally.
The 1990s, dubbed the 'sanctions decade' (Cortright and Lopez
2000), saw the proliferation of the use of unilateral and multilateral
sanctions. Many states have since recognized sanctions as a human
rights issue, in large part as a result of the terrible humanitarian
disaster caused by the economic sanctions on Iraq. Others still see
sanctions as the peaceful middle ground, as demonstrated by the UN
Security Council's use of sanctions to express disapproval of Iranian
nuclear proliferation. While the characterization of sanctions as a
problem of domestic and international security is relatively 'new'
in the post-Cold War security agenda, sanctions and embargoes are

an age-old tactic of war and the subject of much work in strategy and philosophy.[1] Clausewitz famously argued that war is the continuation of politics by other means. I argue that sanctions are the continuation of war by other means; an alternative way of expressing the same sentiments and achieving the same ends. I complement the Clausewitzian argument with a rereading of Bentham's idea of sanction as punishment in order to explore the nature of sanction as an alternative form of war in the 'new' security era.

Economic Sanctions in Post-Cold War Security Discourses

Economic sanctions have featured prominently on the 'new' security agenda, as a bloodless way to inspire shifts in state behavior. James Ngobi explains that 'economic sanctions have gained wide currency and attracted a great deal of attention in the international community, particularly during the last few years,' because 'there is a growing awareness that sanctions can provide an efficacious medium for promoting the commonweal of the international community through peaceful means' (1995: 17). In the security arena, 'sanctions are deployed to deprive an adversary of access to goods and technologies with direct military implications' (Hufbauer et al. 1990: 6). In addition, 'sanctions [as opposed to military means] have also been deployed in pursuit of a number of foreign policy goals' (Hufbauer et al. 1990: 6).

Sanctions have received a substantial amount of scholarly attention, for a number of reasons. First, as Cortright and Lopez (2000) have noted, the 1990s can be characterized at the 'sanctions decade' because of the frequency and duration of economic sanctions regimes applied by various actors in international politics. They explain (1995) that 'in the post-Cold War world, the prominence of economic sanctions as a tool of national and multinational diplomacy has increased.' Second, the economic sanctions regime imposed on Iraq in the 1990s caused substantial concern in global politics about the humanitarian impacts of such measures. Joy Gordon argued that 'sanctions are unacceptable from a utilitarian perspective because their economic effectiveness necessarily entails human damage, while their likelihood of achieving political objectives is low' (1999: 123). As

Mueller and Mueller note, 'the harm caused by [so-called weapons of mass destruction] pales in comparison to the havoc wreaked by a much more popular tool: economic sanctions' (1999: 47). Geoffrey Simons characterized the humanitarian effects of the economic sanctions on Iraq as a 'new holocaust,' explaining that 'details of civilian morbidity and mortality, the scale of sickness and malnutrition, the grim statistics of emaciated babies and dying children' add up to a 'modern genocide' (1998: 214). These humanitarian consequences were caused by the deprivation of food and other essential goods caused by the combination of an import embargo and Iraq's lack of capacity to produce these goods domestically. Third, economic sanctions regimes have caused several quagmires for international law: questions of the authority of the Security Council (Caron 1993), the relationship between sanctions and states' obligations to the World Trade Organization (WTO) (Elliott and Hufbauer 1999), and the punitive implications of sanctions regimes (Nossal 1989). Fourth, the question of whether sanctions are complied with has been one of substantial controversy among political scientists (see Pape 1997, 1998; Elliott 1998). Finally, scholars have wondered about the place of this newly popular security policy in International Relations theory (Drezner 1999; Sjoberg 2002).

It is not only in the academy but also in the policy world that economic sanctions have received a growning degree of attention. In addition to the increased use of sanctions as a tool of security policy, sanctions have been a matter of foreign policy controversy. For example, most recently, 'the six powers dealing with Iran's contested nuclear programme will start work on a resolution for new sanctions against Iran at the UN Security Council' (Agence France Presse 2007), but, among other nations, Italy has expressed skepticism about the value of economic sanctions compared to their possible humanitarian impacts (Press TV 2007). Given the popularity of economic sanctions as a possible answer to the crisis of Iranian nuclear proliferation specifically and the significant role that sanctions have played in the 'new security' discourse generally, this chapter seeks to explore the question of the 'newness' of the sanctions debate, focusing on the view of sanctions as a peaceful alternative to war, and to apply 'old' theoretical tools to analyze its critical questions.

Current Theoretical Approaches to Economic Sanctions[2]

In order to interrogate the 'newness' of the economic sanctions debate, it is necessary to take account of the most successful theoretical approaches to the question in current scholarship. International Relations analyses of the effectiveness of sanctions are informed by a variety of theoretical perspectives. For example, a realist view of sanctions sees economic coercion as a way of raising the cost of non-compliance for the country on which sanctions are imposed until it becomes unacceptable (Baldwin 1985). This approach understands sanctions as an *enforcement* mechanism, a tool of statecraft used to translate relative power advantages into changes in other states' policy choices (Baldwin 1999, 2000; Chan and Drury 2000). Exercising power with sanctions, in this interpretation, is like exercising military power – if an actor can cause substantial enough pain to force an opponent's compliance, sanctions have been successful.

A second generally accepted understanding of sanctions can be seen to fit loosely within the liberal theoretical tradition in International Relations. This approach explains sanctions as a way of depriving the target state of the means to commit a violation of international norms (Martin 1992). In other words, sanctions take away the resources an errant state would use to defy the will of the sanctioner(s). Lisa Martin argues that states cooperate with each other to institute multilateral sanctions regimes that attempt to deprive the target state of the means to act in violation of their demands. In this theoretical approach, sanctions function as institutional constraints on state behavior. The target is not directly forced to cooperate by the degree of suffering, but indirectly forced by the removal of the capacity to engage in the undesirable behavior.

A constructivist approach to sanctions views them as a socializing phenomenon, communicating a message of disapproval through the combination of negative consequences and international shame (Crawford and Klotz 1999). Here, sanctions are not understood as direct or indirect physical force, but as coercive social pressure (Crawford and Klotz 1999; Crawford 2000) According to Crawford and Klotz (1999), sanctions communicate to the target that its behavior is unacceptable, using a combination of negative consequences and shame. They argue that the 'normative communication model' explains the success of sanctions on South Africa (Crawford and Klotz 1999). They explain that, through economic coercion, the international community successfully communicated a norm against apartheid. A similar view sees sanctions as punishment, both for the purposes of social learning and for retribution (Nossal 1989). Sanctions as punishment communicate norm violation and invoke suffering for errant policy choices (Doxey 1987: 4; Leyton-Brown 1987).

A fourth approach to economic sanctions can be seen as having roots in neoliberal institutionalism and linguistic constructivism. This sees economic sanctions as argumentation. T. Clifton Morgan and Valerie Schwebach see economic sanctions as bargaining tools which change the incentive structure states have to reach a negotiated settlement (1997; Morgan 1994). Cortright and Lopez have also characterized sanctions as a tool to be used in bargaining and argumentation for leverage (2002, 2000, 1999). Karen Fierke's (2000) linguistic constructivist approach to economic sanctions also characterizes them as argumentation, describing sanctions as an expression of the strength of one state's opinions about the behavior of another and the reaction to sanctions as the target's response.

These four approaches to the study of economic sanctions draw on traditions in International Relations theory to deal with the 'new' security problem of economic sanctions. Still, this chapter argues that there are two problems with them individually and collectively. First, these approaches have failed to inspire a sophisticated debate about the process by which economic sanctions are or are not effective in the political arena. Second, these approaches have not adequately taken advantage of the 'old' political theorizing that could lend that complexity or of the rich history of the use of economic sanctions in international conflict. For example, the enforcement approach does not take account of the differences between the costs of sanctions to target governments and the cost of sanctions to the civilian populations in target states. Along the same lines, the institutionalist approach analyzes the multilateral nature of some sanctions regimes, but neglects the reasons why states (individually or collectively) obtain an interest in sanctioning other states. The normative communication model does not pay adequate attention to norm formation as a process. The argumentation model ignores the power differentials between the sanctioning power(s) and target state(s). The 'argument' often takes place in an atmosphere of gross power disparity, where sanctions translate economic might into right. Given these issues, this chapter contends that some 'old' theoretical approaches, specifically those of Carl von Clausewitz and Jeremy Bentham, could be the foundation for a more complex approach to economic sanctions as a 'new' security issue.

The 'Old' Problem of Economic Sanctions

While the emphasis on economic sanctions as a part of national security policy and the frequent use of the tool are 'new' in the last two decades, economic sanctions have long been a part of the military and policy arsenals of international actors, and a subject of the analysis of political theory. For example, Thucydides (1998: 61) characterized the Athenians as 'fatigued by blockade' at one point in the Peloponnesian War, and the Peloponnesians at another point as 'at a loss and fearful of winter … [because] it would become impossible to send provisions' through a blockade (1998: 202). Blockades are military installments set up to block the transportation of food and other essential goods into the blockaded areas – an ancient version of economic sanctions used as a weapon in war. In fact, there are eight different blockades in Thucydides' account of the Peloponnesian War.

In the work of Thucydides and other premodern theorists, economic deprivation was seen as a normal tactical choice for actors at war. Works as diverse as those of Machiavelli and Sun Tzu mention economic sanctions as a method of gaining strategic advantage in warfare. Indeed, as Kimberly Elliott and Clyde Hufbauer note, throughout most of history, 'economic sanctions have preceded or accompanied war' (2002). They explain that 'sanctions often have taken the form of a naval blockade intended to weaken the enemy during wartime' (Elliott and Hufbauer 2002). This approach can also be seen in Clausewitz's *On War*, where he discusses the appropriate time to use the tactics of siege and blockade. He describes economic coercion as something which 'can only be decided according to particular circumstances' (1989: 395) and inappropriate 'if the forces opposed were too much on an equality' (1989: 384). Megan O'Sullivan describes sanctions as an 'age-old tool' which has been called upon in many conflicts throughout history, including, most famously, the Napoleonic wars (2003: 1).

Though sanctions had historically been considered a part of the making and fighting of wars, the rhetoric that sanctions may be seen as 'peaceful' is relatively new. As Elliott and Hufbauer document, 'only when the horrors of World War I prompted President Woodrow Wilson to call for new methods of dispute resolution were sanctions seriously considered as an alternative to war. Sanctions were incorporated as a tool of enforcement in ... the League of Nations between the two world wars and the United Nations since World War II' (2002). O'Sullivan notes that from 1914 to 1990 the United States most often used sanctions against states to constrain or influence the external behavior of a country or to destabilize a regime' and 'rarely called upon to alter the internal behavior of regimes,' but treated sanctions as an extra-military tool to achieve strategic goals (2003: 15). Peter Wallensteen explains that 'sanctions policy was a major issue of discussion in the 1930s. In the 1960s a new intensive debate emerged, and in the 1990s there [was] a repeated interest in sanctions issues' (2000: 1). These 'sanctions issues' began to be considered independently of the use of military force.

In the 1930s, the major sanctions debate revolved around handling states' foreign policy aggression. According to Wallensteen, 'one of the conclusions from the First World War was a belief that the economic blockade against Germany had been effective' (2000: 1). Sanctions were then discussed against Japan for its aggression against China, and levied against Italy for its aggression in Ethiopia. The sanctions regime on Italy failed to deter or mitigate Italian aggression, and the policy debate was crippling to the League of Nations.

In the 1960s, a new round of sanctions was implemented: the United States sanctioned Cuba and the Dominican Republic, while the USSR sanctioned Albania and China (Wallensteen 1968). The key determining factor in these sanctions was the state's position in relation to the Cold War superpowers. Two multilateral sanctions regimes also existed during this period: the United Nations sanctions on Southern Rhodesia (to challenge its declaration of independence) and on South Africa in opposition to apartheid. It is widely believed that the sanctions regime against apartheid 'significantly hastened South Africa's historic political transition' (Cortright and Lopez 1995: ix).

Even given these earlier uses of economic sanctions in international policy, the frequency with which states and intergovernmental
organizations use economic sanctions as a tool of policy leverage has
increased exponentially since the end of the Cold War (Cortright
and Lopez 2000). Indeed, as mentioned above, Cortright and Lopez
(2000) have identified the 1990s as the 'sanctions decade' because of
the proliferation of sanctions regimes. As the frequency of the use
of sanctions has changed, the reasons for their application have also
broadened. Since 1990, the majority of sanctions against state actors
have 'had the aim of changing the domestic conduct of a target,'
particularly to promote democracy (O'Sullivan 2003: 15). Wallensteen
notes that 'a mark of the sanctions of the 1990s, as compared to previous periods, is their link to internal war situations' (2000: 5).

Further, the policy rhetoric of sanctions as an alternative to armed
conflict came into its own in this era. While leaders since Woodrow
Wilson had characterized sanctions as a matter outside of military
policy rather than a tactical weapon, the 1990s saw the explicit use
of sanctions as a 'peaceful alternative' to military force in situations
where intervention was deemed necessary. As Cortright and Lopez
explain, the proliferation of sanctions regimes suggests 'a recent
trend to find effective international responses, *short of military action*,
to violations of accepted norms of behavior' (1995: ix).[3] Given these
changes in the intent and understanding of the role of economic
sanctions regimes, the content of the sanctions has changed as well.
While comprehensive embargoes were popular before the twentieth
century, most sanctions after the turn of the century but before the
1990s were targeted and limited in size and scope. There were limitations on humanitarian aid, indirect investment sanctions, or sanctions
that targeted a particular sector of a state's economy. These limited
sanctions were used as an alternative to comprehensive sanctions
regimes reminiscent of old economic embargoes. Since the 1990s,
sanctions regimes have been, for the most part, 'directed against
authoritarian regimes or groupings' and have been, for the most part,
'comprehensive sanctions' (Wallensteen 2000: 8). The comprehensive
nature of these sanctions regimes has revived the question of the
humanitarian implications of (embargoes and/or) sanctions.

The question of humanitarian effects became particularly conten-
tious in the policy debate over one of modern history's most strict

economic sanctions regimes, the United Nations Security Council sanctions against Iraq, which were in place between 1990 and 2003 (Selden 1999). While the actors still disagree on who was responsible for the sanctions regime, most observers agree that the humanitarian implications of the economic deprivation from this sanctions regime was horrific. As Pilger notes:

> When asked on US television if she [Madeleine Albright, US Secretary of State] thought that the death of half a million Iraqi children [from sanctions in Iraq] was a price worth paying, Albright replied: 'This is a very hard choice, but we think the price is worth it.' (Pilger 2000)

Given these humanitarian implications, many states that had initially endorsed the sanctions on Iraq came to oppose the sanctions regime, and expressed wariness about the implementation of others. While economic sanctions regimes are more controversial in the wake of the sanctions on Iraq, there is no 'clear-cut' decrease in the use of unilateral or multilateral economic sanctions regimes in the new millennium (O'Sullivan 2003: 11). Currently, some sort of economic sanctions regime is being enforced against more than three dozen countries in the world. The United Nations Security Council has approved economic sanctions against Iran in the hope that they will deter the country from developing nuclear weapons. As the popularity of economic sanctions as a foreign policy tool increases, sanctions regimes have come to be deemed an appropriate tool for fighting the 'war on terror.' As Meghan O'Sullivan explains, the 'new' use of economic sanctions is 'to deal with one of the greatest challenges of the post-September 11 environment: states that support terrorism and pursue weapons of mass destruction' (O'Sullivan 2003: 1).

Since sanctions came to be seen as an 'alternative' to war, they are 'much explored, but still poorly understood' in the academic and policy arenas (O'Sullivan 2003: 3). Scholars and policymakers have yet to agree on a definition of economic sanctions, on the measure for sanctions' success, or on the humanitarian implications of sanctions as a policy. This picture gets more complex as the 'war on terror' continues. This chapter, relying on the 'old' insights of Carl von Clausewitz, argues that much of that theoretical ambiguity flows from the miscategorization of sanctions as an alternative to war rather than an alternative form of war.

'Old' Solutions to the Economic Sanctions Problem

From a 'tactic' of war to an alternative?

> As Cold War threats have diminished, so-called weapons of mass destruction – nuclear, chemical, and biological weapons and ballistic missiles – have become the new international bugbears. The irony is that the harm caused by these weapons pales in comparison to the havoc wreaked by a much more popular tool: economic sanctions. Tally up the casualties caused by rogue states, terrorists, and unconventional weapons, and the number is surprisingly small. The same cannot be said for deaths inflicted by international sanctions. The math is sobering and should lead the United States to reconsider its current policy of strangling Iraq. (Mueller and Mueller 1999)

In the above passage, Mueller and Mueller argue that the economic sanctions on Iraq (even without any use of military force) caused more human suffering than the combination of all uses of weapons of mass destruction in history. Their implicit argument is that economic sanctions are not only a weapon of war, but one of the most deadly weapons belligerent states can use. This interpretation is squarely at odds with the new security claim that sanctions qualify as a peaceful alternative to war – it argues instead that, under the guise of that peacefulness, sanctions are a deadlier weapon than actual military intervention.

This chapter considers carefully the implied claim in Mueller and Mueller's article that economic sanctions regimes constitute war. It uses Carl von Clausewitz's definition of war to evaluate whether sanctions are 'war' when they are applied outside of the use of any traditional military force. Through Clausewitz's understanding, this section characterizes economic sanctions not as an alternative to war but as an alternative form of war.

Clausewitz, who lived in the late eighteenth and early nineteenth centuries, was a Prussian soldier and military strategist. His *On War* has been characterized by many as the most important single work written on the theory of warfare and strategy. It has been utilized both in policy and political science to identify, disaggregate, and analyze wars in modern times.

Clausewitz defines war as 'an act of [physical] force to compel the enemy to do our will.' He elaborates that 'the political object is the goal, war is the means of reaching it, and means can never be considered in isolation from their purpose' (Clausewitz 1989: 87). Clausewitz understands that 'there is only one means in war: combat. But the multiplicity of forms that combat assumes leads us in as many different directions as are created by the multiplicity of aims' (1989: 96). This definition can be used to characterize economic sanctions (especially in their comprehensive form) as a form of war rather than an alternative to war.

The first element of the Clausewitzian definition of war is the existence of political objects for which the force is being employed. As O'Sullivan and Wallensteen noted, 'new' comprehensive sanctions have often been enacted to inspire domestic political change. For example, the UN Security Council Sanctions regime against Iraq aimed at eliminating Iraq's weapons programs, changing the regional strategic balance, improving the human rights situation in Iraq, ending Saddam Hussein's rule, and/or protecting Kuwaitis from the Saddam Hussein administration. The United States' sanctions regime against Syria under President George W. Bush was in place with the political aims of discouraging the Syrian government from 'supporting terrorism, continuing its occupation of Lebanon, pursuing weapons of mass destruction and missile programs, and undermining the United States and international efforts with respect to the stabilization of reconstruction of Iraq' (Bush 2003). In a speech at the United Nations, Bush made it clear that economic sanctions regimes imposed by the United States and the UN have a political agenda. As Steven Lee Myers reports:

> President Bush, calling on countries to live up to freedoms and rights promised by the United Nations almost six decades ago, ... announced tighter sanctions on Myanmar and denounced the governments of Belarus, Cuba, Iran, North Korea, Syria, and Zimbabwe as 'brutal regimes' that should be confronted for their abuses. (Myers 2007: A8)

These political reasons for economic sanctions regimes, stated and deduced, identify a number of sanctions policies as having political ends that are primary among the reasons for policy implementation. Nevertheless, the existence of political ends is not sufficient to determine the existence of a war in Clausewitz's interpretation. He argues that war is an extension of politics by other means – thus the means of the operation are key to determining the existence of war.

Clausewitz understands that the sole means of war is combat, but explains that it takes many different forms. His extensive treatment of a number of those forms shows no direct evidence that economic coercion (without accompanying military force) qualifies as combat in his interpretation. However, Clausewitz lived in a time when economic coercion generally accompanied military violence, as opposed to a time in which globalized economics and a coordinated intergovernmental organization make economic coercion possible outside the use of military means. Because times have changed, it seems appropriate to consider whether or not economic sanctions on Iraq qualify under Clausewitz's definition of combat even though he does not explicitly consider the possibility. Clausewitz sees combat as the use of physical force for the purpose of making the opponent incapable of further resistance to the intended political purposes. There are two elements, then, of combat: physical force and disabling intent.

Economic sanctions are not physical force in the narrowest of interpretations: military force is not used in sanctions, and therefore it does not appear that the sender is holding the target by the throat and demanding cooperation. A closer look, however, shows that this is often exactly the situation. The economic sanctions regime imposed on the Palestinian territories by Israel and the United States as a result of Hamas winning the 2006 elections, which denied the target $52 million per month, have been called a 'stranglehold' on and 'silent killer' in the fast-deteriorating area (Barrows-Freedman 2007). Likewise, the 2002 economic sanctions punishing North Korea for its acquisition of nuclear weapons were characterized as a 'ruinous economic and political stranglehold' designed to 'bring the impoverished Communist country to its knees' (Buncombe 2002). The Security Council's economic sanctions on Iraq led to the 'slow, preventable deaths' of hundreds of thousands, perhaps millions, of Iraqis in the decade following the first Gulf War (Salter 1999).

The extreme deprivation that these sanctions place on target states is often physical in nature (Hoskins 1997; Weiss et al. 1997). My argument here is that force need not be military to be physical. Comprehensive sanctions regimes deprive citizens of target states of physical goods that they would otherwise have access to, including for basic needs. These are physical deprivations. Sanctions regimes use this physicality to coerce the target to meet a stated set of conditions for the return to normalcy. The physical force of sanctions, then, is not employed with guns, bombs, and tanks but by targeting basic human needs such as nutrition, health care, electricity, and infrastructure.

The other element of Clausewitz's definition, disabling intent, is also invoked by comprehensive economic sanctions regimes. To have disabling intent, physical force must be employed with the intention of making the enemy incapable of further resistance to the stated aims. As Thomas Weiss, David Cortright, George Lopez, and Larry Minear explained, economic sanctions policy on Iraq was put in place to 'exercise sufficient "bite" that the citizens in a targeted country will exert political pressure to force either a change in the behavior of the authorities or removal altogether ... inflicting civilian pain in order to achieve political gain' (1997). In 2000, US economic sanctions against the Taliban in Afghanistan were meant to 'deprive the regime of illicit income,' a move that would be felt and reacted to by the entire Afghan society (Farley 2000: A8).

We can see this disabling intent in several economic sanctions regimes. Sanctions against Iraq were intended to disable Saddam Hussein's resistance to international norms and UN Security Council demands. Sanctions against South Africa were intended to decrease the government's commitment to apartheid by denying citizens essential goods. Sanctions against Cuba were intended to weaken the authoritarian and communist regime there by interrupting its supply chain. This interpretation shares economic sanctions as having disabling intent. However, there is also the discourse of economic sanctions as a more direct tool of deprivation – the intent that sanctions take away the physical capability for developing weapons programs (Niblock 2001; Selden 1999). The economic restrictions placed on Iraq were intended to deprive the government of the money necessary to build weapons of mass destruction (WMD) programs. Economic sanctions against North Korea were intended to prevent the regime further developing and/or deploying nuclear missiles. Economic sanctions against Syria were intended to weaken the country's ability to fund and support Iraqi rebels. Thus, comprehensive economic sanctions regimes can meet all three requirements of Clausewitz's definition of war. The sanctions regimes have clear political ends, are often enacted by physical force (physicality and coercion), and are often enacted with disabling intent.

Wars of sanctions

This reading of Clausewitz's understanding of war, then, uses an 'old theory' to define economic sanctions as an alternative strategy of war rather than a peaceful alternative. In this view, economic sanctions can, like the actual use of military force, be coercive, physical, and disabling. In this 'new' world of a globalized economy, the humanitarian impact of economic sanctions can equal or even surpass that of military force. Viewing (some) sanctions regimes as a different form of war, rather than the absence of war, is an important aspect of understanding the manipulative nature of the 'new' security environment, at once softer and more deadly than ever before. Yet understanding economic sanctions as an alternative form of war-making is only the beginning of a reformulated approach to the sanctions problem – it is also important to understand *why* this form of war is utilized. Certainly, one advantage is that sanctions can be referred to as a 'peaceful alternative,' whether or not that is an accurate description. Nevertheless, the popularity of sanctions as a policy choice has to be due to the belief on the part of the senders that economic deprivation and coercion will be an effective or useful foreign policy tool. While many theorists have, as observed earlier, directly analyzed the causes and consequences of international economic sanctions, particularly in recent decades, this chapter aims to go further. While not intending to discount the validity and importance of this work, I argue that it may be handicapped by its specific attention to the 'newness' and 'uniqueness' of economic sanctions. Having argued that 'old' theories of war can help us to understand the enactment of economic sanctions, I now turn to the argument that an 'old' theory of human incentives can shed some light on why states choose this form of war and what they hope to gain from it. To that end, I employ Jeremy Bentham's theory of sanction to gain some leverage on the question of the nature of sanctions wars.

Bentham's Theory of Sanction[4]

Jeremy Bentham was an English legal and social reformer in the late eighteenth and early nineteenth centuries. Best known for his advocacy of utilitarianism and opposition to a concept of natural rights, Bentham also advocated the separation of the church and state, free expression, animal welfare, women's equality, health insurance, and the decriminalization of homosexuality. Bentham's theory of sanction (or punishment) often receives less scholarly attention than much of his other work, but is interesting and important. Indeed, as Tony Draper (2002) argues, 'Bentham's penal theory has yet to be fully examined,' despite the fact that, according to Gerald Postema (1986), it should inspire a 'jurisprudential debate of historic dimensions and fundamental philosophical significance.'

Unlike the contemporary theorists of economic sanctions reviewed earlier, Bentham is not writing about interstate economic sanctions policies. Instead, his is a theory of 'sanction' or punishment more generally – focusing on the impact of punishment on individuals. Nevertheless, his detailed approach to categories and meanings of inflicted punishments lends substantial insight to the study of economic sanctions. Bentham's approach, like that of some constructivists, is to see sanction largely as a form of punishment, or as expressing disapproval. In *Introduction to the Principles of Morals and Legislation*, Bentham analyzes both the source and the purpose of punishment.

First, Bentham argued that the idea of sanction or punishment presupposes the idea of an offense, since punishment cannot be doled out without consideration of an offense (1948). In other words, the target of the sanction must have done something that the sender of the sanction deems worthy of punishment or redress. The nature of the offense and the actor offended produces four categories of sanction.

According to Bentham, 'there are four distinguishable sources from which pleasure and pain ... flow' (1948: 34). These are the physical, the political, the moral, and the religious. Bentham argues that, 'insomuch as the pleasures and pains belonging to each of them are capable of giving a binding force to any law or rule of conduct; they may all be termed *sanctions*' (1948: 34). In Bentham's definition,

> A sanction, then, is a source of obligatory powers or motives, that is, of pains and pleasures, which, according as they are connected with such or such modes of conduct, operate, and are indeed the only things which can operate, as motives. (Bentham 1948: 34–5)

In the context of international economic sanctions, then, sanction uses material incentive (pain and pleasure) to motivate the target to comply with the will of the sender. The four types of sanction, according to Bentham, correspond to his typology of pleasures and pain. Physical sanction is pleasure or pain 'from the ordinary course of nature, not purposely modified by the interposition of the will of any human being.' Political sanction is pleasure or pain assigned 'at the hands of a ... judge ... chosen for the particular purpose of dispensing it according to the will of the sovereign or supreme ruling power.' Moral sanction is doled out 'according to each man's spontaneous disposition, and not according to any settled or concerted rule.' Religious sanction comes from 'the immediate hand of a superior invisible being, either in present life or in the future' (Bentham 1948: 35).

Bentham argues that sanctions use material and ideational forces in order to socialize the target into the belief that its greatest happiness coincides with the behavioral choice that creates the senders' (the public's) greatest happiness. Sanction, in this interpretation, is a socialization process of creating coincidental preferences in reaction to a deviation from the preferences of the sanctioner.

The source of the sanction, though, is a key distinction for Bentham. He gives examples of each sort of sanction:

> A man's goods, or his person, are consumed by fire. If this happened to him by what is called an accident, it was a calamity. If by reason of his own imprudence (for example, his neglecting to put his candle out) it may be styled a punishment of a physical sanction. If it happened to him by sentence of the political magistrate, a punishment belonging to political sanction, that is, what is commonly called punishment. If for want of any assistance which his neighbour withheld from him out of some dislike for his moral character, a punishment of moral sanction; if by an immediate act of God's displeasure, manifested on account of some sin committed by him, or through any distraction of mind, occasioned by the dread of such displeasure, a punishment of religious sanction. (Bentham 1948: 36)

International economic sanctions are not a physical sanction (directly caused by the target's own imprudence) or religious sanction (directly doled out by a divine source). But it is not immediately clear whether international economic sanctions are political or moral. Political sanctions are distributed by a governing force, as punishment for violation of its laws. Moral sanctions, on the other hand, are distributed by senders without governing authority, by one actor towards another to express moral disapproval.

In Bentham's terms, then, the interesting question about wars of sanctions is whether they are political sanction (law enforcement) or moral sanction (pressure without legal authority). If sanctions wars are political sanction, then they are within the purview of a structure of global governance; if they are moral sanction, then they are the equivalent of 'peer pressure,' without the legitimizing power of governance.

The sanctions regimes discussed in this chapter come from different sources. Some sanctions regimes, like that imposed by the United States on Syria, are unilateral; that is, they are enforced by one government against another. Other regimes, like the NATO sanctions against parts of the former Yugoslavia, are imposed by groups of states, but are not a product of the universal agreement of the members of the international community. Still other regimes, like the UN sanctions agaist Iraq or South Africa, are imposed by an intergovernmental organization and its member-states as a majority or a collective. If we just look at the sender imposing the sanctions, then, unilateral sanctions appear to be moral sanction of one state against another, while United Nations sanctions might carry the power of political sanction with its accompanying legal gravitas.

However, the sender of the sanctions is not the only factor that determines if they are political or moral. For example, economic sanctions could be unilateral and political if the sender state is unilaterally enforcing a legitimate international law espoused by the international governing structure. On the other hand, economic sanctions could be considered moral, not political, even though instituted by the United Nations, if the UN is not considered a structure of governance over its member states.

While I do not intend to rehash the decades of debate about the existence and nature of international anarchy in International Relations, a brief discussion is relevant to the question of whether *any* international economic sanctions are political rather than moral. Realist and liberal scholars propose that the international arena is, to one degree or another, anarchic – that there is no legitimate government over states, and that international organizations serve either a mediating role (liberal approach) or little role at all (realist approach). The English School approach argues that, while the international system is a governmental anarchy, it has a social structure, such that states interact in an international society. Few if any International Relations scholars view the international arena as a place where there is a government with authority over state governments. The norm of national sovereignty, though vulnerable to power politics, is generally strong. The social structure of governance that the English School sees is best interpreted as moral sanction. Bentham's understanding of political sanction is punishment coming from a government towards its citizens or subjects; even economic sanctions instituted by the UN are not universally recognized as backed by governmental authority. It is therefore appropriate to consider international economic sanctions as moral sanction, rather than political sanction.

Some may contend that this is a false distinction, and ask why it is important to determine whether economic sanctions are political or moral. There are, in fact, several important differences. The first is that political sanction comes from a set of laws, established by governmental authority and (in theory) by the consensus of those governed by the laws. Moral sanction, on the other hand, is the expression by one (or more) member(s) of a society of an opinion about the behavior of another member of that society. In other words, political sanction can be seen as closer to objectivity, and moral sanction as closer to subjectivity. The second difference between political and moral sanction is the mechanism through which they influence behavior. Political sanction resembles law enforcement, while moral sanctions uses 'the pains of an ill-name ... pains of ill-repute, pains of dishonor' (Bentham 1948: 47). Moral sanction, according to Bentham, shapes moral sensibility. He explains:

> Moral sensibility seems to regard the average effect or influence of the pains and pleasures of the moral sanction, upon all sorts of occasions to which it is applicable, or happens to be applied. It regards the average force or quantity of the impulses the mind receives from that source during a given period. (Bentham 1948: 57)

The third distinction is how moral sanction impacts behavior. Political sanction often directly and forcibly changes the behavior of citizens (e.g. an imprisoned citizen is unable to continue to commit armed robbery). Moral sanction, on the other hand, does not often directly control the behavior of the target. Bentham explains that a sanctioning power 'must never expect to produce perfect compliance by the mere force of the sanction of which he is himself the author.' Instead, 'all he can hope to do is to increase the efficiency of private ethics, by giving strength and direction to the influence of moral sanction' (Bentham 1948: 290).

Conclusion

Looking back to Bentham's 'old' theory of sanctions and Clausewitz's 'old' theory of war enables us to understand the idea of sanctions as a weapon of war, a tool with millennia of historical precedent. The 'newness' of the economic sanctions regimes in the twentieth century generally and after the Cold War is in the policy rhetoric which proposes that economic sanctions are a 'peaceful' alternative to military intervention in situations in global politics where some intervention will occur. Empirical analysis of these 'peaceful' sanctions regimes, however, demonstrates that they have humanitarian impacts that match or exceed the casualties of military intervention. With reference to the work of Carl von Clausewitz, this chapter has argued that economic sanctions regimes are often not a peaceful alternative to war, but an alternative form of war. This argument demonstrates that the claimed 'newness' of peaceful economic sanctions is rhetorical rather than empirical, and that the 'old' frame of sanctions as within the domain of war-making and war-fighting is nearer to reality. With reference to the work of Jeremy Bentham, this chapter has argued that economic sanctions wars are moral sanction (moral statements) rather than political sanction (law enforcement). Economic sanctions, then, are not only wars but wars of moral disapproval – a level of subjectivity that the Bush administration does not acknowledge when it advocates economic sanctions regimes as solutions to problems in global politics. For example, in discussing the sanctions imposed on the Sudan, the White House explained that the United States, in 2007, 'will more aggressively enforce existing sanctions against Sudan's government' in order to 'prohibit the government of Sudan from conducting military flights over Darfur' because it is essential to restore safety and peace to the region (Bush 2007). This rhetoric, while demonstrating an important moral commitment to fixing the humanitarian situation in the Sudan, fails to acknowledge the subjectivity of that commitment, and the use of a war tactic (sanctions) in order to achieve that moral commitment.

As we as political scientists evaluate sanctions as a 'new' security policy and advise the policy world about the proliferation of sanctions regimes, several lessons can be taken from the historical contextualization of economic sanctions theory and policy. First, the humanitarian impact of many economic sanctions regimes needs to be recognized in determining the utility of sanctions policies. Second, sanctions properly fit *within* the realm of war rather than outside of it, in terms of political aims, coercion, and disabling intent as well as the impact on the target state. This means that the rhetoric of sanctions as a 'peaceful alternative' should be rebutted in the academic and policy worlds. It also highlights the conflictual nature of sanctions, helps to reveal their humanitarian consequences, and links contemporary sanctions regimes with the historical use of sanctions as weapons of war. Third, economic sanctions are moral not political sanction – expressions of social disapproval rather than law enforcement. This ambiguity should be recognized when evaluating economic sanctions regimes, along with 'new' security problems and policies more generally.

10

Pandemic Influenza and Security

Christian Enemark

It is highly likely that the old challenge of pandemic influenza will re-emerge in the twenty-first century, generating an acute health crisis so damaging that it could plausibly be deemed a threat to national security. Framing an issue of human health in such terms would be a means of attracting heightened political attention and mobilising much-needed public health resources. This chapter assesses pandemic influenza as a 'new' security problem and suggests that part of the solution lies in the 'old' economic theory of 'public goods.' It argues that, although the state is the principal focus of vulnerability and action as regards pandemic influenza, domestic responses should be complemented with the production of 'global public goods for health' in order to manage pandemic risks more effectively and fairly into the future. These goods, characterized by non-rivalry in consumption and non-excludability, include sensitive and well-connected disease surveillance systems, and universal access to vaccines.

Pandemic Influenza

The story begins on 12 December 2003, when South Korea's chief veterinary officer advised the World Organization for Animal Health (OIE) that a large number of chickens on a farm near Seoul had suddenly died of highly pathogenic avian influenza. By early January 2004, reports were emerging of a 'mysterious disease' that had killed thousands of chickens in southern Vietnam (Anonymous 2004). In the months that followed, the influenza virus since identified as H5N1 swept through East Asia, forcing government authorities to cull tens of millions of domestic poultry. After the virus infected wild birds at Qinghai Lake in central China in mid-2005, it rapidly spread westward into Europe, India, the Middle East, and Africa. By early 2009, H5N1 outbreaks in birds had occurred in forty-nine countries (OIE 2009). The significance to human health of this avian influenza strain lies in its potential to mutate into a pandemic form capable of sustained person-to-person transmission. The H5N1 virus has repeatedly managed to jump species and successfully infect humans, and every instance of this is a potential mutation opportunity.[1] According to the World Health Organization (WHO), from late 2003 to mid-2008 there had been 393 confirmed cases of human H5N1 infection, including 248 deaths (WHO 2009), a global average case-fatality rate of around 63 percent. To date, H5N1 infections in humans have been caused by close contact with infected birds.

The worst pandemic of the twentieth century was the 1918 'Spanish Flu,' which killed around 50 million people worldwide. Subsequent pandemics in 1957 and 1968 were much less deadly, causing 2 million and 1 million deaths respectively. The conservative estimate of the WHO, using epidemiological modeling based on 1957 data, is that a future influenza pandemic would cause between 2 million and 7.4 million deaths worldwide (WHO 2005). Another estimate, based on 1918–20 data, has predicted 62 million deaths (Murray et al. 2006). Beyond mortality predictions, however, the health damage from pandemic influenza would be manifested more broadly in widespread nonfatal illness and general concern about infection. The WHO anticipates illness affecting around 25 percent of the world's population, more than 1.5 billion people (WHO 2007d: 16). The essence of the global public health challenge of responding to pandemic influenza would thus be scarcity of resources. As the pandemic would cause waves of outbreaks in humans lasting for one to two months in a given region and complete its global spread in eight to twelve months or less (Stöhr and Esveld 2004), there would be a large number of sick people over a large geographical area all requiring care during a short time period.

Alongside high levels of illness and death, an influenza pandemic would also cause immense economic disruption. An Australian study published in 2006 estimated that a mild pandemic would result in 1.4 million deaths worldwide and a cost to the global economy of $330 billion in lost economic output. The worst case scenario was 142 million deaths and a global economic loss of $4.4 trillion (McKibbin and Sidorenko 2006).

The present situation of a looming pandemic, although unfamiliar, is in fact far from new. Around 10,000 years ago, when humans first shifted from the hunter-gatherer existence to farming with domesticated animals, settled communities came into close contact with the infectious microorganisms present in their flocks and herds. This co-existence was the origin of such diseases as smallpox, measles, chickenpox, tuberculosis, leprosy, the common cold, malaria, bubonic plague, and influenza (McMichael 2001: 108–9). In a sense, therefore, the emergence of diseases like H5N1 represents not a new threat but rather a return to business-as-usual between man and microbe. The key difference, however, is that today the stakes are higher because increased human interconnectedness could facilitate the global spread of disease. One way of making the old problem of pandemic influenza new again, in the hope of garnering more response resources, is to characterize this disease as more than simply a health issue.

The Security Dimension

Historically, disciplinary fences have kept security and health segregated from each other largely because they have appeared to represent opposing sets of interests, ideologies, and institutions (Szreter 2003: 31). On one side, the subject matter of security studies has traditionally been death, destruction, and military establishments. On the other side, health studies have been about preventing and treating illness, improving quality of life, and building up healthcare systems. However, the idea of linking health and security concerns, as a matter of academic inquiry and public policy, has more recently received support from both directions. For some members of the public health and human development sectors, the language of security is a means of rallying political support and financial resources to address neglected health issues. In the security sector, some argue that the impact of particular health challenges is sufficiently serious as to warrant the prioritization traditionally accorded to the use of armed force. Most analysis of the links between health and security has favored the constructivist theory of 'securitization' advanced by Barry Buzan, Ole Waever, and Jaap de Wilde (Buzan et al. 1998). According to these authors, the designation of an issue as a security threat is primarily a subjective practice undertaken by policymakers: 'It is a choice to phrase things in security ... terms, not an objective feature of the issue' (Buzan et al. 1998: 211). For threats to count as security issues, they must meet strictly defined criteria that distinguish them from issues that are merely political. Specifically, they have to be 'staged as existential threats to a referent object by a securitizing actor who thereby generates endorsement of emergency measures beyond rules that would otherwise bind' (Buzan et al. 1998: 5).

Elevating pandemic influenza to the security agenda in this way could serve to attract priority political attention, a higher level of resource allocation, and the implementation of extraordinary response measures. A precedent for this is the privileged political treatment accorded to HIV/AIDS, the issue most conspicuous in contemporary academic literature and policy documentation linking infectious diseases to security. The passage in 2000 of United Nations Security Council Resolution 1308 was the first time a health issue had been officially framed as an international security concern.[2] In the same year, HIV/AIDS featured prominently in an influential US National Intelligence Council (NIC) report on the implications for the United States of global infectious disease threats (NIC 2000). Later, as the political momentum to take HIV/AIDS more seriously gained strength, George W. Bush launched his President's Emergency Plan for AIDS Relief (PEPFAR). The original plan (announced in 2003) allocated $15 billion over five years for treatment, prevention, and care. The recent five-year PEPFAR renewal brings an additional $48 billion (Bristol 2008). In arguing HIV/AIDS onto the security agenda, International Relations scholars typically point to how the disease is gradually undermining military capacity, impoverishing millions, and destroying social structures vital to internal state security (Elbe 2003; Prins 2004; Singer 2002). By contrast, the two key elements in the security equation regarding pandemic influenza are speed and dread.

A pandemic of this kind would compress time and space, and the widespread damage caused would seem all the worse because it happened so quickly. On this point, it is worth considering why it is that military threats are traditionally accorded the highest priority among national concerns. For Buzan, the answer lies in the swiftness with which the use of armed force can inflict major undesired changes: 'Military action can wreck the work of centuries in all other sectors. Difficult accomplishments in politics, art, industry, culture and all human activities can be undone by the use of force' (Buzan 1991: 117). More generally, for Richard Ullman, the essence of a security threat is 'an action or sequence of events that ... threatens drastically and over a relatively brief span of time to degrade the quality of life for the inhabitants of a state' (Ullman 1983: 133). Waever defines security problems as things that can, in a particularly rapid or dramatic fashion, undercut the political order within a state, deprive it of the capacity to manage by itself, and thereby 'alter the premises for all other questions' (Waever 1995: 52). Just as states fear military conflict because so many national achievements could be quickly undone, so too an influenza pandemic would set back hard-won economic gains and potentially undermine trust in government. And, like the all-consuming effort of prosecuting a war, defeating 'the flu' would become a first-order issue for governments.

Related to the speed of an influenza pandemic is the dread it would evoke: individual fear of infection and collective fear of contagion. Such dread compromises the day-to-day human interactions which sustain modern societies; civilized humankind functions and survives because people cooperate with and depend upon each other. A pandemic influenza virus would produce disturbing symptoms unfamiliar to most people, and the anxiety this generated would likely be compounded by the inability of medical professionals to provide adequate treatment. By inspiring dread, pandemic influenza is likely to generate a level of societal disruption which is disproportionate to the health burden it poses. All things being equal, any given individual is extremely unlikely to succumb to pandemic influenza, yet the gap between real and perceived risk is likely to remain as a foundation for securitization. Paul Slovic and his co-authors, writing in 1980 about risk perceptions, observed that '[society] appears to react more strongly to infrequent large losses of life than to frequent small losses' (Slovic et al. 1980: 209). They identified 'dread' as a 'higher-order' characteristic of risk, which, they argued, correlated closely with a strong societal desire for risk reduction (Slovic et al. 1980: 211). The 2002 *World Health Report* referred to these findings and acknowledged: 'The higher the dread factor levels and the higher the perceived unknown risks, the more people want action to reduce these risks, including through stricter government regulation and legislative controls' (WHO 2002: 32). As Jessica Stern has observed, fear is disproportionately evoked by certain characteristics of threats, including involuntary exposure, unfamiliarity, and invisibility (Stern 2002: 102). The mutated influenza virus, H_5N_1 or another, which causes the next pandemic would exhibit each of these characteristics.

The consequences and perceptions of pandemic influenza have both an individual and a collective dimension. A pathogenic microorganism constitutes an internal threat in the sense that it is located within state borders, but also because it inhabits the bodies of a state's human population. It is therefore not obvious whether the individual or the state ought to be designated as the referent object of security against pandemic influenza. The fact that pathogenic microorganisms kill individual humans is, on its own, insufficient for the purposes of securitization. Death can come to a person from a variety of sources, but to characterize them all as security threats would be analytically unwieldy. Rather, in order for a threat to acquire heightened political significance, something beyond individual harm is required. In the case of pandemic influenza, factors such as communal dread, contagion, and the cascading social effects of ill health would quickly elevate this issue from one of myriad individual sufferings to one of broad public concern. This is consistent with Buzan's view that the personal security of individual human beings is secondary to the fate of human collectivities (Buzan 1991: 19); a view which tends to emphasize the state as the referent object of security. However, for the purposes of securitizing pandemic influenza, the choice is not so simple.

A key problem identified by Colin McInnes is that, whereas foreign and security policy focus on the state as the referent object, public health policy focuses on communities: 'Though the state may form a community, communities with distinct health security issues may exist within a state. Thus the state is not necessarily the referent object, rather it is the community, which may or may not be a state' (McInnes 2004: 53). According to such reasoning, the referent objects for security against pandemic influenza may include individuals, states, and communities of individuals that exist inside and across state boundaries. For the purposes of this chapter, even if it is impossible to establish a unitary referent object of security, it is reasonable to proceed on the assumption that states will be the principal rallying points for action. At the practical level, national governments are the main providers of healthcare services, and state-based institutions and resources will be of primary importance in responding to an influenza pandemic. This does not, however, preclude involvement by non-state entities or cooperation between states, the importance of which is highlighted in the last section.

To the extent that state vulnerability is a valid sphere of analysis, historical experience suggests strongly that pandemic influenza would endanger internal security. Under circumstances in which a fast-spreading and unfamiliar disease was inspiring dread within national populations, the social contract under which citizens rely on governments to protect them during times of crisis would be subjected to severe pressure. The severe acute respiratory syndrome (SARS) outbreak of 2003 provided a glimpse of this phenomenon when, in parts of China, there were riots caused by rumors of government plans to establish local SARS patient isolation wards (Eckholm 2003). In 1994, an epidemic of plague in the Indian city of Surat engendered such terror that a quarter of the population fled within four days. This exodus, as Peter Chalk observed, 'fuelled an unprecedented level of anxiety across India, with fear and ignorance combining to freeze out even basic inter-personal sentiments of caring and civility.... So great was this national hysteria that the Delhi government was forced to bring in a police Rapid Reaction Force to effectively quarantine Surat' (Chalk 2006: 127). Such incidents demonstrate the panic caused when populations imagine a disease out of control, and where governments are seemingly incapable of securing the safety of their citizens.

Although it is impossible to predict precisely how the public would behave in response to the next influenza pandemic, it is clear that some governments expect severe social disruption as national health systems come under unprecedented pressure. In the United Kingdom, for example, domestic contingency plans for a pandemic include posting police at doctors' surgeries and health clinics to stop panicking crowds from stealing medication (Tendler 2005). In the United States, the Pentagon's plan for pandemic influenza includes the provision: 'When directed by the President, DoD will provide support to civil authorities in the event of a civil disturbance' (Department of Defense 2006: 16). And the chief medical officer at the US Department of Homeland Security, Jeffrey W. Runge, has stated that National Guard troops could be dispatched to cities facing possible insurrection (Connolly 2006). The envisaged use by the state of instruments of force is indicative of the depth of political concern surrounding pandemic influenza, although national responses to this threat would for the most part involve medical and public health interventions.

Domestic Responses to Pandemic Influenza

Responses to an influenza pandemic, once it is under way, generally fall into two categories: pharmaceutical (vaccines and antiviral drugs) and non-pharmaceutical (infection control and social distancing). Governments preparing for an influenza pandemic tend to focus on non-pharmaceutical responses as the most immediate. This is unsurprising as antiviral drugs to treat influenza and prevent its spread are in short supply, and a matching vaccine would not be available for several months after a pandemic started. Non-pharmaceutical interventions recommended by the US government, for example, include: isolation in the home or a healthcare setting of all persons with confirmed or probable pandemic influenza; voluntary home quarantine of members of households with confirmed or probable influenza cases; dismissal of students from school and school-based activities, and closure of childcare programs; and the use of social distancing measures to reduce contact between adults in the community and workplace, including cancellation of large public gatherings (DHHS 2007).

In 2003 the governments of affected countries in Asia and North America confronted the threat of SARS by implementing strict societal controls. Because no specific vaccine or treatment for the disease existed, the only interventions that seemed effective were those that minimized human contact. Transmission of SARS was quickly discovered to be containable using basic measures such as isolation of all infected patients and quarantine of close contacts, but government action also extended to the closure of interstate borders and the use of military personnel to assist in enforcing containment orders (Prescott 2003: 218). There is a risk, however, that governments seeking to securitize pandemic influenza may look to the SARS experience as a precedent for imposing similarly strict controls. It is important to note that non-pharmaceutical measures such as quarantine and isolation are likely to be less effective against influenza than they were against SARS. This is largely because the microorganisms that cause each disease behave differently; influenza is far more contagious than SARS, it has a shorter incubation period, and it can be transmitted before the onset of symptoms (WHO Writing Group 2006a: 83). Advice commissioned by the WHO on responding to pandemic influenza goes so far as to state that 'forced isolation and quarantine are ineffective and impractical' (WHO Writing Group 2006b: 88).

To the extent that extraordinary efforts and additional resources should be directed to addressing the threat of a pandemic, it makes sense for governments to place greater emphasis on pharmaceutical responses, as these are more promising for disease control purposes. Of immediate use are antiviral drugs which, if taken shortly before or after a person is exposed to an influenza virus, can prevent that person from becoming infected and spreading disease to others.[3] A vaccine matched to the pandemic virus, once produced, would thereafter be the single most effective defense. The problem with pharmaceutical defenses, however, is that individual states cannot deploy them at will within their territory in the way they can non-pharmaceutical defenses. Rather, states as well as non-state entities must compete in a global market for antivirals and vaccines. Under these circumstances, even the wealthiest of states are unlikely to acquire as much medicine as they require as soon as they require it. As for the developing world, where 96 percent of all pandemic influenza deaths are predicted to occur (Editorial 2007), pharmaceutical defenses are for the most part inaccessible.

In circumstances where non-pharmaceutical measures implemented domestically are of limited utility, and where acquiring national stockpiles of pharmaceuticals is difficult, a focus on national security alone is inadequate. Against the worldwide threat of pandemic influenza, security needs also to be pursued cooperatively among state and non-state entities. As the WHO stated on World Heath Day 2007, 'In today's world, health security needs to be provided through coordinated action and cooperation between and within governments, the corporate sector, civil society, media and individuals' (WHO 2007b: 2). This statement resonates with a basic principle contained in the original WHO Constitution of 1946 that 'The health of all peoples is fundamental to the attainment of peace and security and is dependent upon the fullest co-operation of individuals and States' (WHO 1946). Today, in the context of a looming pandemic, the aim of such cooperation should be to strengthen global systems of defense tailored to a security threat which transcends political borders. Accordingly, the final section of this chapter assesses the importance of producing global public goods for health in two areas: sensitive and well-connected disease surveillance systems; and universal access to pandemic influenza vaccines. The analysis adopts Mely Caballero-Anthony's 'two-track approach of complementing the securitization framework with the more inclusive global public goods approach' (Caballero-Anthony 2006: 108). However, whereas that author focused on East Asia in suggesting a more efficient and sustainable system for addressing infectious disease threats generally, the following discussion considers pandemic influenza only and takes a worldwide view.

Global Public Goods for Health

In economic theory, public goods are the result of market failures. They are goods that cannot be produced without government intervention because the incentives or resources for private actors to do so are not sufficient. Once a public good is provided, no one can readily be excluded from its consumption, and one person's consumption does not prevent anyone else from consuming it. Classic examples include lighthouses, traffic lights, and street lighting. The concept of public goods traces its origins to such eighteenth-century writers as David Hume and Adam Smith. In *The Wealth of Nations* Smith argued that 'the Sovereign or Commonwealth' is duty-bound to cover expenses in three areas: defense of the society through military force; the administration of justice; and

> erecting and maintaining those public institutions and those public works, which, though they may be in the highest degree advantageous to a great

society, are, however, of such a nature, that the profit could never repay the expense to any individual or small number of individuals, and which it therefore cannot be expected that any individual or small number of individuals should erect or maintain. (Smith 1937: 681)

For Smith, such works and institutions were chiefly for the purpose of facilitating the commerce of the society, and he noted the example that 'In China, and in several other governments of Asia, the executive power charges itself both with the reparation of the high roads, and with the maintenance of the navigable canals' (Smith 1937: 687). Economic theorists have traditionally analysed public goods at the level of national government policy. However, globalization has transformed many matters once confined to national policy into issues of global impact and concern. As Inge Kaul and her co-authors argued in 1999, 'A concept of global public goods is crucial to effective public policy under conditions of increasing economic openness and interdependence among countries' (Kaul et al. 1999: 9). They defined such goods as 'outcomes (or intermediate products) that tend toward universality in the sense that they benefit all countries, populations groups and generations' (Kaul et al. 1999: 16).

In the area of human health, the idea of producing global public goods for health (GPGH) has its origins in mid-nineteenth-century efforts by European countries to confront collectively the common threat posed by cholera. From 1851 to 1900, ten international sanitary conferences were convened, with successive meetings attracting more delegates and considering additional diseases like plague and yellow fever (Stern and Markel 2004: 1474–6). In the same way that Smith regarded public goods as essential for facilitating commerce *within* a given society, early international efforts to control infectious diseases were aimed at 'simultaneously curtailing the transnational importation of diseases and upholding the imperatives of trade and commerce' (Stern and Markel 2004: 1475). The international sanitary conferences were the precursor to the WHO, established in 1945, and the first International Health Regulations (1969) which sought to 'ensure the maximum security against the international spread of diseases with a minimum interference with world traffic' (WHO 1983).

A contemporary example of the production of GPGH is the response to SARS. In 2003, as David Fidler explains, states, inter-governmental organizations (including the WHO), and non-state actors collaborated in 'the crisis production of globally accessible "public goods" [in three major areas] that contributed to the successful containment of this outbreak': (1) surveillance data on SARS cases; (2) information on the best clinical practices for patient treatment and management; and (3) basic scientific research about the pathogen which caused the disease (Fidler 2004). The same kinds of goods would likewise be of great importance in minimizing the damage caused by an influenza pandemic. Arguably, because the stakes are so high, state and non-state actors need to intervene cooperatively rather than wait for market failure. Two areas that require special political attention, and that would otherwise be unlikely to attract resources through normal commercial mechanisms, are global disease surveillance and vaccine production capacity.

Disease surveillance

Mark Zacher explains the GPGH status of disease surveillance as follows: 'all countries benefit in some way from knowledge of foreign outbreaks of infectious diseases because it allows countries to take measures to protect their people and prepare their medical institutions to cope with threatening diseases' (Zacher 1999: 268–9). With regard to pandemic influenza, early warning of the commencement of human-to-human transmission of a new virus will be vital in order to maximize time to deploy pharmaceutical and non-pharmaceutical defenses. The effectiveness of disease surveillance is measured in terms of sensitivity and connectivity. The former refers to the capability to identify quickly and accurately an illness that is out of the ordinary. The latter refers to the speed and accuracy with which this and related information is passed among medical professionals, public health authorities and relevant international bodies. Global electronic disease surveillance systems provide for a high level of connectivity, although the sensitivity and effectiveness of such systems depends largely upon local surveillance.

One factor working against good local surveillance is the traditional reluctance of affected countries to publicize an outbreak and thus incur national and private costs in the form of trade embargoes or faltering tourism (Zacher 1999: 267). A key lesson from the experience of SARS was the importance of government transparency. In particular,

China's initial bungled response to that outbreak demonstrated how the withholding of information only compounds the damage from a contagious disease, hinders the task of containing an outbreak, and heightens the risk posed to other countries. The following year, the UN secretary general's High-Level Panel on Threats, Challenges and Change acknowledged that 'the security of the most affluent State can be held hostage to the ability of the poorest State to contain an emerging disease' (UN 2004: 14). Some scholars have gone so far as to argue that 'Government failures to cooperate and participate in rapid and transparent [disease] surveillance need to be addressed by the political organs of the United Nations, including the Security Council, given the importance of surveillance to the achievement of global health security' (Lee and Fidler 2007: 228–9). On the whole, however, global disease surveillance is hindered more by lack of local capacity than by deliberate blindness, and global electronic inter-connectedness is gradually circumventing the traditional reluctance to report outbreaks.

The WHO Global Outbreak Alert and Response Network, for example, is a highly sensitive network of over a hundred laboratories and disease-reporting systems, providing timely reports of infectious disease outbreaks. It is supported by a computer-driven tool for real-time gathering of disease intelligence, the Global Public Health Intelligence Network. This network continuously and systematically trawls websites, newswires, local online newspapers, public health email services, and electronic discussion groups for rumors of out-breaks. This in turn allows the WHO to scan the world for news that might raise suspicions of an unusual disease event. Under the revised International Health Regulations which entered into force in June 2007, the WHO is authorized to use a range of non-official intel-ligence sources to raise an alarm and begin a process of verification with countries that have not voluntarily reported significant outbreak events. Nevertheless, developing countries with little or no disease surveillance capacity continue to be the weak links in the electronic chain. In Laos and Cambodia, for example, none of the national or provincial surveillance units has reliable Internet access or email, and there is no system for laboratory-based surveillance (Cao et al. 2004: 65–6). In August 2006 the Chinese government revealed that its first human death from H5N1 avian influenza occurred in late 2003, two years before China first publicly acknowledged a human infection (Macartney 2006). This means H5N1 was present in China before the outbreak of the virus was disclosed elsewhere in Asia. Although this revelation provoked accusations about the government's poor commitment to transparency, it is more likely that China's ability to detect locally emerging diseases is simply inadequate. Effective disease surveillance is particularly dependent upon adequate diagnostic laboratory capacity. Testing for H5N1 antibodies in a human tissue sample is technically difficult, time-consuming, and expensive. And because it involves the use of live H5N1 virus, it should be carried out in high-containment laboratories, of which the developing world has few. In 2005, laboratory facilities in Hanoi (Vietnam) were so limited that it was taking up to a week for the return of blood-test results, by which time H5N1 influenza patients were sometimes already dead (Watts 2005).

Despite the continuing deficiencies of many local disease surveillance systems, there are some promising indications that the developed world is supportive of the production of GPGH to meet the threat of pandemic influenza. The stated goals of the International Partnership on Avian and Pandemic Influenza (IPAPI), announced by then US President Bush in September 2005, include: elevating the avian influenza issue on national agendas; coordinating efforts among donor and affected nations; mobilizing and leveraging resources; increasing transparency in disease reporting and improving surveillance; and building local capacity to identify, contain, and respond to an influenza pandemic (Anonymous 2007b). At a conference in Beijing in January 2006, the world's major aid donors, led by the United States and the European Union, pledged $1.9 billion toward preventing an influenza pandemic. About half of this sum was to be spent in Vietnam, Laos, Cambodia, Indonesia, and Thailand on strengthening disease surveillance, improving laboratory and health services, and boosting the communication capacity of these countries (Cheng 2006). The total amount pledged so far does not, however, appear commensurate with the gravity of the global threat presented in official pronouncements. Despite rhetoric from the US government, for example, that it is seeking to 'heighten awareness' of the pandemic threat, 'promote the development' of other nations' health capacity, and 'encourage transparency' in disease reporting, the US share of the January 2006 pledge was a mere $334 million (Anonymous 2006: 4). On the other hand, as of May 2007 the United States had pledged an additional $100 million to support international efforts in preparedness and communication, surveillance and detection, and response and containment (Anonymous 2007c). And it planned to pledge further funds at the IPAPI meeting in India in December 2007 (Lange 2007).

Notwithstanding the importance of disease surveillance as a GPGH to provide universal early warning of an incipient influenza pandemic, the data provided would be of much less benefit to countries that lack the medical, technological and financial resources to respond to new outbreaks. The single most effective defense during a pandemic would be a vaccine matched to the causative virus, yet most developing countries are likely to miss out entirely unless there is a large expansion in global vaccine manufacturing capacity.

Vaccines

Only once a pandemic virus had started to spread could the process of developing a strain-specific influenza vaccine begin. Thereafter, the number of lives saved would depend largely upon how quickly and on what scale vaccine manufacturing could be initiated. David Woodward and Richard Smith explain the GPGH status of universal vaccination as follows: 'if the effect [of vaccination] on the risk of person-to-person or cross-border transmission of communicable disease is sufficient, it is not rational either to exclude an individual or nation from consumption, or to limit production to a level at which consumption is rivalrous' (Woodward and Smith 2003: 10). At present, however, no global plan exists for rationing influenza vaccine across countries: 'the governance regime for protection remains primarily focused on satisfaction of national interests rather than production of global public goods' (Lee and Fidler 2007: 223). The amount of seasonal influenza vaccine able to be produced each year is extremely limited, and doses are delivered almost exclusively to the developed world where the major vaccine manufacturers operate. Facing the prospect of an influenza pandemic, many developing countries regard the existing situation as profoundly inequitable and have become more assertive in their demand for fairer vaccine distribution arrangements.

In January 2007 Indonesia, the country most heavily afflicted by human H5N1 infections, started withholding samples of H5N1 virus from the WHO Global Influenza Network. This network compiles information for influenza vaccine formulation based on the analysis of viral isolates collected in participating countries, and it also serves as a mechanism for alerting countries to the emergence of strains with unusual pathogenicity or pandemic potential. For the network to serve its purpose, however, virus samples must be supplied in a timely fashion. Indonesia's government claimed that the WHO was transferring viral samples to pharmaceutical companies to make influenza vaccines for which the Indonesian people would have to pay an unacceptably high price. In a somewhat ruthless attempt to secure an affordable vaccine supply in the event of an influenza pandemic, Indonesia subsequently commenced negotiations to sell H5N1 virus samples exclusively to the US-based company Baxter International (Aglionby and Jack 2007). This move highlighted the fear among poorer countries that they may be unable to benefit from new vaccines and drugs that result from their cooperation with influenza researchers worldwide. At a meeting with WHO officials in March 2007, the Indonesian health minister sought assurances that her country would get a vaccine if a pandemic occurred, reportedly calling the current vaccine supply scheme 'more dangerous that the threat of an H5N1 pandemic itself' (Normile 2007). Indonesia subsequently agreed to negotiate on resuming the supply of virus samples to the WHO, subject to the agency seeking Indonesia's authorization before sharing these with other researchers (Anonymous 2007a).

In formal recognition of the concern represented by Indonesia's drastic action, the WHO member states at the Sixtieth World Health Assembly in May 2007 passed a resolution requesting that the WHO 'establish an international stockpile of vaccines for H5N1 or other influenza viruses of pandemic potential, and ... formulate mechanisms and guidelines aimed at ensuring fair and equitable distribution of pandemic influenza vaccines at affordable prices in the event of a pandemic.' (WHO 2007e). Notwithstanding this gesture of international solidarity, the practicalities of producing and distributing vaccine are primarily the function of pharmaceuticals companies rather than states. Even where there is political support for international cooperation, the achievement of universal vaccine availability faces formidable commercial obstacles. For the most part, the production of this GPGH requires national governments to provide incentives to industry. For an expansion in global vaccine manufacturing capacity to be commercially worthwhile, there needs to be a long-term increase in consumer demand for vaccines against regular influenza from one year to the next. In essence, a healthy influenza vaccine market would be one constantly primed for a pandemic emergency.

In 2006 global manufacturing capacity for seasonal influenza vaccine was reportedly around 900 million single doses every six months (Stephenson 2006). Recent scientific advances and increased capacity for vaccine manufacturing may see the global availability of pandemic influenza vaccine courses rise to 4.5 billion courses per year in 2010. However, the director of the WHO Initiative for Vaccine Research, Marie-Paule Kieny, has cautioned that 'it is still far from the 6.7 billion immunization courses that would be needed in a six month period to protect the whole world' (WHO 2007c). Also, some evidence suggests that two doses of pandemic vaccine at a higher dose than seasonal vaccine will be required to optimize protection in humans (Booy et al. 2006). In any event, achieving or exceeding this projected increase in supply is contingent on corresponding demand for seasonal influenza vaccine.

The WHO *Global Pandemic Influenza Action Plan to Increase Vaccine Supply* recommends that states: (a) develop seasonal influenza vaccination programs if they can afford to; and (b) increase influenza vaccine coverage in existing programs. The intended effect would be to 'provide industry with the clear forecast of demand that is integral to ensuring an incremental increase in seasonal vaccine production-capacity' (WHO 2006: v). Improving seasonal influenza vaccine coverage or establishing vaccine production capacity in resource-constrained countries would be the responsibility of 'the international community,' which implies financial assistance from the developed to the developing world, and the estimated cost of implementing the plan is $3–10 billion (WHO 2006: v, viii). Specific incentives to boost global supply which wealthy governments could provide to vaccine manufacturers include: boosting demand through seasonal vaccine awareness programs; issuing purchasing contracts; providing price guarantees or subsidies; tax incentives; streamlining the regulatory process for licensing vaccines; and strengthening protection against litigation. States could also consider paying vaccine manufacturers for unused excess capacity of vaccines.

Conclusion

This chapter has addressed an old problem, pandemic influenza, the twenty-first-century manifestation of which is likely to generate an acute health crisis so damaging as to endanger national security. If H5N1 or some other influenza virus mutates into a form transmissible between humans, the result would be widespread illness and death, severe economic disruption, and the undermining of societal functioning. A severe pandemic would swiftly set back hard-won economic gains, undermine public confidence, and become a first-order issue for governments which would alter the premiss for all other activity. In framing this problem anew as a security issue, there is potential to attract heightened political attention and mobilize much-needed public health resources. However, it is not enough to focus on the vulnerability of individual states to pandemic influenza and on domestic state actions taken in response. In addition, the solution to this global challenge for health and security lies in the production of global public goods for health which will reduce pandemic risks worldwide in the long term. To this end, states, international organizations and non-government entities need to cooperate in the key areas of disease surveillance systems and access to influenza vaccines.

11

Natural Disasters

Lisa Burke

Natural disasters are not new phenomena, nor are they new issues; however, the framing of what is a natural disaster and the politiciza- tion and securitization of responses in the aftermath of the failed levees in Hurricane Katrina raises questions about the role of the political in providing security. While natural disasters are as old as the planet itself, they have been recently introduced to the security agenda, and have captured much attention as a 'new' *security* problem (Cooper and Block 2006; Huxley 2005). The new securitization of natural disasters has led to militarized policies to address them. For example, much of the work after Hurricane Katrina in New Orleans was delegated to the United States military and to the Department of Homeland Security. In response to the 2004 tsunami, United States and Thai military units were charged with providing health care in the immediate aftermath.

Many of these securitizing efforts emphasize the newness of natural disasters as security problems, and fail to take notice of centuries and even millennia of political theorizing about the relationship between humanity, nature, and governance that could serve as interpretive lenses and policy guidance for dealing with present-day natural disasters. For example, as Michael Ignatieff points out, the image of the residents in New Orleans waiting for some response or adequate offer of government assistance implicated the question of what citizens could expect from their governments, an age-old issue in political theory. (Ignatieff, 2005). Other political theories have addressed the relationship between humanity and nature. This chapter supplements insights of Machiavelli and Rousseau with twentieth-century political theory in order to trace the frameworks of meaning making sense of the moral geographies of post-disaster assistance.

These questions point to the interrelationship and mutual construction of the natural and the social in specific resolutions of the paradox associated with state sovereignty (for example, see Connolly 2004). This paradox includes the status of the rule of law in democratic polities and how one can account for the authority that founds itself. The role of the Legislator in Rousseau is an example of such a figure who embodies the authority to make law and to found the state that is intertwined from a corresponding legal framework. If the authority to make meaning is equally intertwined with the assertion of regulatory frameworks, then the construction of norms echoes many of the same themes touched upon by various figures such as Rousseau, Agamben, Foucault, and Deleuze. The construction and simultaneous selection of which 'events' that occur 'out there' qualify as natural disasters is a political process. Actions designating an event as a natural disaster set into play a host of normative imperatives and narratives of intervention intended to mitigate the effects of disasters and alleviate suffering. The construction of natural disasters is embedded with assumptions about nature versus culture, and the role of the sovereign state in protecting citizens from insecurity. This chapter is an attempt to trace the evolution of the norm of international assistance in the case of 'out of the blue' natural disasters from expectations of self-help to international governments more readily responding to such events with assistance of money, resources and logistics. It is an analysis of the changing nature of intervention in the international community through a genealogical exegesis of how the concept of natural disaster is constructed and how it relates to articulations of political community.

The question of how natural disasters are constructed, in turn, leads to conclusions about how certain events are structured as justifying mobilization by the international community. The sovereignty of the individual and the state is reproduced in the sovereignty of the system of sovereign states (Walker, 2006). A form of sovereignty is attributed to the international system, whether it is Waltz's system and unit answer to the question, or the assumption of anarchy and insecurity critiqued by Alexander Wendt that creates a specific form of state–interstate society (Waltz 1979; Wendt 1999). This underlines the importance of debates about the constitutive nature of power, interaction, order, and the search for security as a cut into international politics. Conventional answers to these questions found in international relations do not appear to offer solutions to the 'problem' of nature and its role in international politics unless it is a problem of instability. The usual story is that nature and its effects are problems to be solved within the boundaries of the state. It is a matter of domestic administration and national capacity. Thus, Finnemore, in *The Purpose of Intervention*, explicitly separates out interstate cooperation during periods of natural catastrophe from her analysis of humanitarian intervention as two conditions are satisfied (Finnemore 2003: 53–4). The first is that the assistance is consensual as the affected government requests assistance from those capable of assisting. The requirement of consent of the affected government is based on the exercise of state sovereignty. The second is that the form of assistance is confined to the temporary borrowing or loaning of (domestic) state capacity, specifically that of technical or logistical capacities. Finnemore's discussion does not cover post-natural disaster assistance as her focus is the use of force, which, for some, is the distinctive character of international politics. The evolution of this norm, it is argued here, in many ways is an evolution of a hierarchy based on the ability to assert control over nature. This hierarchy becomes spatialized in a world of sovereign states. Those portrayed at risk are defined as those who have not yet achieved adequate mastery over *fortuna* in order to better provide security for their citizens.

Norms and Sovereignty

The relationship of nature/culture to articulations of sovereignty can be highlighted through a reading of Machiavelli. The prince was advised to draw on the strength of both man and beast to achieve power and glory (Machiavelli 1979: 134). This is significant, as the sovereign is to balance and draw strength from both that which is natural and that which is cultural. Similarly, Chiron the Centaur is the model of political education as both the man and the beast are required for successful governance and the erection of institutions that would weather the storms and tempests of *fortuna*. *Virtù*, in this reading, is the ability to create the institutions that would buttress culture against the destructive forces of nature. Machiavelli opposes *virtù* to *fortuna* and defines the former as the ability to properly organize civic life to resist the river's incursion:

> The same things happen where Fortune is concerned: She shows her force where there is no organized strength to resist her; and she directs her impact there where she knows that dikes and embankments are not constructed to hold her. (Machiavelli 1979: 159)

Machiavelli's categories were intended to be metaphors used to make sense of early modern forms of political community. However, utilizing these categories of meaning highlights the tension within sovereignty itself between that which is natural and that which is explicitly created as cultural artifact. Sovereign forms of political community involve both the man and the beast, both the cultural and the natural. The tension between the competing demands is a rich source for making sense of how out-of-the-blue disasters threaten the capacity of certain forms of political communities.

The relationship between culture and nature within later forms of sovereignty resonate with themes elaborated by Machiavelli. The work of 'men' can be challenged by the advent of a natural disaster. During a crisis, the institutions and the functions of the various levels of government are overwhelmed by various forces of 'nature.' Machiavelli's prince is no longer successful at erecting a dike to control the rising waters of *fortuna*. *Virtù* is eclipsed.

The tension between culture and nature is transformed in late modernity. Institutions of the state that Machiavelli conceptualized as controlling nature to achieve glory become a vehicle for progress. The erections of culture continue to be overwhelmed by the forces of nature during a natural disaster (Berman 1982: 73). It is important to distinguish the controlled and constant dynamic of destruction, obsolescence, and re-creation of institutions associated with Berman's vision of modernity (Berman 1982: 68–71) from the destructive forces associated with a natural disaster. Crucially, this distinction hangs upon the differences in types of destruction. One is undertaken in the name of progress, and the other is the destruction of the conditions of possibility for progress by nature. Ironically, and as implied by Berman, the paradox is that the Faustian bargain of development can never release Faust from his deal with the devil (Berman 1988: 84–5). Once the drive to develop is triggered, it becomes an increasingly hungry drive. The irony, of course, is that culture can never fully incorporate and dominate nature, although that is the Sisyphean task of progress. It is almost as if nature is portrayed as intervening in state sovereignty from outside and problematizes political control, territorial integrity, and security. The guarantee provided by various iterations of the social contract fails during the advent of natural disasters. It does not protect against incursions by the state of nature and problematizes the boundaries of the state that both define the specific institution of a state and the meaning associated with state sovereignty more generally.

This brings the discussion to the articulation of *Homo sacer* outlined by Agamben. If sovereignty as a social construct requires the apparent negation of itself in the construction of the animalistic, bare life of the state of nature, then the social construction of natural disasters is implied in the articulation and development of state sovereignty itself. One reading of Agamben is that the sovereign constructs both the power of the law and simultaneously this power to create the law in the same paradoxical act (Connolly 2004: 26). This paradox becomes more apparent as the bare life, the life that is both inside and on the border of power, culture and the law, is more deeply penetrated by sovereignty as biopolitical power (Connolly 2004: 26). Agamben states that 'One of the essential characteristics of modern biopolitics (which will continue to increase in our century) is its constant need to redefine the threshold in life that distinguishes and separates what is inside from what is outside' (1998: 132). Thus, the tension between *fortuna* and *virtu*, which became a relationship between nature and culture characterized as oscillating between progress and destruction, becomes one of biopolitics in which various articulations of sovereignty hinge on the distinction between the rights of men and the rights of citizens (Agamben 1998: 132).

Agamben traces this disjuncture at the border of the city of political life to two phenomena whereby the right of entry into the city based purely on birth and nationality is eroded. First, the power of the sovereign in the form of the nation-state becomes more and more focused on 'natural life,' which enables a distinction between a life that is not valued enough to live and the rights of the citizens who have earned entry into the walls of the city (Agamben 1998: 132). A second tendency noted by Agamben is that the rights of the citizen are separated from and opposed to the rights of man. This allows for the re-creation of a bare life that is infused with biopolitical power and is the path by which nature attempts to re-enter the city and is apparently blocked by the power of the sovereign. This power allows for the killing of those outside the walls as they are separated from and opposed to the legal context that would turn this killing into homicide. Effectively it is the spatial removal of the animalistic aspects of humanity to the state of nature that defines and continually rewrites the boundaries of civil political life. It is a constant process of drawing boundaries which define the political.

Interestingly and ironically, Agamben also reads humanitarian assistance as reproducing the figure of bare life and reproducing the effects of power of the sovereign that humanitarian organizations are attempting to ameliorate or mitigate. This tension plays on the relationship between nature and culture that supports a specific iteration of late-modern sovereignty and a normative structure that it supports. The figures populating the bare life, stripped of all rights of citizenship during crises such as natural disasters, expose some of the contradictions of sovereignty and modern political life more generally. The changing nature of the norm of assistance associated with emerging and developing forms of humanitarian assistance are also developments in forms of biopolitics that support and reinforce the boundary between 'man' and citizen, in this context between refugees who live outside the wall of the city and the citizens who provide assistance to those displaced to the state of nature.

Norms and Meaning

The concept of norm utilized in this discussion is not one of positivist causality (Kratochwil 1989: 5), but is embedded within the larger structures of identity and meaning that define and characterize international society. Norms are used not only to signal action, but assume some form of mutually comprehensible intersubjective framework of meaning (Kratochwil 1989: 11). They create meaning, structure actions, and create expectations around consequences of actions. Norms, as concepts used in the analysis, play a key policing role in the discourses of meaning that animate international society and the sovereign states and other actors that are comprised by this interaction and that, in turn, construct the international system.

Thus, the conceptualizations of norms and identity used to analyze the construction of natural disasters are embedded within specific iterations of the sovereign state. It is important to sketch how the instantiation of the sovereign state appears to offer a resolution to ontological problems of nature/culture, necessity/freedom, and security/order. The answers to these questions provided by the naturalized institution of state sovereignty (Campbell 1992) are situated within a tradition of modernity and sovereignty defined by terms found in Western thought. The questions, answers, and debates about appropriate ways to frame discourses of natural disaster and debates about assistance have a conceptual history embedded within the chronology of occurrences that have come to be labeled natural disasters. Sovereignty has been defined by various scholars of International Relations as, first, political control associated with authority and the consequential ability to make and enforce law, and, second, as control over a defined territory (Walker 2005; Waltz 1979: 74–6). Sovereignty, in this reading, is the creation of boundaries and conditions of possibility for political life existing with a specific view of the world.

A Succession of Dangerous Spaces and an Ideology of Putrefaction

The boundaries between states, and between the inside and the outside of the state, are not the only ontological distinctions challenged by the construction of natural disasters. Discourses of modernity also create a historical relationship between the knowing subject and the object of knowledge. The creation of the sovereign individual echoes the dynamics touched upon in the distinction of sovereign state. The position of the knowing subject radically separated from its object of knowledge is a crucial factor in the construction of the nature from which sovereign individuals have been abstracted. This process of separation creates a discourse of knowledge as control and mastery over nature and the natural (Berman 1988: 40–41). Berman points to the link sketched by Goethe's *Faust* between self-development and economic development as characteristic of the promise of modernity. The two paths of social 'progress' and individual development are transformed into a larger maelstrom that provides a unifying narrative. This gives direction to a larger series of projects characterized by frenetic destruction and re-creation in the various images of modernity.

Economic development, which necessitates and is based upon a social, intellectual and spiritual foundation erected in the modern quicksand of constant change and shifting boundaries, requires the affirmation and naturalization of boundaries to create both meaning and a sense of fixity. The link between the development of individual and state forms of sovereignty is played in various chords through diverse iterations of the modern project.

> Some writers identify modernity in relation to characteristic claims about evolutionary teleology and progressive history. Impressed by the speed and accelerations of the contemporary era, they speak of a new spatial awareness, characterising postmodernity as a transition from time to space, from temporal continuities to spatial dislocations. Others, focusing more on the constitutive moments of early-modern thought, analyse modernity primarily in spatial terms, notably in relation to the spatial separation of the self-conscious ego from the objective world of nature, the aesthetics of three dimensional perspective, and the demarcations of the territorial state. (Walker 1993: 10)[1]

The distinction between the knowing subject and the object allegedly 'found' out there allows for the perception of foundations in reason and certainty in progress, defined as increasing control over the object constructed as nature (Haraway 1989). This distinction allows for, and grounds, a faith in both reason and the Enlightenment and creates what Foucault famously termed the blackmail of the Enlightenment (Foucault 1984: 42–3). The form of rationality associated with the Enlightenment as an undifferentiated pantheon allowed one either to accept the terms of rationality, which were dictated in part by the separation of the subject from the object of knowledge, or to reject them entirely and be considered non-rational or irrational

(Foucault 1984: 43). Reason is to be considered both universal and universalizable. The challenge that Foucault took upon himself, as did Berman using a different set of analytical tools, was to untangle the different and varied components of the modern project and to take it seriously as a condition of possibility for knowing ourselves and transgressing the boundary between the material, or nature, and reason, or forms of knowing. Humanity no longer was part of a unified cosmos between nature and the heavens, but was separated from and opposed to it by virtue of reason.

More specifically, for the purposes of this chapter, the crucial axis upon which progress through reason manifested itself was the belief in development defined as mastery of that which is natural. This allowed for the development of a hierarchy of societies/communities along this axis. This construction was not restricted to political communities but also included other groups such as women. Thus, according to this logic, women are thought to be closer to nature, and thus less rational when defined by one type of patriarchical hierarchy (Haraway 1989: 279–303). The same logic is applied to colonial possessions when utilizing the logic of progress as mastery over a specifically constructed nature. Those who are less able to master nature are closer to it and constructed as embedded within the natural and outside of the boundaries of the city and political life through a complex range of epistemological moves. The colonies are constructed as objects of knowledge by Western reason.[2] The radical separation of knowing subject from the objects and 'reality' of nature is an important source of scientific power in the pursuit of progress. Reason must trump emotion, and the natural within human beings, to create a more powerful and efficient world. And, as pointed out by Berman (1988), the tragedy of development is that the knowing subject becomes hollow and obsolete as the last vestiges of the premodern world are successfully destroyed and the task of 'burning bridges' with the world that nurtured Faust is complete. The knowing subject has become the object of his[3] own knowledge, and the dynamics of the division of society and the division of labor continue on in an unceasing manner to ensure constant change and constant development.

Exacerbating the separation of the knowing subject from the object of rational knowledge (Cox 1986: 88–90; Horkheimer 1999) is the construction of threat around natural disasters and concomitant conceptions of both vulnerability and contagion (Bankoff 2001). Natural disasters are constructed as something that happens outside and in the Third World, possibly due to the lack of technical knowledge and mastery over nature that animates one tale about progress (McGrane 1989; Fabian 2002). Those societies portrayed, for example, by anthropological discourses as non-Western are portrayed as non-rational or irrational vis-à-vis control over nature and the ability to successfully mitigate risks posed by nature. The answer to the problem of vulnerability becomes, in this story, one of development, and a development in the model articulated by modernity with the implications for both sovereignty and progress noted above. Not only are these non-Western societies a challenge to the ontological monopoly of modernity's answer to political community, but many areas of the globe were rendered safe for Westerners through a discourse of danger. It is not safe 'out there' for Westerners (Bankoff 2001: 25).

Bankoff argues that this discourse of danger has had three iterations that have structured relationships between Western states and the rest of the world since the seventeenth century. Early contact by Westerners with the different diseases, animals and warmer climes resulted in the creation of a vision of out-of-control climate, such as drought, flood, and storms of the magnitude of typhoons and hurricanes (Bankoff 2005: 20). Even the animals that were encountered, such as lions, tigers, and elephants, were perceived as being much more of a risk than those inhabiting Western Europe. The blush of early exploration and discovery, with all of the attendant exhilaration felt by some, was transformed to a perception of threat to Europeans. This perception appeared to be confirmed due to the high mortality rates of Europeans through the eighteenth century (Arnold 1996: 6). Arnold terms this discourse the invention of tropicality (Arnold 1996: 5), which interpreted the tropics as being threatening to Europeans. Everything was constructed as different and threatening (Arnold 1996: 7–10). Arnold defines tropicality as: 'a Western way of defining something culturally and politically alien, as well as environmentally distinctive, from Europe and other parts of the temperate zone' (Arnold 1996: 6).

The development and mastery of modern science in the specific form of schools of tropical medicine allowed the West to continue to colonize the tropical areas, with less mortality. Bankoff points to the creation of the London School of Hygiene and Tropical Medicine in 1899. A corollary to the development of the discourse of tropicality was the creation of a medical geography theorizing that placed and contained races in specific climatic zones (Bankoff 2001: 21). The function of science underscores the creation of different, hierarchically ranked political communities. The goal of Western science was to make the troublesome regions afflicted by malaria and characterized by climate differences more safe for Westerners to inhabit. The only subjects in this story are the Westerners.

The next stage in creating otherness out of non-Western political communities through the construction of hazard, according to Bankoff, was structured by the Cold War. The economic and social goals of recently decolonized Third World states could now be met through two options: capitalism or communism. Development theory became the site of insertion of Western technical reasoning into the Third World. Modernization theory, in particular, was embedded with teleological, notions of both the stages and the necessity for non-Western states to become 'modern.' This discourse effectively creates the Third World (Bankoff 2001: 23), defined in opposition to the First and the Second Worlds. Development was offered as the solution to the problems of poverty, death, production, and other ailments of recently independent states. The offers of aid and various forms of investment made by both parties of the Cold War were designed to foster the needs of national interest by swaying different states to one side or the other.

The hierarchical ranking of various political communities on the globe shifted in the period of decolonization from an axis based on the construction and administration of colonies to a continuum of those less and more developed. Assumptions about the path to progress and Enlightenment that characterize the modern project were recast into development as a form of technical knowledge to be applied to the state members of the Third World as the concept of state sovereignty had been effectively universalized. The white man's burden is recast more in terms of a scientific and technical knowledge to husband the administration of aid and investment (Bankoff 2001: 28) than as the administration of colonies.

Legal decolonization within the context of the Cold War results in a change in the sites of identity that foster norms of development.[4]

This process is reflected in the universal applicability of the norms of legal equality, sovereignty and territorial integrity to the relevant members of the international society: sovereign states. Once formal legality of the dominant form of political community was institutionalized, and the norm subsequently universalized, then other dimensions of political life became the sites of hierarchy and the confrontation of identity with its other. Different norms were articulated as sites of contestation and discrimination. The tension between sovereign equality and the practice of power institutionalized in the differential architecture of the United Nations – that is, the General Assembly and the Security Council – highlighted the tension between the need for legitimacy and the pursuit of the national interest, particularly as defined during the Cold War. As states had become the monopolistic site of legitimate political behavior in the international system, the pursuit of national interest subsequently became the lens through which identities were asserted, defined, and defended. Thus, development is pursued through and with the consent of the sovereign governments.

The third iteration of the discourse constructing the Third World as danger is the construction of hazard and vulnerability. The death tolls of those in the Third World from 'natural' disasters are cited as a threat constructed of space, rather than disease or more systemic societal issues associated with poverty, hunger, and developmental malaise. Bankoff notes that demographics also play an important role in determining death rates (Bankoff 2001: 24). Thus, not only is identity structured spatially, but it is also defined by the construction of populations. Western space and population are constructed as very different to those in the Third World. This claim is reinforced by statistics which show that from 1963 to 1992 more than 93 percent of all global 'hazards' occurred outside North America and Europe (Smith 1996: 24). Science and technological/bureaucratic administration reinforces the separation of the knowing subject from the object of knowledge. This separation is further enhanced by the form of assistance provided for the West to mitigate risks associated with natural disasters. The assumption is that societies are to engineer an infrastructure to minimize risk and provide security for citizens, sovereign functions that the states in the Third World are not able to perform.

Thus, Western states intervene, through such agencies as the United Nations' International Strategy for Disaster Reduction. The organization was founded in 1999 by a Geneva mandate whose introductory paragraph bears repeating:

> We, participants in the IDNDR International Programme Forum – Towards Partnerships for Disaster Reduction in the 21st Century, – recognise that the world is increasingly being threatened by large scale disasters triggered by hazards, which will have long term negative social, economic, and environmental consequences on our societies and hamper our capacity to ensure sustainable development and investment, particularly in developing countries.[5]

The mandate builds upon the 1994 Yokohama Strategy and specifies the need for scientific and technical knowledge to prevent risks and minimize hazards and to provide security for the processes of development as well as economic and social well-being. Development has expanded to include disaster reduction. Thus, it can be argued that the role of sovereign political communities for the Third World has been expanded to both promote and enhance development and to fortify various state institutions to mitigate risks posed by the natural disasters that happen from 'out' there. The fortifications of risk management will allow the processes of development to continue. The interrelationship between the two – that is, how development facilitated vulnerability – is not assessed or addressed (Bankoff 2001: 24). Natural disasters are portrayed as something that happens, not as something that is created. Thus the disjuncture between subjectivity and objectivity plays into the discourse of risk mitigation. The western subjects assist and intervene with modern scientific bureaucratic and technical expertise in the objects of this knowledge: states in the Third World. Also, importantly, the mandate specifies the need for resources, financial aid, and technical know-how from a variety of existing bilateral and multilateral bodies, particularly for those who are most vulnerable – that is, the constitutive members of the Third World.[6] This mandate indicates an expectation that vulnerable and poor governments will ask the West for technical expertise, funds, and resources to minimize the risks posed by the natural hazards that threaten the world. The threat to normalcy posed by 'defenseless spaces' (Hewitt 1997: 121–2) requires alleviation by the defended spaces whose appropriate application of technical and bureaucratic knowledges safeguards the security of political community, the project of modernity, and demonstrates the triumph of *virtù* over *fortuna*.

Humanitarianism, Biopolitics, and Global Space

Developments of a global space include the bureaucratization of humanitarian assistance (Barnett 2005). This bureaucratization includes the development of a division of labor to control, mitigate, and reduce the risk of fatalities and destruction of property. This is associated with and characterized by the creation of categories such as populations of refugees who have been placed outside of the bonds of citizenship, refugee camps that are also placed outside of the civic political life, and the effects of the natural disaster that has the ability to juxtapose and contrast the rights of citizens with the existence of humanity. The forms of knowledge employed to construct spaces of hazard and vulnerable populations increasingly rely on specialists with scientific knowledge and project managers who identify and mitigate risks to the operation.

As an explanation and possible indication of how increasingly bureaucratized humanitarianism is becoming, Barnett points to two characteristics that signal the transformation and redefinition of humanitarianism: politicization and institutionalization (Barnett 2005: 724). Humanitarian operations have become more overtly political and involved with the promotion of various goals such as human rights, democratization and healthcare (Barnett 2005: 724). Humanitarian assistance becomes more acceptably a tool of statecraft. Furthermore, the institutionalization of humanitarian organizations takes the form of permanent structures, increasing budgets, and professionalized staff, rather than building piecemeal coalitions on an ad hoc basis. Barnett also traces a transformation in the goal of humanitarian relief that stems from the two aspects of change noted above. A more careful analysis of these drivers of change reveals the increasing presence of biopolitical power in the space of relief efforts through a changing relationship between the space of politics and humanitarian efforts.

The drivers of this change are fourfold. The first is a change in perception of threats to peace and security from the Cold War's state-centricity that resulted in the 1992 UN resolution that made the United Nations the overarching and responsible authority for humanitarian efforts to ensure coordination and rationalization (Barnett 2005: 726). This resolution creates a structure of authority and presence that exceeds the space of the sovereign state. Second, the concept of the complex humanitarian emergencies was developed (Barnett 2005: 726). These events were multifaceted and often included state failure, militarized violence, and refugee movement, necessitating the development of a corresponding and specialized set of knowledges to address the underlying causes of such events. The type of intervention required included a more obviously politicized insertion into the space of crisis to ensure the safety of the aid workers, to bargain with various factions to ensure the movement of goods and supplies (Barnett 2005: 726–7). The definition of humanitarian crisis was transformed and correspondingly expanded the set of available tools and techniques utilized by the aid workers on the objects of their efforts. Third, Barnett touches upon a transformation of the economics behind the funding of various humanitarian missions. The primary source of funding was no longer private organizations, but states. Finally, a transformation of the normative structure, including moral and legal frameworks, questioned the sacred and inviolable nature of state sovereignty. An example of this transformation is the Responsibility to Protect, which outlines a responsibility to protect those whose governments are not providing basic security, or who are in fact the violators. All of these transformations signal a change in the political space within which natural disasters are constructed and in the power and tools available to mitigate or mediate the categories which allow for the construction of natural disasters and their relationship to state sovereignty.

Humanitarian relief is no longer focused solely on mitigating the effects of various catastrophic events. Relief efforts are now also targeting and transforming the perceived causes of the disasters (Barnett 2005: 724). Thus, response to the victims of the 2004 Boxing Day tsumani was triggered within hours of the tidal wave (Barnett 2005: 724). The contrast between the international responses to China's Yellow River flood of 1931 and the 2004 tsunami illustrate the increased bureaucratization of biopolitics and its penetration into international space. The Yellow River flood saw almost 4 million dead from direct and indirect causes, and the destruction of a quarter of China's agricultural production (Hughes 2002: 137); some 14 million refugees were created. The 1931 flood was significant in its magnitude, even in the flood-prone region, causing 300 dams to burst.[7] Starving peasants were not the stuff of high politics during the 1930s when the Depression was at its height and the Japanese were advancing to Manchuria. Charles Lindbergh and his wife flew their plane over the devastation and took photographs.[8] They tried to bring a physician to assist survivors but were mobbed by the starving peasants. However, an American missionary also provided invaluable assistance. Some 2,000 tons of rice were sent by the United States. Herbert Hoover expressed his condolences to Chiang Kai-Shek. The assistance was piecemeal and localized. In 1931 there was a lack of humanitarian infrastructure, communications and transportation capacity. Although organizations such as the Red Cross, founded in the nineteenth century, were operational on the ground, they were insufficiently developed and bureaucratized for the scale of the emergency, and their reach much more limited.

Consider now the strong contrast with the response to the tsunami of 2004, where donations to aid agencies exceeded the capacity of the organizations to absorb funds. Relief efforts were triggered within hours of the tidal wave. Relief organizations continue their presence with the building and rebuilding of state capacity and infrastructure. The tsunami not only changed the physical landscape but also resulted in a corresponding transformation of the political space. In Thailand, for example, the king issued a proclamation outlawing the erection of buildings close to the shoreline. USAID is experimenting with new types of seaweed farming in an attempt to create more environmentally sustainable industries. The infrastructure is being rebuilt, associated in part with the rapid erection of large hotels as part of the reconstructive process. The World Health Organization questioned whether 2005 was the year of the disaster, with 97,490 people estimated killed in events around the world, most of which were natural disasters.[9]

The knowledge, techniques, and capacity brought to the reconstruction efforts in Thailand and Banda Aceh, Indonesia, complete with assistance in re-creating living space, indicate a degree of professionalization and the application of scientific and bureaucratic discourses aimed at creating and responding to specific articulations of culture and nature that are embedded within changing notions of sovereignty.

This is not to imply that all natural disasters are treated equally or trigger the same type of response and mobilization. An attempt to untie the relationship between nature and culture, various forms of sovereignty, and the construction of dangerous spaces reveals the social construction of natural disasters as a political set of discourses establishing developments in humanitarian assistance increasingly infused with biopolitical power. This allows for an insight into why some disasters trigger vast international mobilization and some do not. The evolution of the norm of assistance during periods of natural disasters is attributable to a specific construction of hazard and the scientific discourse that, in part, constructs the spatialized danger and the biopolitical techniques utilized to mitigate this threat.

Conclusion

Natural disasters are certainly not new issues – one thinks of such events as the Plague of Athens (430–426 BC) and the San Francisco earthquake of 1906. Their newness, though, lies in their construction as not merely natural but as political/security events which justify military and humanitarian assistance from outside the state. But despite this newness, these issues are not so unprecedented that normative traditions dealing with the adversity of natural disasters cannot speak to their politicization. The key distinction between the prior apolitical view of natural disasters and the treatment of these disasters as political issues is the recognition that *fortuna* is not the domain of the prince alone but of the international community. There is an expansion of moral space beyond the border of the state which fosters a broader sense of obligation and a corresponding desire to alleviate suffering. Political theory, from Machiavelli to Agamben, can be an important tool for unpacking and understanding these changes.

Conclusion

Amy Eckert and Laura Sjoberg

The first years of the twenty-first century have, according to some, been a time of unprecedented threats to both human and national security. According to this view, the dangers in this first century of the new millennium are so unique that they render the inherited normative and theoretical traditions irrelevant for the purposes of addressing what are presented as 'new' security problems. The chapters in this book have interrogated the purported newness of emerging twenty-first-century security problems, arguing that, despite their novelty, existing traditions of social and political theory have important contributions to make to debates regarding their possible resolution. Collectively, we have established that the available 'old' solutions can be used to rethink and recontextualize discourses of international security in the twenty-first century.

New Problems

None of these problems is so new that it is without some degree of historical precedent. The types of new problems that we confront within this book fall into three categories in terms of their balance between new and old elements. The first are issues that have been significant in other respects but are just becoming recognized as involving security; the second are re-manifestations of problems that have been historically significant; and the third are problems that, although characterized as new, in reality enjoy significant points of continuity with the recent past. These three categories possess new and old attributes in different proportions and combine them in different ways, but ultimately none of these problems is so new as to be completely beyond the reach of the 'old' theoretical traditions that we have inherited from our intellectual ancestors.

In the first category, some issues are in fact new security problems in the sense that they are old issues being recognized for the first time as involving security. This is the case, for example, with natural disasters and the transformation of their treatment, as outlined in Lisa Burke's chapter. The disasters themselves are not new, but the international community now sees them in a fundamentally different way and, as such, has developed a different set of responses. Events once accorded low priority by the international community have come to be constructed as suitable for intervention by outside states. Likewise, argues Laura Sjoberg, sanctions, once treated as a non-violent alternative to waging war, now share more with war than with peace, as such are perhaps more usefully analyzed as a type of war. Such shifts in perception and practice reflect the changing normative structure of international society and the identities of the states that inhabit that system. This category of new issues also reflects, in the case of natural disasters and health issues like avian flu, a recognition that the focus of security (in both policy and academic terms) has become rather broader than it once was. While such matters were previously considered to be of purely domestic concern, they are now reconceived as problems of international security. That is, they are not themselves new, but their conceptualization has changed so significantly that they now belong in the security realm.

The second category consists of problems with elements of both oldness and newness, like terrorism and the reprivatization of force. That is, they have historical precedents, but also contain novel components, thereby rendering them only partially new. Contemporary terrorist networks, the subject of Caron Gentry's chapter, possess novel characteristics, but they also reflect traits of the pre-state system in which non-state actors played a more significant role. Likewise states' reliance on private force, the norm in the pre-Westphalian system, all but disappeared with the rise of national armies following the French Revolution. Changes in the international system have again created an opening for private military companies to sell their services to states and other actors. This has been a driving factor in the related problem of individuals becoming alienated from the fighting of war, as Cheyney Ryan contends. These types of issues are not entirely new, then, inasmuch as they have historical precedents. At the same time, the current incarnations of these problems differ in key respects from earlier manifestations – most particularly in the political culture of statism that infuses the international system in its current form. The presence of private actors in a statist system carries significantly different meaning than does the presence of such actors in a system without a presumption in favor of the state. Despite such differences, these new problems have not entirely outgrown the relevance of older ethical and normative traditions.

The third, and most troubling, type of 'new' issues is those that are so characterized for the express purpose of breaking free of previously existing normative rules or perhaps from any restraints whatsoever. Such issues, like the related questions of pre-emptive and preventive war, are treated as novel or as existing within a new and unprecedented framework. In reality, they are continuations of security issues from the nineteenth and twentieth centuries. Indeed, Dan Lindley has argued that 29 percent of wars between 1816 and 1997 were pre-emptive or preventive in nature (2007: 22). Anticipatory war is clearly not new; it has both significant historical precedents and a set of regulatory principles. This significant degree of continuity with the past suggests that the construction of the problems in this category as being new is somewhat disingenuous. The newness of this category, rather than being substantive, is instead rhetorical or representational; its purpose is to sever contemporary consideration of issues from their historical antecedents and, more particularly, from the normative traditions that have grown out of them. The issue of preventive war itself is framed as so radically different from what has happened in the past that the old rules are treated as unsuitable and irrelevant. The assumed inapplicability of these old rules leaves a blank page on which new (and undoubtedly more permissive) rules can be written. Such new rules might conflate preventive war – traditionally forbidden – with pre-emptive war, which is permitted in the face of a special class of threat, thereby conferring a veneer of legitimacy on an act that would have been impermissible under the old rules. While there may indeed be an element of newness, its nature is exaggerated for a particular purpose. Specifically, the newness is constructed for the purpose of avoiding scrutiny under a more restrictive set of rules, not because the threats under consideration are genuinely without precedence.

These categories of 'new' security problems strike differing balances of new and old elements with respect to the existence of historical precedents. Each is the product of specific transformations within the international system, including the growing significance of new actors (Ferguson and Mansbach 2004). Yet the type of newness of the particular problems considered in this book does not pose a problem regarding the application of earlier traditions of thought in the effort to make sense of them. For example, while understanding health as a global public good may involve fresh thinking, there have nevertheless been such public goods in the past. The principles that evolved out of the preservation of those public goods can help us preserve global health as a public good enjoyed across the world. In other words, the newness poses questions of strategy rather than raising normative or intellectual problems that challenge inherited traditions.

These traditions have the authority to speak to the security problems of the twenty-first century, particularly when these are understood to be more substantive than is allowed for in the narrow definitions prescribed by neorealism. Even the security of states is not easily separated from issues of individual well-being or even, as Michael Klare's work on resource wars demonstrates, from issues of environmental degradation and resource scarcity as growing competition for resources drives states into conflict with one another (Klare 2001). To the extent that wars cannot be separated from the context in which they occur, old definitions of security cannot be divided from new security problems, despite the fact that the latter have not always been recognized as such. Even if we adopt a rather conventional sense of security, then, 'new' issues can factor into national security. What such security issues suggest, however, is that the distinction between national security and human security is rapidly disappearing.

Even when maintaining a focus on the security of the state, engagement with the concept of human security is essential if we are to make sense of the threats posed. The connection between the survival of states and of their individual members creates what Liotta calls a 'boomerang effect,' whereby the line between traditional and non-traditional security issues becomes increasingly blurred. This argument suggests that the September 11 attacks on the US demonstrated not only that a relatively powerless actor could now strike a powerful state, but also that 'non-traditional' security issues affecting mostly individuals (human security concerns, in other words) could become issues of state security (Liotta 2002). Extending the concept of security beyond a narrow focus on the survival of states underscores even more clearly the relevance of old traditions to the understanding of new problems.

Beyond a concern exclusively or even primarily with the well-being of the state, 'new' security issues, to the extent that they concern the individual, recognize that security cannot stop at the boundaries of the state but must encompass an understanding of the individuals who make up that state. As the work of Buzan (1991) and Tickner (1992) shows, an exclusive focus on the state precludes a perspective on the other aspect of security, the place of individuals, which should lie at the heart of the discipline. While the state remains the dominant actor within the international system, it has never been the only actor. Integrating an understanding of human security into security studies recognizes the importance of the other actors who exist alongside the state and underscores the extent to which their security is interrelated.

The chapters in this book and the 'new' security problems they raise suggest that the concept of security can and should include within its purview issues as diverse as health, natural disasters, and terrorism, in addition to more conventional concerns about national security. These new twenty-first-century issues have traditionally fallen within the purview of political theory and ethical approaches within this field, including justice and concern for collective goods. Bringing them within the framework of security, particularly to the extent that they reach beyond the state, means recognizing the continuing relevance of the 'old' theoretical traditions to a productive intellectual engagement in our era. Indeed, these moral traditions are arguably better qualified to address certain twenty-first-century issues than are the new discourses employed and the standards proposed in the new century.

Old Solutions

In each of these chapters, the newness of the security problems is not normative newness that would render 'old' solutions irrelevant or unhelpful in addressing them. Their newness is representational or perhaps strategic, but it is not normative newness that requires a break from earlier traditions. As the chapters in this book have demonstrated, these 'new' security issues – even those that do possess genuine elements of newness – are not beyond the reach of the ethical and social theory traditions that had been developing for centuries prior to their emergence on the security agenda. On the contrary, such traditions provide an essential context for the problems, even those that contain significant new elements.

The value of ethical traditions provides a model for the contributions that such a context can make to understanding a new problem. An ethical tradition is a set of beliefs or customs that is handed down the generations (Nardin 1992: 6). These traditions, whether ancient (like the strategizing of Sun Tzu) or more contemporary (the psychological theory of cognitive dissonance), have the potential to provide at least partial solutions to the ethical dilemmas posed by the security problems of the twenty-first century. While the theoretical traditions tapped here may not provide preformed answers to the new security problems of today – in part because they contain genuine elements of newness uncontemplated at the time – they do furnish the values and methods necessary to engage in moral reasoning about these problems. They are 'traditions of argument' rather than 'uniform and unchanging doctrines' (Nardin 1992: 1). They do not provide ready-made answers to new security problems, but offer methods and principles that can be applied to them and that may yield productive outcomes. Hence, these traditions can be utilized to provide moral guidance even in the case of problems wholly unanticipated at the time of their emergence.

The traditions applied to the 'new' security problems addressed in this book, then, provide enduring frameworks for the process of moral decision-making. As such, they provide guidance that is as relevant in the twenty-first century as at the time of their formation. The chapters apply a wide variety of normative and social frameworks, which provide different, and in some cases conflicting, answers to the

various twenty-first-century security problems. Bentham's utilitarianism, for example, is a moral tradition that assesses justice based on
the consequences of particular decisions, for example the decision to
impose sanctions. By contrast, the social contract tradition exemplified
by Locke and Rousseau applies a set of rules without reference to
the consequences. These moral traditions are likely to yield different
responses to the same problem. This conflict among moral orienta-
tions is a manifestation of what Rawls terms 'reasonable pluralism,'
and follows naturally from the free exercise of reason (Rawls 1993:
144). The plurality of normative traditions, as the normal outgrowth
of free reason, does not discount the relevance of these traditions
to security problems, but instead makes the moral analysis richer
and more capable of engaging the range of such problems that have
emerged in this new century.

These intellectual and normative traditions and their 'old' solutions
are capable of providing normative guidance in addressing all three
categories of 'new' twenty-first-century problems. Their continuing
to do so is imperative if we are to make moral sense of the emerging
and re-emerging dangers of our time. Traditions of moral analysis
and social theory endure in part because of their value as analytical
tools. While the problems of the twenty-first century may be to
varying degrees new and unprecedented, new principles with which
to analyze them are not a necessity; the existing moral traditions are
quite capable of providing this moral analysis.

Applying old solutions to new problems will necessarily involve
extending the former beyond their previous confines, given that the
problems do possess genuinely novel elements. This does not serve
to negate the validity or relevance of the traditions or even to dilute
them. To the extent that an ethical tradition is an evolving process and
a thought community rather than a static doctrine, it can be applied
to new problems as they emerge. The contention that new problems
require new solutions rather than answers from existing traditions
should be met with skepticism. As several of the chapters in this book
have established, the claim that these old traditions cannot apply or
that new rules are necessary is often driven by a political agenda that
seeks to discard old restraints in favor of new permissiveness.

Furthermore, 'old' traditions offer important advantages over new
sets of standards that might be felt to be applicable to the new

problems. For a set of moral principles or social theory to be applicable to security issues, they must be seen as enjoying a degree of legitimacy. In the particular case of moral traditions, principles derive their legitimacy from two possible sources – a common commitment to a set of values or the political culture of the relevant community (Wenar 2002: 83). In the case of the community of states, the 'old' moral traditions drawn upon in the chapters of this book enjoy a degree of legitimacy that newly proposed principles cannot. These principles represent values that are the subject of consensus within the state system. Proposed 'new' solutions to emerging security problems, particularly where they conflict with the political culture of the international community, do not enjoy the same degree of legitimacy as the values that have been the subject of reflection and consensus. As such, they cannot speak to the moral aspects of the new security problems in the same way that the old traditions oriented around considered moral judgements can. The same is true with respect to intellectual traditions within the social sciences. Discarding 'old' traditions that offer compelling explanations in favor of new traditions that lack new wisdom is both unnecessary and inappropriate if our goal is the accumulation of knowledge in these fields.

While the twenty-first century does present some new security problems – as well as some old ones with new dimensions – their novelty is insufficient to warrant removing them from the domain of the 'old' moral and intellectual traditions that have historically been depended upon. Indeed, these new problems are at once an essential step in the evolution of the relevant moral and social traditions, which grow through the application of their core principles to new circumstances. Furthermore, the 'old' solutions provide answers that resonate with a greater degree of legitimacy than the new sets of standards that have been proposed for emerging security problems.

The characterization of many of the twenty-first-century problems as too 'new' for our inherited normative traditions may be accounted for by a number of factors. Transformations within the international system have again put individuals and transnational actors into a more prominent position relative to the state, creating an element of change within the system of states. Some may wish to exaggerate this newness for the purpose of avoiding the moral or legal rules that have applied in the past. This instrumental treatment of security problems and their newness threatens to create a world in which the alleged uniqueness of the end justifies any means necessary to achieve it, and renders considerations of justice beside the point.

In any case, the moral traditions discussed in this book have a unique ability to speak to new problems even where they may be truly unprecedented. Disregarding such insights is both unnecessary and unwise. They have endured for as long as they have in large part because of their ability to reflect with wisdom on the problems societies have faced. They also form the basis of a moral consensus – which cannot be said for many of the new solutions proposed by those who would discard the old. Particularly in a time of such profound systemic change, these traditions and the degree of consensus they enjoy provide a valuable source of social legitimacy as well as the balm of accrued wisdom. In a world where these intellectual currents are consulted for their wisdom, rather than ignored as useless impediments to progress, they may bring solutions to 'new' problems are justified and understood as part of a deeper, lasting tradition.

Notes

Chapter 1

1. Gaddis (2002) describes the Bush administration's grand strategy as one of 'transformation' of Middle Eastern states to Western liberal democracies, arguing that Bush justifies this (apparently) radical break from the past in terms of the combined newness and urgency of the problem of global terrorism.

2. Before the 1990s, most Security Council resolutions took their titles from the area of the world in which the conflict they were addressing was located. While the majority of resolutions continue this tradition, a new trend has also arisen, addressing human rights, humanitarianism, food security, and individual security. These include S/RES/1208 (1998) on refugee camps; S/RES/1261 (1999), S/RES/1314 (2000), S/RES/1379 (2001), S/RES/1460 (2003), S/RES/1539 (2004), and S/RES/1612 (2005) on children and armed conflict; S/RES/1265 (1999), S/RES/1296 (2000), S/RES/1674 (2006), and S/RES 1738 (2006) on civilians in armed conflict; S/RES/1325 (2000) on women, peace, and security; and S/RES/1308 on HIV/AIDS.

Chapter 2

1. This chapter uses the terms 'radical Islamic' or 'radical Islam' in contradistinction to moderate and secular Muslims. In 1992, Bilgrami identified three groups within Islam. First, the absolutists (he disagrees with the term 'fundamentalist' because even moderates may have a fundamental belief in Islamic teachings), who believe in an 'antisecular polity based on Islamic personal and public law (the *Sharia*)' (Bilgrami 1992: 824). Second, the moderate Muslims, who are still committed to their faith but are

averse to the 'antisecular absolutist forces' (Bilgrami 1992: 829). Finally, the
secular Muslims, with whom he self-identifies, are those without a belief
in Islamic theology but who are ethnically Muslim (Bilgrami 1992: 822).
While Bilgrami does not use the term 'radical' in his article, it is the more
common term used to distinguish between the various groupings within
the larger Muslim population.

2. See also Ganor 2002: 292; Wilkinson 2000: 13; Dugard 1974: 72.

3. Cronin argues that this is in part because terrorism is '*intended* to be
a matter of perception' and the complications in defining it arise from
this (Cronin 2002: 121). This chapter does not fully agree with her point,
but maintains that terrorist organizations are not hesitant in their beliefs
– thus, there is little room for intended perception or not, only for perceived truth and rightness on both sides of the conflict.

4. This chapter does not mean to isolate or make singular Islamic radical
thought, as opposed to radical thought in other traditions. Given the space
limitations, only Islamic radicalism is covered here in depth because of its
direct relevance to al-Qaeda.

5. The Thugs, a group in India between the seventh and thirteenth centuries AD, worshipped the Hindu god Kali, and killed travelers as a part of
their worship. The Zealots-Sicarii were Jews rebelling against the Greek
population and Roman rule in Judea in the first century AD (Rapoport
1984: 660–62, 669).

6. *Ummah* is Islamic for nation or community. In this sense, it is an 'international Muslim community' (Wright 2006: 186).

7. Al-Zawahiri, an Egyptian-born physician, is 'al-Qaeda's principal ideo-
logue and Osama bin Laden's mentor' (Kepel 2004: 1).

8. I differentiate al-Qaeda from sub-state actors because of the various groups
(sub-state themselves) that are self-identified with the larger, global al-
Qaeda network (Hoffman 2005).

9. Wahhabism, also known as Salafism, is a reformed Sunni sect that believes
in the literal translation of the Koran (Global Security 2007).

10. These references cite the Cambridge edition (Locke 1963), but are refer-
enced by Treatise (I or II) and paragraph number for ease of location in
other editions.

11. Although Seliger does raise a pertinent issue: both secessionists and revo-
lutionaries alike 'claim to have the people on [their] side, without this
being actually the case' (Seliger 1963: 555).

12. I would argue that, due to the subjective nature of the term, there are
some so-called 'terrorist groups' that represent a large proportion of their
populations and that are fighting for self-determination. One such group is
arguably the Chechens in the 1990s before they began to target noncombatant populations.

13. Al-Zarqawi, a Jordanian-born Palestinian, was the leader of al-Qaeda
in the Land of Two Rivers in Iraq (MIPT Terrorism Knowledge Base
2007).

14. This view was also expressed by Ayatollah Ali al-Sistani, the preeminent
Iraqi Shia religious leader, who said 'the sons of the Arab and Islamic na-

tions to close ranks, unite and work hard for the liberation of the usurped lands and restore rights' (Plett 2004).

15. Many Muslims in Europe live in dense pockets in urban areas (see Savage 2004).

16. The 'unemployment rate among Muslims is generally double that of non-Muslims, and it is worse than that of non-Muslim immigrants' (Savage 2004: 31).

17. Although, it must be stated once again, Locke would strenuously object to the use of terrorism, as it is a form of violence that targets the people. The population must always be protected according to his theory.

Chapter 3

1. Webster-Ashburton Treaty, The Avalon Project, www.yale.edu/lawweb/avalon/diplomacy/britain/br-1842d.htm.

2. Some may object that states do not feel the kind of love of which Augustine speaks, and indeed Augustine lived and wrote many centuries before the rise of the state system. As such, he probably had individual rulers in mind rather than the state. However, the state has an existence of its own independent of that of the individuals and groups who make up the state. However, collective entities such as the state are also capable of possessing intention and emotion in addition to more advanced moral attributes such as a sense of justice (Reidy 2004; Erskine 2003a; Rawls 1999; Wendt 1999).

3. Citations for Vattel have three numbers, indicating the book, chapter and paragraph.

4. Additionally, as is clear in Vattel's introduction, states do not have to go any further than that – because states have the right to behave however they see fit, and the justice of their conduct is another issue entirely, and one which other states do not have the right to judge.

Chapter 4

1. See United Nations Commission on Human Rights, Resolution 2003/66, CHR 59th, E/CN.4/RES/2003/66, April 25, 2003.

2. The term 'obligation' is often used in political theory to mean a responsibility citizens have as members of a society to their government (Simmons 1979). This is not the meaning used in this chapter. For accessibility and ease of reading, I use the term 'obligation' as synonymous with duty.

3. For a more complete discussion, see Sjoberg 2006.

4. Passage from *Quaestionum in Heptateuchum*, Q.x, on Joshua), cited in Johnson 2001.

5. The examples of different types of moral standards given in this section are drawn from the Western, Christian tradition. This is done for consistency's sake, as the principles of Just War theory as they are understood today are largely based on a Western, Christian morality. Similar examples could likely be taken from a number of moral traditions.

Chapter 5

1. While cognitive dissonance is not an ethical theory per se, it has ethical implications, and thus fits within the scope of this volume.
2. The nature of state sovereignty has been increasingly debated since the end of the Cold War. See, for example, Barry Buzan and Richard Little, 'Beyond Westphalia: Capitalism after the "Fall",' *Review of International Studies* 25: 89–104.
3. Of course, by a strictly legal definition, a state either has sovereignty or not.
4. I locate 'contingent' sovereignty in the middle of the diagram for simplicity. However, it could lie anywhere between the two poles, depending on the number of contingencies that sovereignty encompasses.
5. Also underlying this debate are concerns of material emancipation, as reflected in events in Kosovo (1999).
6. President Jiang Zemin, UN Millennium Summit, September 7, 2000.
7. President Jiang Zemin, 'Promote Disarmament Process and Safeguard World Security,' Conference on Disarmament, March 26, 1999.
8. President Jiang Zemin, UN Millennium Summit, September 7, 2000.
9. President Putin, 'The Foreign Policy Concept of the Russia Federation,' June 28, 2000.
10. Ibid.
11. Secretary of State Condoleezza Rice, 'Remarks at the InterAction 2007 Annual Forum.' L'Enfant Plaza Hotel, Washington DC, April 18, 2007.
12. UK Foreign Secretary Robin Cook, 'Human Rights – A Priority of Britain's Foreign Policy,' March 28, 2001.
13. Some have questioned whether sovereignty in this sense has been a constant, or even a 'norm' in the international system (Krasner 1999), compliance with the norm has arguably occurred more often than not. For example, Krasner asserts that sovereignty covaries over time with power and interests and is frequently violated. However, he provides no baseline from which to judge this (potential number of violations) and thereby his work suffers from selection bias. I would argue that state sovereignty has more often than not served as an inviolate norm governing international relations.
14. An additional area to explore outside the scope of this chapter is vertical reproduction of norms – how norms are passed down through generations within states – which reflect status quo behavior.
15. For an excellent account of how secondary states come to be socialized by the hegemon, see Ikenberry and Kupchan 1990. Leading powers are those states with the power relative to other states to determine which norms prevail through their actions.
16. I remain agnostic as to whether the norm change is a good thing.
17. A state's decisions can be regarded as the collective decision of the key decision-makers of that state (Snyder et al. 1962: 65), and hence subject to psychological analysis.
18. I recognize that states may say other things in their justifications not necessarily related to sovereignty.

19. Following North et al. (1963), to capture changes in the sovereignty norm, I
    construct a coding protocol based on references to (1) state rights; (2) state
    obligations; (3) the international community's rights; and (4) the inter-
    national community's obligations. These categories map onto the concept
    of state sovereignty, which necessarily implies the relationship between a
    state's rights and obligations and the international community's rights and
    obligations. While reference to a state's right connotes *absolute sovereignty*,
    discussion of the other categories signifies adherence to *contingent sovereignty*.
    Coding is done with the object of contention being a state's internal affairs
    and in whom authority is vested over it in matters related to counterterror-
    ism. If a statement is normative, in that it discusses what a state ought to do,
    then I code it as discussing a 'state's obligations.' If a statement mentions
    that state sovereignty must be respected, I code this as a mention of 'states'
    rights.' The same is applied to coding the international community's rights
    and obligations. If a speech refers to the idea that the international commu-
    nity is allowed to interfere in the internal affairs of a state, this is coded as
    a reference to 'international community's rights,' and a speech that points
    out what the international community *should* do to aid a state is coded as a
    mention of the 'international community's obligations.'
20. United Nations Bibliographic Information System. This is an online cata-
    logue of United Nations documents and publications, which includes bib-
    liographic records, voting records, and an index to speeches. Available at
    http://unbisnet.un.org/.
21. Compared to before 9/11, the topic of terrorism is more common on the
    UNSC's agenda after 9/11.
22. I recognize that the number of speeches in the period prior to the war in
    Afghanistan is small, but they represent the universe of speeches, rather
    than a sample, that deal with global terrorism at this level of analysis.
    One would expect the number of speeches to be small in this issue area
    because the United Nations Security Council, as representatives of the
    international community, did not recognize the challenges of terrorism as
    an international threat to peace and security until 1999, shortly before the
    terrorist attacks of 9/11.
23. MIPT Terrorism Knowledge Base, 2007, www.mipt.org.
24. See Department of Defense 2006. The five-year report on the conflict in
    Afghanistan states that there were fewer than 10,000 US troops in 2002,
    13,000 in 2003, and around 21,000 in 2004–06.
25. Statistics on casualties from the war in Afghanistan are available at http://
    icasualties.org/oef/DeathsByYear.aspx.
26. Thomas Pickering on behalf of the United States to the United Nations
    Security Council as recorded in the provisional verbatim record of the
    three thousand and thirty-third meeting, 21 January 1992, S/PV.3033/1992;
    Thomas Pickering on behalf of the United States to the United Nations
    Security Council as recorded in the provisional verbatim record of the
    three thousand and sixty-third meeting, 31 March 1992, S/PV.3063/1992.
27. Madeline Korbel Albright on behalf of the United States to the United
    Nations Security Council as recorded in the provisional verbatim record

of the three thousand six hundred and twenty-seventh meeting, 31 January 1996, S/PV.3627/1996.

28. Edward Gnehm on behalf of the United States to the United Nations Security Council as recorded in the provisional verbatim record of the three thousand six hundred and ninetieth meeting, 16 August 1996, S/PV.3690/1996.

29. Peter Burleigh on behalf of the United States to the United Nations Security Council as recorded in the provisional verbatim record of the three thousand nine hundred and sixteenth meeting, 13 August 1998, S/PV.3916/1998.

30. Richard Holbrooke on behalf of the United States to the United Nations Security Council as recorded in the provisional verbatim record of the four thousand and fifty-third meeting, 19 October 1999, S/PV.4053/1999.

31. Nancy Soderberg on behalf of the United States to the United Nations Security Council as recorded in the provisional verbatim record of the four thousand two hundred and forty-second meeting, 6 December 2000, S/PV.4242/2000.

32. Ibid.

33. James Cunningham on behalf of the United States to the United Nations Security Council as recorded in the provisional verbatim record of the four thousand three hundred and seventieth meeting, 12 September 2001, S/PV.4370/2001.

34. Colin Powell on behalf of the United States to the United Nations Security Council as recorded in the provisional verbatim record of the four thousand four hundred and thirteenth meeting, 12 November 2001, S/PV.4413/2001.

35. James Cunningham on behalf of the United States to the United Nations Security Council as recorded in the provisional verbatim record of the four thousand four hundred and fifty-third meeting, 18 January 2002, S/PV.4453/2002.

36. Colin Powell on behalf of the United States to the United Nations Security Council as recorded in the provisional verbatim record of the four thousand six hundred and seventh meeting, 11 September 2002, S/PV.4607/2002.

37. Colin Powell on behalf of the United States to the United Nations Security Council as recorded in the provisional verbatim record of the four thousand six hundred and eighty-eighth meeting, 20 January 2003, S/PV.4688/2003.

38. Richard S. Williamson on behalf of the United States to the United Nations Security Council as recorded in the provisional verbatim record of the four thousand seven hundred and thirty-fourth meeting, 4 April 2003, S/PV.4734/2003; John D. Negroponte on behalf of the United States to the United Nations Security Council as recorded in the provisional verbatim record of the four thousand seven hundred and ninety-second meeting, 23 July 2003, S/PV.4792/2003.

39. John D. Negroponte on behalf of the United States to the United Nations Security Council as recorded in the provisional verbatim record of the four thousand seven hundred and fifty-second meeting, 6 May 2003, S/PV.4752/2003.

40. John D. Negroponte on behalf of the United States to the United Nations Security Council as recorded in the provisional verbatim record of the four thousand seven hundred and ninety-eighth meeting, 29 July 2003, S/PV.4798/2003.

41. Nicholas Rostow on behalf of the United States to the United Nations Security Council as recorded in the provisional verbatim record of the five thousand one hundred and thirteenth meeting, 18 January 2005, S/PV.5113/2005.

Chapter 6

1. See, for example, Hare and Joynt 1982: 6; Regan 1996: 96.

2. Most legal traditions distinguish on the basis of intention.

3. For simplicity and the fact that an individual has to be either male or female, I assume each of the combatants in my examples is male. Gender can certainly affect motivations for service in war and the effects of war upon participants. The substantive content of some women's and some men's motives can supplement or even supersede more gender-neutral motivations shared by both women and men, but the moral weight derived from them can serve the same function when applying the principle of double effect.

4. Proportionality would still be an issue in a real war, but in this section we are only considering the effects of one criterion at a time.

5. See 'How Prospects Can Be Improved in the "Difficult Days Ahead"', *New York Times*, December 7, 2006: A24. Robin Wright and Ann Scott Tyson, 'Joint Chiefs Advise Change In War Strategy; Leaders Seek No Major Troop Increase, Urge Shift in Focus to Support of Iraqi Army,' *Washington Post*, December 14, 2006: A1.

6. Since ground forces were not used during the Kosovo campaign, it did not raise the same kinds of issues for the infantry.

7. See Michael R. Gordon, 'Blurring Political Lines in Iraq,' *New York Times*, December 4, 2006: A8; Jennifer Medina, 'General Endorses Lamont, Faults Lieberman on Iraq,' *New York Times*, October 7, 2006: B3; Margaret Talev, 'Former Officers Criticize Rumsfeld Democrats Seek to Put Focus on Iraq,' *Pittsburgh Post–Gazette* (Pennsylvania), September 26, 2006: A-4.

8. See also, for example, Bennett 1966.

Chapter 7

1. Peter Singer uses a spear analogy to describe the functions performed by PMCs, with functions being closer to the tip of the spear being closer to combat (2001). Furthest from the tip, PMCs now perform a number of logistical tasks that were once performed by military personnel, including the construction and dismantling of camps, transport, and so on. Closer to the tip of the spear, PMCs now train military personnel and plan campaigns. Finally, they can also engage in combat and functions adjacent to combat, particularly in a conflict like Iraq with no discernible front or rear.

2. Additionally, *jus in bello* norms of the type I consider here were considerably less developed in this earlier time period (Aristotle 1984).

3. The patchwork of political authority during this era was so complex that during the Hundred Years War the king of England was both a vassal to the king of France and a claimant to his throne (Johnson 1981: 152). Alongside this very complicated system of secular authority, the Church also claimed political authority over the faithful and maintained that it also had the right to declare war.
4. For a contemporary translation of this work, see Gratian 1993.

Chapter 8

1. Chief Justice White, US Supreme Court Selective Draft Law Cases, 245 U.S. 366 (1918).
2. Polls indicated that popular support for the draft was 90 percent in December 1965, dropping to 79 percent in August 1966, and to 50 percent by May 1968. See Useem 1973: 115.
3. See Friedberg 2000: 193–4; D. Smith 1974: 89; Flynn 1993.
4. See also Glover 2000: 47.
5. Woodrow Wilson's words about World War I.
6. Army Recruiting Commander Briefing by Major General Michael D. Rochelle, Office of the Assistant Secretary of Defense (Public Affairs), May 20, 2005, www.defenselink.mil/transcripts/transcript.aspx?transcriptid=3274. An excellent collection of articles on problems in minority recruiting in today's military can be found at www.countermilitary.org/Articles/MilitaryRecruiting/PeopleOfColor/article_list.html.
7. See also MacPherson 2008.
8. 'Army Recruits' "Moral Waivers",' Rick Sallinger, CBS News, http://cbs4 denver.com/investigates/Colorado.News.Denver.2.554096.html.

Chapter 9

1. The divide seems to be 'old' sanctions as a tactic of war and 'new' sanctions as a peaceful alternative to war, despite no real change in the methods of implementation of sanctions or the sorts of offenses for which they are applied. 'New' is in scare quotes throughout the chapter to indicate the author's skepticism regarding the legitimacy of these claims of newness.
2. I first laid out this typology of theories in *Gender, Justice, and the Wars in Iraq* (2006).
3. The question of whether sanctions are 'short of' military force depends on how you define the continuum of violence. Mueller and Mueller (1999, cited above) would argue that sanctions are not 'short of' military force because of their high casualty rate. A number of political scientists have pointed out that the United States' invasion of Iraq caused fewer fatalities among Iraqis than the sanctions regime. Others, however, see sanctions as 'short of military force' by measuring on the actions, and commitment, required of the sanctioner(s).
4. I would like to express my thanks to Nick Onuf, who in my first year in

graduate school read my Bachelor's thesis, which re-theorized the economic sanctions regime on Iraq through gender lenses. He ended each of our conversations on the topic with the advice that I should read Bentham to understand sanctions. Of course, it took me a few more years than perhaps Nick would have liked.

Chapter 10

1. It is important to acknowledge that H5N1 mutation is not certain to occur. At present, the virus attaches to cells in the lower respiratory tract of humans. It is possible that scientists might discover a feature of this particular virus which prevents it from attaching to upper respiratory tract cells and thus transmitting to others through coughing and sneezing.
2. This Resolution expressed concern about the potential adverse effects of HIV/AIDS on UN peacekeeping personnel, but it also stressed more generally that this disease, 'if unchecked, may pose a risk to stability and security.'
3. It is possible, however, that antiviral drugs will become less effective or ineffective. In early 2005, H5N1 virus with high-level resistance to oseltamivir (Tamiflu®) was isolated from two Vietnamese patients, both of whom died despite being treated with the antiviral drug.

Chapter 11

1. See also Nietzsche 1974.
2. Said 1978 is a good example of this analysis.
3. The gendered 'his' is intentional and reflects a specific construction of individual sovereignty fostered by modernity.
4. The theories of colonization and decolonization are vast and complex. This chapter is not meant to suggest that the period of granting formal sovereignty to previously colonized regions of the world is a simple or finished process. Rather, the argument is the reverse. The shift from formal imperialism to other axes of identity and discrimination is based on different sites of identity that have currency. The unequal status of many states in various forms is related to the unequal structure of power and embedded within the international system itself.
5. www.unisdr.org/eng/about_isdr/bd-geneva-mandate-eng.htm.
6. The strength of this construction of defenseless spaces as something that happens in the Third World was underlined during Hurricane Katrina and the careful messaging of displaced persons and the delay in accepting aid from other jurisdictions. The United States as global hegemon could not be seen as lacking in *virtù* and thus vulnerable.
7. See Takeuchi 2002: 17; Hughes 2002, 137–8; and www.unisdr.org/country-inform/china-disaster.htm.
8. www.charleslindbergh.com/history/china.asp.
9. www.who.int/bulletin/volumes/ 84/1/news/10106/en/index.html.

References

Agamben, G. (1998) *Homo Sacer: Sovereign Power and Bare Life*, trans. Daniel Heller-Roazen, Stanford University Press, Stanford.

Agence France Presse (2007) 'Major Powers to Seek Sanctions against Iran,' December 1, http://afp.google.com/article/ALeqM5imrPGfVd6_72mVV8Sub Nln FOePoQ

Aglionby, J., and A. Jack (2007) 'Indonesia Blames WHO for Bird Flu Deal,' Business Day, February 8; accessed May 22, 2007 from http://businessdayonline. com/?c=125&a=11127.

al-Zawahiri, A. (2007a) 'Loyalty and Enmity,' in R. Ibrahim, ed. and trans., *The Al Qaeda Reader*, Broadway Books, New York.

al-Zawahiri, A. (2007b) '*Sharia* and Democracy,' in R. Ibrahim, ed. and trans., *The Al Qaeda Reader*, Broadway Books, New York.

Allison, G., and P. Zelikow (1999) *Essence of Decision: Explaining the Cuban Missile Crisis*, 2nd edn, Longman, New York.

American Friends Service Committee (2008) 'Eight things you need to know about the draft,' www.afsc.org/youthmil/thinking-of-enlisting/poverty-draft.htm.

Angell, N. (1913) *The Great Illusion*, G.P. Putnam's Sons, London and New York.

Anonymous (2007a) 'Indonesia Edges Closer to Sharing Bird-Flu Samples,' *Nature*, vol. 450, no. 7170.

Anonymous (2007b) 'US Government Support to Combat Avian and Pandemic Influenza,' US Department of State, June 4, from www.state.gov/r/pa/scp/86190.htm; accessed November 19, 1997.

Anonymous (2006) 'Implementation Plan for the National Strategy for Pandemic Influenza,' Homeland Security Council, Washington DC.

Anonymous (2004) 'Mysterious Disease Kills Thousands of Vietnamese

Chickens,' *Sydney Morning Herald*, January 7, www.smh.com.au/articles/ 2004/01/06/1073268033540.html; accessed January 12, 2004.

Ansah, T.B. (2005) 'A Terrible Purity: International Law, Morality, Religion, and Exclusion,' *Cornell International Law Journal*, vol. 38, no. 1.

Anscombe, G.E.M. (1990) 'Comments on Coughlan's "Using People",' *Bioethics*, vol. 4, no. 1.

Anscombe, G.E.M. (1970) 'War and Massacre,' in R.A. Wasserstrom, ed., *War and Morality*, Wadsworth, Belmont CA.

Aquinas, T. (2006) *Summa Theologiae*, Volume 13: *Man Made to God's Image*, ed. Edmund Hill, Cambridge University Press, Cambridge.

Aquinas, T. (1959) 'On Princely Government,' in *Aquinas: Selected Political Writings*, trans. and ed. A.P. d'Entreves, Barnes & Noble, New York.

Aristotle (1984 [1270]) *The Politics*, trans. C. Lord, University of Chicago Press, Chicago.

Arnold, D. (1996) *Warm Climates and Western Medicine: The Emergence of Tropical Medicine 1500–1930*, Editions Rodopi, Atlanta GA and Amsterdam.

Aronson, E., and J.M. Carlsmith. (1963) 'Effect of Severity of Threat on the Valuation of Forbidden Behavior,' *Journal of Abnormal and Social Psychology*, vol. 66, no. 6, June.

Aronson, E., and J. Mills (1959) 'The Effect of Severity of Initiation on Liking for a Group,' *Journal of Abnormal Social Psychology* 59.

Ashley, R.K. (1984) 'The Poverty of Neorealism,' *International Organization*, vol. 38, no. 2.

Atran, S. (2004) 'Mishandling Suicide Terrorism,' *Washington Quarterly*, vol. 27, no. 3, Summer.

Augustine, Saint (1998) *The City of God against the Pagans*, trans. R.W. Dyson, Cambridge University Press, Cambridge.

Augustine, Saint (1956) 'Contra faustum,' in *Nicene and post-Nicene Fathers*, ed. P. Schaff, Eerdmans, Grand Rapids MI.

Augustine, Saint (1955) *The Problem of Free Choice*, trans. Dom Mark Pontifex, Newman Press, Westminster MD.

Augustine, Saint (1950) *The City of God*, Modern Library, New York.

Avant, D.D. (2005) *The Market for Force: The Consequences of Privatizing Security*, Cambridge University Press, Cambridge.

Avant, D.D. (2004) 'The Privatization of Security and Change in the Control of Force,' *International Studies Perspectives*, vol. 5, no. 4, November.

Baldor, L. (2007) 'Military May Ease Standards for Recruits,' Associated Press, November 6.

Baldwin, D. (1999/2000) 'The Sanctions Debate and the Logic of Choice,' *International Security*, vol. 24, no. 3.

Baldwin, D. (1985) *Economic Statecraft*, Princeton University Press, Princeton NJ.

Bandura, A. (1998) 'Mechanisms of Moral Disengagement,' in W. Reich, ed., *Origins of Terrorism: Psychologies, Ideologies, Theologies, States of Mind*, Woodrow Wilson Center Press, Washington DC.

Banerjee, S. (1997) 'Reproduction of Social Structures,' working paper.

Bankoff, G. (2001) 'Rendering the World Unsafe: "Vulnerability" as Western Discourse,' *Disaster*, vol. 25, no. 1.

Barkin, J.S., and B. Cronin (1994) 'The State and the Nation: Changing Norms and the Rules of Sovereignty in International Relations,' *International Organization*, vol. 48, no. 1.

Barnett, J. (2001) *The Meaning of Environmental Security: Ecological Politics and Policy in the New Security Era*, Zed Books, London.

Barnett, M.N. (2005) 'Humanitarianism Transformed,' *Perspectives on Politics*, vol. 3, no. 4.

Barnett, M.N. (2003) 'Bureaucratizing the Duty to Aid: The United Nations and Rwandan Genocide,' in A.F. Lang, Jr., ed., *Just Intervention*, Georgetown University Press, Washington DC.

Barnett, M.N. (2002) *Eyewitness to a Genocide: The United Nations and Rwanda*, Cornell University Press, Ithaca NY. June

Barnett, M.N. (1997) 'The UN Security Council, a Difference, and Genocide in Rwanda,' *Cultural Anthropology*, vol. 12, no. 4.

Barnett, M.N. (1993) 'Institutions, Roles, and Disorder: The Case of the Arab States System,' *International Studies Quarterly*, vol. 37, no.3.

Barrows-Friedman, N. (2007) 'Mideast: Israel's Economic Strangehold a Silent Killer,' Interpress, January 31, www.ipsnews.net/news.asp?idnews=36379; accessed January 1, 2008.

BBC News (2004) Excerpts: Bush and Blair on Iraq,' 28 June, news.bbc.co.uk/2/hi/middle_east/3847751.stm; accessed March 14, 2008.

Beauvois, J.-L., and R.V. Joule (1996) *A Radical Dissonance Theory*, Taylor & Francis, London.

Bellamy, A.J. (2006) *Just Wars: From Cicero to Iraq*, Polity Press, Cambridge.

Bennett, J. (1966) 'Whatever the Consequences,' *Analysis* 26, January.

Benson, J.A. (1999) 'Trends: End of Life Issues,' *Public Opinion Quarterly*, vol. 63, no. 2, Summer.

Bentham, J. (1948 [1780]) *Introduction to the Principles of Morals and Legislation*, Hafner, New York.

Berger, K. (2007) 'The Iraqi Insurgency for Beginners,' Salon.com, http://web.lexis-nexis.com/universe; accessed April 1, 2007.

Berlin, I. (1969) *Four Essays on Liberty*, Oxford University Press, Oxford.

Berman, M. (1988) *All That Is Solid Melts into Air: The Experience of Modernity*, Penguin, New York.

Betts, R.K. (2003) 'Striking First: A History of Thankfully Lost Opportunities,' *Ethics and International Affairs*, vol. 17, no. 1.

Bica, C.C. (1997) 'Collateral Violence and the Doctrine of Double Effect,' *Public Affairs Quarterly*, vol. 11 no. 1, January.

Biersteker, T.J., and C. Weber (1996) 'The Social Construction of State Sovereignty,' in T.J. Biersteker and C. Weber, eds., *State Sovereignty as a Social Construct*, Cambridge University Press, Cambridge.

Bilgrami, Akeel (1992) 'What is a Muslim?' *Critical Inquiry*, vol. 18, no. 4.

bin Laden, O. (2007) 'Israel, Oil, and Iraq,' in R. Ibrahim, ed. and trans., *The Al Qaeda Reader*, Broadway Books, New York.

bin Laden, O., A. al-Zawahiri, A.B.R.A. Taha, M. Hamza, and F. Rahman. (2007) 'Declaration of War against Americans,' in R. Ibrahim, ed. and trans., *The Al Qaeda Reader*, Broadway Books, New York.

Black, D. (1999) 'The Long and Winding Road: International Norms and Domestic Political Change in South Africa,' in T. Risse, S.C. Ropp, and K. Sikkink, eds., *The Power of Human Rights: International Norms and Domestic Change*, Cambridge University Press, Cambridge.

Blumenthal, S. (2006) *How Bush Rules: Chronicles of a Radical Regime*, Princeton University Press, Princeton NJ.

Bolton, J.R. (2002) 'The New Strategic Framework: A Response to 21st Century Security Threats,' *United States Foreign Policy*, vol. 7, no. 2, July.

Booth, K. (1997) 'Security and Self: Reflections of a Fallen Realist,' in K. Krause and M.C. Williams, eds., *Critical Security Studies*, University of Minnesota Press, Minneapolis.

Booy, R., L.E. Brown, G.S. Grohmann and C.R. MacIntyre (2006) 'Pandemic Vaccines: Promises and Pitfalls,' *Medical Journal of Australia*, vol. 185, no. 10.

Bourne, R. (1917) 'A War Diary,' *Seven Arts* 2.

Boyle, J.M. (1980) 'Toward Understanding the Principle of Double Effect,' *Ethics*, vol. 90, no. 4, July.

Bradford, W.C. (2004) '"The Duty to Defend Them": A Natural Law Justification for the Bush Doctrine of Preventive War,' *Notre Dame Law Review* 79.

Brayton, S. (2002) 'Outsourcing War: Mercenaries and the Privatization of Peacekeeping,' *Journal of International Affairs*, vol. 55, no. 2.

Brehm, J.W. (1956) 'Postdecision Changes in the Desirability of Alternatives,' *Journal of Abnormal and Social Psychology* 52.

Brigety, R. (2006) 'The Moral Influence of *Jus ad Bellum* for Modern Warriors,' Keynote Address, Joint Services Conference on Military Ethics, Springfield VA, January 26.

Brinkley, J., and J. Glanz (2004) 'Contract Workers Implicated in February Army Report on Prison Abuse Remain on the Job,' *New York Times*, May 4, 6.

Bristol, N. (2008) 'US Senate Passes New PEPFAR Bill,' *The Lancet*, vol. 372, no. 9635.

Broder, J.M., and J. Risen (2007), 'Blackwater Mounts a Defense with Top Talent,' *New York Times*, November 5.

Brown, C. (2003) 'Selective Humanitarianism: In Defense of Inconsistency,' in D.K. Chatterjee and D.E. Scheid, eds., *Ethics and Foreign Intervention*, Cambridge University Press, Cambridge.

Bueno de Mesquita, B. (2000) *Principles of International Politics*, CQ Press, Washington DC.

Bueno de Mesquita, B. (1981) *The War Trap*, Yale University Press, New Haven CT.

Bull, H. (1977) *The Anarchical Society: A Study of Order in World Politics*, Macmillan, London.

Buncombe A. (2002) 'US Threatens North Korea with Ruinous Economic Stranglehold,' *Independent*, December 30.

Bures, O. (2005) 'Private Military Companies: A Second Best Peacekeeping Option?' *International Peacekeeping*, vol. 12, no. 4.

Burris, C.T., E. Harmon-Jones and W.R. Tarpley (1997) 'By Faith Alone: Religious Agitation and Cognitive Dissonance,' *Basic and Applied Social Psychology* 19.

Bush, G.W. (2007) 'President Bush Discusses Genocide in Darfur, Implements

Sanctions,' White House Press Release, www.whitehouse.gov/news/releases/2007/05/20070529.html; accessed January 1, 2008.

Bush, G.W. (2003) 'Executive Order Blocking Property of Certain Persons and Prohibiting the Export of Certain Goods to Syria,' Office of Foreign Assets Control, US Department of the Treasury, www.treas.gov/offices/enforcement/ofac/programs/ascii/syria.txt.

Bush, G.W. (2002a) 'President Delivers State of the Union Address,' January 29, www.whitehouse.gov/news/releases/2002/01/20020129–11.html; accessed November 13, 2007.

Bush, G.W. (2002b) 'The National Security Strategy of the United States of America,' White House, Washington DC, www.whitehouse.gov/nsc/nss.html; accessed March 16, 2008.

Bush, G.W. (2002c) 'West Point Graduation Speech (June 1, 2002),' www.whitehouse.gov/news/releases/2002/06/20020601–3.html.

Bush, G.W. (2001a) 'Address to a Joint Session of Congress and the American People,' September 20, www.whitehouse.gov/ news/releases/2001/09/20010920–8.html; accessed November 13, 2007).

Bush, G.W. (2001b) 'Press Conference by President Bush and Prime Minister Tony Blair,' July 19, Office of the Press Secretary.

Buzan, B. (1991) *People, States and Fear: An Agenda for International Security Studies in the Post-Cold War Era*, Harvester Wheatsheaf, Hemel Hempstead.

Buzan, B. (1982) *People, States, and Fear: An Agenda for International Security Studies in the Post-Cold War Era*, Lynne Rienner, Boulder CO.

Buzan, B., O. Waever and J. de Wilde (1998) *Security: A New Framework for Analysis*, Lynne Rienner, Boulder CO.

Byman, D., and K. Pollack (2001) 'Let Us Now Praise Great Men: Bringing the Statesman Back In,' *International Security*, vol. 25, no. 4.

Caballero-Anthony, M. (2006) 'Combating Infectious Diseases in East Asia: Securitization and Global Public Goods for Health,' *Journal of International Affairs*, vol. 59, no. 2.

Cable, V. (1995) 'What is International Economic Security?' *International Affairs*, vol. 71, no. 2.

Cahill, T. (1999) *Desire of the Everlasting Hills: The World Before and After Jesus*, Doubleday, New York.

Campbell, D. (1992) *Writing Security: United States Foreign Policy and the Politics of Identity*, University of Minnesota Press, Minneapolis.

Cao, H., T. Nguyen and N. Daniels (2004) 'HIV/AIDS and Public Health Care in the Greater Mekong River Region,' in Y. Lu and M. Essex, eds., *AIDS in Asia*, Kluwer, New York.

Caron, D.D. (1993) 'The Legitimacy of the Collective Authority of the Security Council,' *American Journal of International Law*, vol. 87, no. 4.

Carroll, J. (2007) 'Slim Majority Supports Anti-Terrorism Action in Afghanistan, Pakistan,' Gallop Poll, August 31, www.galloppoll.com/content/?ci=38333.

Carver, T. (2003) 'Bush Puts God on His Side,' BBC News, April 6, news.bbc.co.uk/2/hi/Americas/2921345.stm; accessed March 22, 2007.

Cave, D. (2005) 'Growing Problem for Military Recruiters: Parents,' *New York Times*, June 3.

Chalk, P. (2006) 'Disease and the Complex Processes of Securitization in the Asia–Pacific,' in M. Caballero-Anthony, R. Emmers, and A. Acharya, eds., *Non-Traditional Security in Asia: Dilemmas in Securitization*, Ashgate, Aldershot.

Chan, S, and A.C. Drury (2000) *Sanctions as Economic Statecraft: Theory and Practice*, St. Martin's Press, New York.

Charlesworth, H. (1999) 'Feminist Methods in International Law,' *American Journal of International Law*, vol. 93, no. 2.

Chatterjee, D.K., and, D.E. Scheid, eds. (2003) *Ethics and Foreign Intervention*, Cambridge University Press, Cambridge.

Chen, L., and V. Narasimhan (2004) 'Human Security and Global Health,' *Journal of Human Development*, vol. 4, no. 2.

Cheng, M.H. (2006) 'Cash Boost for Avian Influenza Exceeds Expectations,' *The Lancet*, vol. 367, no. 9507.

Chinyaeva, E. (2001) 'A New Partisanship or Another Political Bargain?' *Transitions Online*, Prague, www.worldpress.org/Europe/267.cfm; accessed March 16, 2008.

Chivers, C.J. (2006) 'Contractor's Boss in Iraq Shot at Civilians, Workers' Suit Says,' *New York Times*, November 17.

Clausewitz, C. von (1989 [1830]) *On War*, trans. M. Howard and P. Paret, Princeton University Press, Princeton NJ.

Clinton, W.J. (1994) Remarks at the United States Naval Academy Commencement Ceremony in Annapolis, Maryland, May 25.

Coates A.J. (1997) *The Ethics of War*, Manchester University Press, Manchester.

Coker, C. (1999) 'Outsourcing War,' *Cambridge Review of International Affairs*, vol. 13, no. 1.

Connolly, C. (2006) 'U.S. Plan for Flu Pandemic Revealed,' *Washington Post*, April 16, A01.

Connolly, W. (2004) 'The Complexity of Sovereignty,' in J. Edkins, V. Pin-Fat and M. Shapiro, eds., *Sovereign Lives: Power in Global Politics*, Routledge, London.

Convention on the Prevention and Punishment of the Crime of Genocide (1948) 78 U.N.T.S. 277.

Cook, M.L. (2004) 'Ethical and Legal Dimentions of the Bush Preemption Strategy,' *Harvard Journal of Law and Public Policy*, vol. 27, no. 3.

Cook, M.L. (2003) '"Immaculate War": Constraints on Humanitarian Intervention,' in A.F. Lang Jr., ed., *Just Intervention*, Georgetown University Press, Washington DC.

Cooper, A. (1997) 'Niche Diplomacy: A Conceptual Overview,' in A. Cooper, ed., *Niche Diplomacy: Middle Powers after the Cold War*, Macmillan, London.

Cooper, C., and R. Block (2006) *Disaster: Hurricane Katrina and the Failure of Homeland Security*, Macmillan, London.

Cortright, D., and G. Lopez (2002) *Sanctions and the Search for Security*, Lynne Rienner, Boulder CO.

Cortright, D., and G. Lopez (2000) *The Sanctions Decade: Assessing UN Strategies in the 1990s*, Lynne Rienner, Boulder CO.

Cortright, D., and G. Lopez (1995) *Economic Sanctions, Panacea or Peacebuilding in the Post-Cold War World*, Westview Press, Boulder CO.

Cox, R.W. (1996) *Approaches to World Order*, Cambridge University Press, Cambridge.

Cox, R.W. (1986) 'Social Forces, States, and World Orders: Beyond International Relations Theory,' in R.O. Keohane, ed., *Neorealism and its Critics*, Columbia University Press, New York.

Crawford, N.C. (2003) 'The Slippery Slope to Preventive War,' *Ethics & International Affairs*, vol. 17, no. 1.

Crawford, N.C. (2000) 'The Passion of World Politics: Propositions on Emotion and Emotional Relationships,' *International Security*, vol. 24, no. 4.

Crawford, N.C., and A. Klotz (1999) *How Sanctions Work: Lessons from South Africa*, Palgrave Macmillan, New York.

Creswell, M.J. (2004) 'Legitimizing Force: A Lockean Account,' *Armed Forces and Society*, vol. 30, no. 4, Summer.

Cronin, A.K. (2002/3) 'Behind the Curve: Globalization and International Terrorism,' *International Security*, vol. 27, no. 3, Winter.

Cronin, A.K. (2002) 'Rethinking Sovereignty: American Strategy in the Age of Terrorism,' *Survival*, vol. 44, no. 2, Summer.

Cuellar, J.P. de (1995) 'Reflecting on the Past,' *Global Governance*, vol. 1, no. 2, May/August.

Cushman Jr., J. (2004) 'Private Company Finds No Evidence Its Interrogators Took Part in Prison Abuse,' *New York Times*, August 13.

Cutler, A.C., V. Haufler, and T. Porter (1999) 'Private Authority and International Affairs,' in A.C. Cutler, V. Haufler and T. Porter, eds, *Private Authority and International Affairs*, State University of New York Press, Albany.

Daalder, I.H., and J.B. Steinberg (2005) 'Preventative War: A Useful Tool,' *Los Angeles Times*, December 4.

Dalby, S. (2002) *Environmental Security*, University of Minnesota Press, Minneapolis.

Dalby, S. (1997) 'Contesting an Essential Concept: Reading the Dilemmas of Contemporary Security Discourse,' in K. Krause and M.C. Williams, eds., *Critical Security Studies*, University of Minnesota Press, Minneapolis.

Darling, D. (2005) 'Letter From Ayman al-Zawahiri to Abu Mussab Zarqawi,' Manhattan Institute Center for Policy Terrorism, www.cpt-mi.org/pdf_secure.php?pdffilenameFLetter_from_Ayman_al_Zawahiri; accessed November 13, 2007.

Deane, H.A. (1963) *The Political and Social Ideas of St. Augustine*, Columbia University Press, New York.

Deng, F.M., and T. Lyons, eds. (1998) *Africa Reckoning: A Quest for Good Governance*, Brookings Institution Press, Washington DC.

d'Entreves, A.P. (1959) *The Medieval Contribution to Political Thought*, Humanities Press, New York.

Department of Defense (2006a) 'Five-Year Afghanistan Report,' www.defenselink.mil/home/dodupdate/For-the-record/documents/20062006d.html; accessed October 14, 2007.

Department of Defense (2006b) *Department of Defense Implementation Plan for Pandemic Influenza*, Office of the Assistant Secretary of Defense for Homeland Defense, Washington DC.

Department of State (1994) Action Memorandum from Assistant Secretary of State George Moose to Secretary of State Warren Christopher, 'Has Genocide Occurred in Rwanda?' May 21.

Destexhe, A. (1994/5) 'The Third Genocide,' *Foreign Policy* 97, Winter.

Dewey, J. (1929) *The Quest for Certainty: A Study of the Relation of Knowledge and Action*, Milton, Balch, New York.

DHHS (Department of Health and Human Services) (2007) 'Community Strategy for Pandemic Influenza Mitigation,' US Department of Health and Human Services, February, www.pandemicflu.gov/plan/community/commitigation.html; accessed September 10, 2007.

Dolan, C.J. (2005) *In War We Trust: The Bush Doctrine and the Pursuit of Just War*, Ashgate, Burlington VA.

Donnelley, T. (2003) 'The Underpinnings of the Bush Doctrine,' *National Security Outlook: AEI Online*, www.aei.org/publications/pub13.15845/.

Donnelly, J. (1995) 'State Sovereignty and International Intervention: The Case of Human Rights,' in G.M. Lyons and M. Mastanduno, eds., *Beyond Westphalia? State Sovereignty and International Intervention*, Johns Hopkins University Press, Baltimore.

Doxey, M. (1987) *International Sanctions in Contemporary Perspective*, Macmillan, London.

Drake, C.J.M. (1998) 'The Role of Ideology in Terrorists' Target Selection,' *Terrorism and Political Violence*, vol. 10, issue 2, Summer.

Draper, T. (2002) 'Introduction to Jeremy Bentham's Theory of Punishment,' *Journal of Bentham Studies* 5.

Drezner, D. (1999) *The Sanctions Paradox: Economic Statecraft and International Relations*, Cambridge University Press, Cambridge.

Dugard, J. (1974) 'International Terrorism: Problems in Defining,' *International Affairs*, vol. 50, no. 1, January.

Dyson, M.E. (2006) *Come Hell or High Water: Hurricane Katrina and the Color of Disaster*, Basic Books, New York.

Eckholm, E. (2003) 'SARS is the Spark for a Riot in China,' *New York Times*, April 29, A1.

Editorial (2007) 'International Health Regulations: the Challenges Ahead,' *The Lancet*, vol. 369, no. 9575.

Edmonds, M. (1999) 'Defence Privatisation: From State Enterprise to Commercialism,' *Cambridge Review of International Affairs*, vol. 13, no. 1.

Elbe, S. (2003) *Strategic Implications of HIV/AIDS*, Oxford University Press, New York.

Elliott, K.A. (1998) 'The Sanctions Glass: Half Full or Completely Empty,' *International Security*, vol. 23, no. 1.

Elliott, K.A., and G.C. Hufbauer (2002) 'Sanctions,' *The Concise Encyclopedia of Economics*, www.econlib.org/library/nc/Sanctions.html; accessed January 1, 2008.

Elliott, K.A., and G.C. Hufbauer (1999) 'Same Song, Same Refrain? Economic Sanctions in the 1990s,' *American Economic Review*, vol. 89, no. 2.

Erskine, T., ed. (2004) *Assigning Duties to Institutions: Debating Hard Cases*, special issue of *Global Society*, vol. 18, no. 1, January.

Erskine, T. (2003a) 'Making Sense of "Responsibility" in International Relations

- Key Questions and Concepts,' in *Can Institutions Have Responsibilities? Collective Moral Agency and International Relations*, Palgrave Macmillian, New York.

Erskine, T., ed. (2003b) *Can Institutions Have Responsibilities? Collective Moral Agency and International Relations*, Palgrave Macmillian, New York.

Etzioni, A. (2004) *From Empire to Community: A New Approach to International Relations*, Palgrave Macmillan, New York.

Fabian, J. (2002) *Time and the Other: How Anthropology Makes it Object*, Columbia University Press, New York.

Falk, R. (2003) *The Great Terror War*, Interlink, New York.

Falk, R. (2002) 'The New Bush Doctrine,' *The Nation*, July 15.

Falk, R. (1998) 'Sovereignty and Human Dignity: The Search for Reconciliation,' in F.M. Deng and T. Lyons, eds., *Africa Reckoning: A Quest for Good Governance*, Brookings Institution Press, Washington DC.

Farer, T.J. (1991) 'An Inquiry into the Legitimacy of Humanitarian Intervention,' in L.F. Damrosch and D.J. Scheffer, eds., *Law and Force in the New International Order*, Westview Press, San Francisco.

Farley, M. (2000) 'UN to Tighten Afghan Sanctions,' *Los Angeles Times*, December 20.

Feil, S.R. (1998) *Preventing Genocide: A Report to the Carnegie Commission on Preventing Deadly Conflict*, Carnegie Corporation, New York.

Ferguson, N. (1995) *The Cash Nexus*, Basic Books, New York.

Ferguson, Y.H., and R.W. Mansbach (2004) *Remapping Global Politics: History's Revenge and Future Shock*, Cambridge University Press, Cambridge.

Festinger, L. (1957) *A Theory of Cognitive Dissonance*, Row, Peterson, Evanston IL.

Festinger, L., and J.M. Carlsmith (1959) 'Cognitive Consequences of Forced Compliance,' *Journal of Abnormal and Social Psychology*, vol. 58, no. 2, March.

Festinger, L., H.W. Riecken, and S. Schachter (1956) *When Prophecy Fails: A Social and Psychological Study of a Modern Group That Predicted the Destruction of the World*, Harper & Row, New York.

Fidler, D.P. (2004) 'Germs, Norms and Power: Global Health's Political Revolution,' *Law, Social Justice & Global Development*, June 4, www2.warwick.ac.uk/fac/soc/law/elj/lgd/2004_1/fidler/; accessed October 15, 2007.

Fierke, K.M. (2000) 'Logics of Force and Dialogue: the Iraq/UNSCOM Crisis as Social Interaction,' *European Journal of International Relations*, vol. 6, no. 3.

Fierke, K.M. (1997) 'Changing Worlds of Security,' in K. Krause and M.C. Williams, eds., *Critical Security Studies*, University of Minnesota Press, Minneapolis.

Finnemore, M. (2003) *The Purpose of Intervention: Changing Beliefs about the United States of Force*, Cornell University Press, Ithaca.

Finnemore, M. (1998) 'Military Intervention and the Organization of International Politics,' in, J. Lepgold and T.G. Weiss, eds., *Collective Conflict Management and Changing World Politics*, State University of New York Press, Albany.

Fischer, M. (1992) 'Feudal Europe: 800–1300. Communal Discourse and Conflictual Practices,' *International Organization* 46, Spring.

Fixdal, M., and D. Smith (1998) 'Humanitarian Intervention and Just War,' *Mershon International Studies Review* 42.

Flax, J. (1987) 'Postmodernism and Gender Relations in Feminist Theory,' *Signs: Journal of Women in Culture and Society*, vol. 12, no. 4.

Fleischer, A. (2001) 'Press Briefing by Ari Fleischer,' September 12, www.whitehouse. gov/news/releases/2001/09/20010912-8.html; accessed November 13, 2007.

Flynn, G.Q. (1993) *The Draft, 1940–1973*, University Press of Kansas, Lawrence.

Forbes, I., and M. Hoffman, eds. (1993) *Political Theory, International Relations, and the Ethics of Interventions*, St. Martin's Press, Basingstoke.

Fotion, N. (2000) 'Reactions to War: Pacifism, Realism, Just War Theory,' in Andrew Valls, ed., *Ethics in International Affairs*, Rowman & Littlefield.

Foucault, M. (1984) 'What is Enlightenment?', in P. Rabinow, ed., *The Foucault Reader*, Pantheon Books, New York.

Friedberg, A.L. (2000) *In the Shadow of the Garrison State: America's Anti-Statism and Its Cold War Grand Strategy*, Princeton University Press, Princeton NJ.

Fromkin, David (1974) 'The Strategy of Terrorism,' *Foreign Affairs*, vol. 53, no. 4.

Frost, M. (1996) *Ethics in International Relations: A Constitutive Theory*, Cambridge University Press, Cambridge.

Fukuyama, F. (1992) *The End of History and the Last Man*, Free Press, New York.

Fullinwider, R. (1999) *Civil Society, Democracy, and Civic Renewal*, Rowman & Littlefield, Lanham MD.

Gaddis, J.L. (2002) 'A Grand Strategy of Transformation,' *Foreign Policy* 133, November–December.

Ganor, B. (2002) 'Defining Terrorism: Is One Man's Terrorist Another Man's Freedom Fighter?,' *Police Practice and Research*, vol. 3, no. 4.

Gelb, L.H. (1995) 'Quelling the Teacup Wars: The New World's Constant Challenge,' *Foreign Affairs*, vol. 73, no. 6.

Gibson-Graham, J.K. (1994) '"Stuffed if I Know!": Reflections on Post-Modern Feminist Social Research,' *Gender, Place, and Culture: A Journal of Feminist Geography*, vol. 1, no. 2.

Global Security (2007) 'Wahhabi,' www.globalsecurity.org/military/world/gulf/ wahhabi.htm; accessed December 8, 2007.

Glover, J. (2000) *Humanity*, Yale University Press, New Haven CT.

Gordon, J. (1999) 'A Peaceful, Silent, Deadly Remedy: The Ethics of Economic Sanctions,' *Ethics and International Affairs*, vol. 13, no. 1.

Gourevitch, P. (1998) *We Wish to Inform You That Tomorrow We Will be Killed With Our Families*, Picador Press, London.

Gratian (1993) *The Treatise on Laws*, trans. Augustine Thompson, O.P., Catholic University of America Press, Washington DC.

Greenwood, C. (1993) 'Is There a Right of Humanitarian Intervention?' *The World Today* 49.

Grier, P. (2006) 'Is War in Iraq a Shield against Attacks at Home?' *Christian Science Monitor*, September 18, Ebscohost.com; accessed April 5, 2007.

Griffith, S.B. (1963) 'Introduction,' in Samuel Griffith, ed., *Sun Tzu: The Art of War*, Oxford University Press, London.

Grotius, Hugo ([1952] 1625) *De Iure Belli ac Pacis*, Martinus Nijhoff, Dordrecht.

Gunaratna, R. (2005a) 'The Prospects of Global Terrorism,' *Society*, September.

Gunaratna, R. (2005b) 'Responding to the Post 9/11 Structural and Operational Challenges of Global Jihad,' *Quarterly Journal*, Spring.

Haass, R.N. (1999) *Intervention: The Use of American Military Force in the Post-Cold War World*, Brookings Institution Press, Washington DC.

Hall, R.B. (1999) *National Collective Identity: Social Constructs and International Systems*, Columbia University Press, New York.

Hall, R.B., and T.J. Biersteker (2002) 'The Emergence of Private Authority in the International System,' in R.B. Hall and T. J. Biersteker, eds., *The Emergence of Private Authority in Global Governance*, Cambridge University Press, Cambridge.

Halperin, M.H., and Scheffer, D.J. (1992) *Self-Determination in the New World Order*, Carnegie Endowment for International Peace, Washington DC.

Hansen, L. (2000) 'Gender, Nation, Rape: Bosnia and the Construction of Security', *International Feminist Journal of Politics*, vol. 3, no. 1.

Haraway, D. (1989) *Primate Visions: Gender, Race and Nature in the World of Modern Science*, Routledge, New York.

Hare, John E., and C.B. Joynt. (1982) *International Ethics*, Palgrave Macmillan, London.

Harff, B. (2003) 'No Lessons Learned from the Holocaust? Assessing Risks of Genocide and Political Mass Murder since 1955,' *American Political Science Review* 97.

Harmon-Jones, E., and J. Mills, eds. (1999) *Cognitive Dissonance: Progress on a Pivotal Theory in Social Psychology*, American Psychological Association, Washington DC.

Hart, H.L.A. (1990) *The Concept of Law*, Clarendon Press, Oxford.

Hayasaki, E. (2005) 'Military Recruiters Targeting Minority Teens,' *Los Angeles Times*, April 5.

Hayes, S.S. (2007) *The Brain: Paul Wolfowitz and the Making of the Bush Doctrine*, HarperCollins, New York.

Henzel, C. (2005) 'The Origins of al Qaeda's Ideology: Implications for U.S. Strategy,' *Parameters*, Spring.

Hess, H. (2003) 'Like Zealots and Romans: Terrorism and Empire in the 21st Century,' *Crime, Law and Social Change* 39.

Hewitt, K. (1997) *Regions of Revolt: A Geographical Introduction to Disasters*, Longman, Edinburgh.

Hirsch, H. (1995) *Genocide and the Politics of Memory: Studying Death to Preserve Life*, University of North Carolina Press, Chapel Hill.

Hobsbawm, E. (1994) *Age of Extremes*, Pantheon Books, New York.

Hoffman, B. (2006) *Inside Terrorism*, Columbia University Press, New York.

Hoffman, B. (2005) 'Does Our Counter-Terrorism Strategy Match the Threat?,' Report Before the Committee on International Relations, Subcommittee on International Terrorism and Nonproliferation, United States House of Representatives, September 29.

Hoffman, B. (1995) '"Holy Terror": The Implications of Terrorism Motivated by a Religious Imperative,' *Studies in Conflict and Terrorism*, vol. 18, no. 4.

Hoffman, S. (2003) 'Intervention: Should It Go On, Can It Go On?' in D.K. Chatterjee and D.E. Scheid, eds., *Ethics and Foreign Intervention*, Cambridge: Cambridge University Press, Cambridge.

Holmes, R.L. (1989) *War and Morality*, Princeton University Press, Princeton NJ.

Holthouse, D. (2006) 'A Few Bad Men: Ten Years after the Scandal over Neo-

Nazis in the Armed Forces, Extremists Are Once Again Worming Their Way into a Recruit-starved Military,' Southern Poverty Law Center, July 6, at www.splcenter.org/intel/news/item.jsp?aid=66; accessed March 14, 2008.

Hopf, T. (2002) *Social Construction of International Politics: Identities and Foreign Policies*, Cornell University Press, Ithaca.

Horkheimer, M. (1999) 'Traditional and Critical Theory,' in *Critical Theory: Selected Essays*, Continuum, New York.

Hoskins, E. (1997) 'The Humanitarian Impacts of Sanctions and War on Iraq,' in *Political Gain and Civilian Pain: Humanitarian Impacts of Economic Sanctions*, ed. T.G. Weiss, D. Cortright, G.A. Lopez, and L. Minear, Rowman & Littlefield, Lanham MD.

Hufbauer, G.C., J.J. Schott, and K.A. Elliott (1990) *Economic Sanctions Reconsidered: History and Current Policy*, Institute for International Economics, Washington DC.

Hughes, N.C. (2002) *China's Economic Challenge: Smashing the Iron Rice Bowl*, Eastgate, New York.

Human Security Centre (2007) *Human Security Report*, University of British Columbia, Vancouver, www.hsgroup.org; accessed April 1, 2007.

Huntington, S.P. (1996) *The Clash of Civilizations and the Remaking of the World Order*, Simon & Schuster, London.

Hussain, A. (2000) 'Joy Harjo and Her Poetics as Praxis,' *Wicazo Sa Review*.

Huston, N. (1983) 'Tales of War and Tears of Women,' in J. Stiehm, ed., *Women and Men's Wars*, Pergamon Press, Oxford.

Huxley, T. (2005) 'The Tsunami and Security: Asian 9/11?' *Survival*, vol. 47, no. 1.

Hwang, B.Y. (2005) 'Japan's New Security Outlook: Implications for the U.S.,' Heritage Foundation Backgrounder 1865, www.heritage.org/research/asiaand thepacific/bg1865.cfm; accessed March 15, 2008.

Ibrahim, R., ed. and trans. (2007) *The Al Qaeda Reader*, Broadway Books, New York.

ICISS (2001) *The Responsibility to Protect: The Report of the International Commission on Intervention in State Sovereignty*, International Development Research Centre, Ottawa.

Ignatieff, M. (2005) 'The Broken Contract,' *New York Times*, September 25.

Ikenberry, G.J., and C. Kupchan (1990) 'Socialization and Hegemonic Power,' *International Organization*, vol. 44, no. 3.

International Strategy for Disaster Reduction (1999) *Declaration of Intent: The Geneva Mandate On Disaster Reduction*, Geneva, www.unisdr.org/eng/about_isdr/bd-geneva-mandate-eng.htm.

International Strategy for Disaster Reduction (2008) *Country Profile: China*, Geneva, www.unisdr.org/eng/country-inform/china-disaster.htm.

Islamic Center of Beverly Hills (2007) 'Muslim Unity,' www.icbh.org/topics/muslimu.htm; accessed December 15, 2007.

Jackson, R.H. (1990) *Quasi-States: Sovereignty, International Relations, and the Third World*, Cambridge University Press, Cambridge.

Jehl, D., and K. Zernike (2004) 'Greater Urgency on Prison Interrogation Led to Use of Untrained Workers,' *New York Times*, May 28.

Jenkins, B.M. (2003) 'International Terrorism: The Other World War,' in C.W. Kegley, ed., *The New Global Terrorism: Characteristics, Causes, Controls*, Prentice Hall, Upper Saddle River NJ.

Jervis, R. (1976) *Perception and Misperception in International Politics*, Princeton University Press, Princeton.

Johnson, J.T. (2001) 'Just War Tradition and the New War on Terrorism,' *Pew Forum on Religion and Public Life*, http://pewforum.org/publications/reports/PFJustWar.pdf, accessed January 8, 2009.

Johnson, J.T. (1999) *Morality & Contemporary Warfare*, Yale University Press, New Haven CT.

Johnson, J.T. (1981) *Just War Tradition and the Restraint of War: A Moral and Historical Inquiry*, Princeton University Press, Princeton NJ.

Jurgensmeyer, M. (2000) *Terrorism in the Mind of God: The Global Rise of Religious Violence*, University of California Press, Los Angeles.

Kahler, M. (2005) 'Economic Security in an Era of Globalization,' *Pacific Review*, vol. 17, no. 4.

Kaldor, M. (2006) *New and Old Wars: Organized Violence in a Global Era*, Polity Press, Cambridge.

Kaldor, M. (2000) 'Cosmopolitanism and Organized Violence,' paper prepared for conference on 'Conceiving Cosmopolitanism,' Warwick, April 27–29.

Kaldor, M. (1999) *New and Old Wars: Organized Violence in a Global Era*, Stanford University Press, Stanford CA.

Kant, I. (1987) *Fundamental Principles of the Metaphysics of Morals*, Prometheus Books, Buffalo.

Kant, I. (1970) *Perpetual Peace: A Philosophical Sketch*, in *Kant's Political Writings*, ed. Hans Reiss, Cambridge University Press, Cambridge.

Kaufmann, C. (2004) 'Intervention in Ethnic and Ideological Civil Wars,' in R.J. Art and K.N. Waltz, eds., *The Use of Force: Military Power and International Ethics*, Rowman & Littlefield, New York.

Kaul, I., I. Grunberg, and M. Stern (1999) 'Defining Global Public Goods,' in I. Kaul, I. Grunberg, and M. Stern, eds., *Global Public Goods: International Cooperation in the 21st Century*, Oxford University Press, New York.

Kavka, G.S. (1988) *The Moral Paradoxes of Nuclear Deterrence*, Cambridge University Press, Cambridge.

Keith, T. (2001) 'Courtesy of the Red, White, and Blue: The Angry American,' Show Dog Records, Nashville.

Kellogg, D. (2006) 'Coopting Lawfare as a Strategy in the War on Terrorism,' Joint Services Conference on Professional Ethics, Springfield VA, January 27.

Keohane, R., and J. Nye (1977) *Power and Interdependence*, Little, Brown, Toronto.

Kepel, G. (2002) 'The Trail of Political Islam,' *OpenDemocracy*, July 3, www.opendemocracy.net/content/articles/PDF/421.pdf; accessed December 1, 2007.

Keren, M., and D.A. Sylvan (2002) *International Intervention: Sovereignty versus Responsibility*, Routledge, New York.

Kifner, J. (2006) 'Hate Groups Are Infiltrating the Military, Group Asserts,' *New York Times*, July 7.

Klare, M.T. (2001) *Resource Wars: The New Landscape of Global Conflict*, Henry Holt, New York.

Kleinschmidt, H. (2000) *The Nemesis of Power: A History of International Relations Theories*, Reaction Books, Chicago.

Krasner, S.D. (1999) *Sovereignty: Organized Hypocrisy*, Princeton University Press, Princeton NJ.

Krasner, S.D. (1988) 'Sovereignty: An Institutional Perspective,' *Comparative Political Studies* 2, April.

Kratochwil, F.V. (1989) *Rules, Norms, and Decisions: On the Conditions of Practical Reasoning in International Relations and Domestic Affairs*, Cambridge University Press, Cambridge.

Krause, K., and M.C. Williams (1997a) 'Preface: Towards Critical Security Studies,' in K. Krause and M.C. Williams, eds., *Critical Security Studies*, University of Minnesota Press, Minneapolis.

Krause, K., and M.C. Williams (1997b) 'From Strategy to Security: Foundations of Critical Security Studies,' in K. Krause and M.C. Williams, eds., *Critical Security Studies*, University of Minnesota Press, Minneapolis.

Kuperman, A. (2001) *The Limits of Humanitarian Intervention in Genocide*, Brookings Institution Press, Washington DC.

Lackey, D.P. (1988) *The Ethics of War and Peace*, Prentice Hall, Upper Saddle River.

Lang Jr., A.F., ed. (2003) *Just Intervention*, Georgetown University Press, Washington DC.

Lange, J.E. (2007) 'Pandemic Flu: Towards an Effective Global Preparedness Policy,' US Department of State, 17 October, www.state.gov/g/avianflu/93627.htm; accessed November 19, 2007.

Lapidus, Gail W. (1998) 'Contested Sovereignty: The Tragedy of Chechnya,' *International Security*, vol. 23, no. 1, Summer.

Lav, D. (2007) '"The Al-Qaeda Organization in the Islamic Maghreb": The Evolving Terrorist Presence in North Africa,' *MEMRI: Inquiry and Analysis Series* 332, March 7, http://memri.org/bin/opener.cgi? Page=archives&ID=IA33207; accessed November 13, 2007.

Lee, K., and D. Fidler (2007) 'Avian and Pandemic Influenza: Progress and Problems with Global Health Governance,' *Global Public Health*, vol. 2, no. 3.

Lee, S. (2004) 'Double Effect, Double Intention, and Assymetric Warfare,' *Journal of Military Ethics*, vol. 3, no. 3.

Legro, J. (1997) 'Which Norms Matter? Revisiting the 'Failure' of Internationalism,' *International Organization* 51.

Lepard, B. (2002) *Rethinking Humanitarian Intervention*, Pennsylvania State University Press, University Park PA.

Leyton-Brown, D. (1987) *The Utility of Economic Sanctions*, Helm, London.

Lindley, D. (2007) 'The Practice of Pre-emptive and Preventive Wars: What is the Custom?,' paper presented at the Midwest Political Science Association meeting in Chicago, April 4.

Liotta, P.H. (2002) 'Boomerang Effect: the Convergence of National and Human Security,' *Security Dialogue*, vol. 33, no. 4.

Lipset, S.M. (1996) *American Exceptionalism: A Double-Edged Sword*, W.W. Norton, New York.

Litfon, R.J. (2000) *Destroying the World to Save it: Aumshiniku, Apocalyptic Violence, and New Global Terrorism*, Owl, New York.

Locke, J. (2005) *Two Treatises of Government and A Letter Concerning Toleration*, Digireads.com Books, Stillwell KS.

Locke, J. (1963 [1690]) *Two Treatises of Government*, Cambridge University Press, New York.

Lucas, Jr., G.R. (2003) 'From *jus ad bellum* to *jus ad pacem*: Re-thinking Just-war Criteria for the Use of Military Force for Humanitarian Ends,' in D.K. Chatterjee and D.E., Scheid, eds., *Ethics and Foreign Intervention*, Cambridge University Press, Cambridge.

Lynd, S. (2006) 'Soldiers of Conscience,' *The Nation*, October 19.

Macartney, J. (2006) 'China Admits Concealing First Human Bird Flu Death,' *The Times*, August 8, www.timesonline.co.uk/tol/news/world/asia/article 603492.ece; accessed May 22, 2007.

Machiavelli, N. (1979) *The Portable Machiavelli*, Penguin Books, New York.

McDermott, R. (1992) 'Prospect Theory in International Relations: The Iranian Rescue Mission,' *Political Psychology*, vol. 13, no. 2.

McGrane, B. (1989) *Beyond Anthropology: Society and the Other*, Columbia University Press, New York.

McInnes, C. (2004) 'Health and Security Studies,' in A, Ingram, ed., *Health, Foreign Policy and Security*, Nuffield Trust, London.

McInnes, C., and K. Lee (2006) 'Health, Security, and Foreign Policy,' *Review of International Studies*, vol. 32, no. 1.

McKibbin, W., and A. Sidorenko (2006) *Global Macroeconomic Consequences of Pandemic Influenza*, Lowy Institute for International Policy, Sydney.

McMichael, A.J. (2001) 'Human Culture, Ecological Change, and Infectious Disease: Are We Experiencing History's Fourth Great Transition?' *Ecosystem Health*, vol. 7, no. 2.

McNeilly, M. (2001) *Sun Tzu and the Art of Modern Warfare*, Oxford University Press, New York.

MacPherson, M. (2008) 'McNamara's "Moron Corps",' Salon.com, March 26.

MacPherson, M. (2002) *Long Time Passing: Vietnam and the Haunted Generation*, Indiana University Press, Bloomington.

McRae, R.G., and D. Hubert (2001) *Human Security and New Diplomacy: Protecting People, Promoting Peace*, McGill-Queens University Press, Montreal.

Mandel, R. (2001) 'The Privatization of Security,' *Armed Forces*, vol. 38, no. 1.

Mao Tse-tung (1938) *On Protracted War*, Foreign Language Press, Beijing.

March, J.G., and J.P. Olsen (1998) 'The Institutional Dynamics of International Political Order,' *International Organization*, vol. 52, no. 4.

Martin, L. (1992) *Coercive Cooperation: Explaining Multilateral Economic Sanctions*, Princeton University Press, Princeton NJ.

Matthews, W. (2007) 'Lawmaker: Recruiting Criminals Unwise,' *Army Times*, November 9.

Mayerfeld, J. (1999) *Suffering and Moral Responsibility*, Oxford University Press, Oxford.

Melvern, L. (2004) *Conspiracy to Murder: The Rwandan Genocide*, Verso, London.

Merle, R., and E. McCarthy (2004) '6 Employees From CACI International, Titan Referred for Prosecution,' *Washington Post*, August 26.

Miller, M.A. (1995) 'The Intellectual Origin of Modern Terrorism in Europe,' in M. Crenshaw, ed., *Terrorism in Context*, Penn State University Press, University Park.

Military Balance (2006) 'Complex Irregular Warfare: The Privatisation of Force,' *The Military Balance*, vol. 106, no. 1.

MIPT Terrorism Knowledge Base (2007) www.tkb.org/KeyLeader.jsp?memID =5872; accessed December 8, 2007.

MIPT Terrorism Knowledge Database (2006) 'Assessment Tools,' www.tkb.org; accessed November 18, 2006.

Moniz, D. (2005) 'Black Americans Make Up Smaller Share of Military,' *USA Today*, November 4, www.usatoday.com/news/nation/2005–11–04–army-blacks_x.htm; accessed March 14, 2008.

Moose, G. (1994) 'Has Genocide Occurred in Rwanda?' Action Memorandum from Assistant Secretary of State George Moose to Secretary of State Warren Christopher, May 21.

Morgan, T.C. (1994) *Untying the Knot of War*, University of Michigan Press, Ann Arbor MI.

Morgan, T.C., and V.L. Schwebach (1997) 'Fools Suffer Gladly: The Use of Economic Sanctions in International Crises,' *International Studies Quarterly* 41.

Morgenthau, H.J. (1948) *Politics Among Nations*, McGraw-Hill, New York.

Mueller, J., and K. Mueller (1999) 'Sanctions of Mass Destruction,' *Foreign Affairs*, vol. 78, no. 3.

Murphy, S.D. (1996) *Humanitarian Intervention: The United Nations in an Evolving World Order*, University of Pennsylvania Press, Philadelphia.

Murray, C.J.L., A.D. Lopez, B. Chin, D. Feehan and K.H. Hill (2006) 'Estimation of Potential Global Pandemic Influenza Mortality on the Basis of Vital Registry Data from the 1918–20 Pandemic: A Quantitative Analysis,' *The Lancet*, vol. 368, no. 9554.

Muthien, B., and I. Taylor (2002) 'The Return of the Dogs of War? The Privatization of Security in Africa,' in by R.B. Hall and T.J. Biersteker, eds., *The Emergence of Private Authority in Global Governance*, Cambridge University Press, Cambridge.

Myers, S.L. (2007) 'Bush, at UN, Announces Stricter Burmese Sanctions,' *New York Times*, September 26.

Nagel, T. (1989) *The View from Nowhere*, Oxford University Press, Oxford.

Nardin, T. (1992) 'Ethical Traditions in International Affairs,' in T. Nardin and D.R. Mapel, *Traditions of International Ethics*, Cambridge University Press, Cambridge.

Narula, S. (2003) 'Overlooked Danger: The Security and Rights Implication of Hindu Nationalism in India,' *Harvard Human Rights Journal*, vol. 16, no. 41.

New York Times (2005) 'Pentagon Proposes Rise in Age Limits for Recruits,' July 22.

Ngobi, J. (1995) 'The United Nations Experience with Economic Sanctions,' in D. Cortright and G. Lopez, *Economic Sanctions: Panacea or Peacebuilding in the Post-Cold War World*, Westview Press, Boulder CO.

Niblock, T. (2001) *Pariah States and Sanctions in the Middle East: Iraq, Libya, and Sudan*, Lynne Rienner, Boulder CO.

NIC (2000) 'The Global Infectious Disease Threat and its Implications for the

United States,' National Intelligence Council, January, www.cia.gov/cia/reports/nie/report/nie99–17d.html; accessed November 18, 2003.

Nichols, T.M. (2003) 'Just War, not Prevention,' *Ethics and International Affairs*, vol. 17, no. 1.

Nietzsche, F. (1974 [1882]) *Gay Science: With a Prelude in Rhymes and an Appendix of Songs*, trans. Walter Kaufmann, Random House, New York.

Normile, D. (2007) 'Indonesia to Share Flu Samples Under New Terms,' *Science*, vol. 316, no. 5821.

North, R.C., O.R. Holsti, M.G. Zaninovich, and D.A. Zinnes (1963) *Content Analysis: A Handbook with Applications for the Study of International Relations*, Northwestern University Press, Evanston IL.

Nossal, K.R. (1989) 'International Sanctions as International Punishment,' *International Organization*, vol. 43, no. 2.

O'Hanlon, M., and P.W. Singer (2004) 'The Humanitarian Transformation: Expanding Global Intervention Capacity,' *Survival* 46.

OIE (2009) 'Update on Avian Influenza in Animals (Type H5),' OIE, January 7, www.oie.int/downld/avian%20influenza/A_AI-Asia.htm; accessed January 8, 2009.

Onuf, N. (2002) 'Worlds of our Making: The Strange Career of Constructivism in IR,' in Donald J. Puchala, ed., *Visions of International Relations*, University of South Carolina, Charleston.

Onuf, N. (1989) *World of Our Making: Rules and Rule in Social Theory and International Relations*, University of South Carolina Press, Charleston.

Orend, B. (2006) *The Morality of War*, Broadview Press, Peterborough ON.

O'Sullivan, M. (2003) *Shrewd Sanctions*, Brookings Institution Press, Washington DC.

Oye, K. (1985) 'Explaining Cooperation under Anarchy: Hypotheses and Strategies,' *World Politics*, vol. 38, no. 1.

Pape, R. (1998) 'Why Economic Sanctions Still Do Not Work,' *International Security*, vol. 23, no. 1.

Pape, R. (1997) 'Why Economic Sanctions Do Not Work,' *International Security*, vol. 22, no. 2.

Paris, R. (2001) 'Human Security, Paradigm Shift or Hot Air?,' *International Security*, vol. 26, no. 2.

Paul, R. (2001) Speech in the House of Representatives, September 25, www.house.gov/paul/congrec/congrec2001/cr092501.htm.

People's Daily (2004) 'China to Continue to Pursue a New Security Concept for World Peace,' *People's Daily Online*, December 27, English.peopledaily.com.cn/200412/27/eng20041227–168809.html; accessed March 14, 2008.

Peterson, V.S., and A.S. Runyan (1999) *Global Gender Issues*, Westview Press, Boulder CO.

Philpott, D. (2001) *Revolutions in Sovereignty: How Ideas Shaped Modern International Relations*, Princeton University Press, Princeton NJ.

Pilger, J. (2000) 'Squeezed to Death,' *Guardian*, March 4.

Pillar, P.R. (2004) 'Counterterrorism after Al Qaeda,' *Washington Quarterly*, vol. 27, no. 3, Summer.

Plant, R. (1993) 'The Justification for Intervention: Needs before Contexts,' in I.

Forbes and M. Hoffman, eds., *Political Theory, International Relations, and the Ethics of Interventions*, St. Martin's Press, New York.

Plett, B. (2004) 'Yassin Killing Brings Calls for Islamic Unity,' BBC News, March 24, http://news.bbc.co.uk/1/hi/world/middle_east/3564957.stm.

Postema, G.J. (1986) *Bentham and the Common Law Tradition*, Oxford University Press, Oxford.

Pound, E.T., and J. El-Tahri (1994) 'Sanctions: the Pluses and Minuses,' *U.S. News and World Report*, 31 October.

Power, J. (1994) 'Sanctions are Not Always the Answer,' *Calgary Herald*, February 21.

Power, S. (2002) *A Problem from Hell: America in an Age of Genocide*, HarperPerennial, New York.

Power, S. (2001) 'Bystanders to Genocide,' *Atlantic Monthly*, September.

Prescott, E.M. (2003) 'SARS: A Warning,' *Survival*, vol. 45, no. 3.

Press TV (2007) 'Italy Skeptical about Iran Sanctions,' November 30, www.presstv.ir/detail.aspx?id=33187&sectionid=351020104; accessed December 2, 2007.

Prins, G. (2004) 'AIDS and Global Security,' *International Affairs*, vol. 80, no. 5.

Program on International Policy Attitudes (2006) *The Iraqi Public on the U.S. Presence and the Future of Iraq*, September 27, www.worldpublicopinion.org/pipa/pdf/sep06/Iraq_Sep06_rpt.pdf; accessed December 14, 2007.

Ramsbotham, O., and Woodson, T., eds. (1996) *Humanitarian Intervention in Contemporary Conflict*, Polity Press, Cambridge.

Ramsey, P. (1992) 'The Just War According to St. Augustine,' in J.B. Elshtain, ed., *Just War Theory*, New York University Press, New York.

Ramsey, P. (1961) *War and the Christian Conscience: How Shall Modern War Be Conducted Justly?*, Duke University Press, Durham NC.

Ranstorp, M. (1996) 'Terrorism in the Name of Religion,' *Journal of International Affairs*, vol. 50, no. 1, Summer.

Rapoport, D.C. (1984) 'Fear and Trembling: Terrorism in Three Religious Traditions,' *American Political Science Review*, vol. 78, no. 3, September.

Rauchhaus, R. (2006) 'Asymmetric Information, Mediation, and Conflict Management,' *World Politics*, vol. 58, no. 2.

Rawls J. (1999) *The Law of Peoples with 'The Idea of Public Reason Revisited'*, Harvard University Press, Cambridge MA.

Rawls, J. (1993) *Political Liberalism*, Columbia University Press, New York.

Ray, J.L. (1998) *Global Politics*, Houghton Mifflin, Boston MA.

Regan, P.M. (1998) 'Choosing to Intervene: Outside Interventions in Internal Conflicts,' *Journal of Politics* 60.

Regan, R.J. (1996) *Just War: Principles and Cases*, Catholic University of America Press, Washington DC.

Reidy, D.A. (2004) 'Rawls on International Justice: A Defense,' *Political Theory* 32.

Reynolds, D. (2003), 'Lindbergh's Stay in Nanking, September 1931,' www.charleslindbergh.com/history/china.asp.

Richards, N. (1984) 'Double Effect and Moral Character,' *Mind* 93.

Richter, P., R. Wright, and M. Farley (2003) 'U.S., Britain to Tell U.N. It Has 3 Weeks on Iraq,' *Los Angeles Times*, 22 February, A1.

Risse, T. (2000) 'Let's Argue: Communicative Action in World Politics,' *International Organization*, vol. 54, no. 1.

Risse, T., S.C. Ropp and K. Sikkink (1999) *The Power of Human Rights: International Norms and Domestic Change*, Cambridge University Press, Cambridge.

Rivkin Jr., D.B., L.A. Casey, and M.W. DeLaquil (2005) 'Preemption and Law in the Twenty-First Century,' *Chicago Journal of International Law*, vol. 5, no. 2.

Roberts, A. (2003) 'Law and the Use of Force After Iraq,' *Survival* 45.

Ronayne, P. (2001) *Never Again: The United States and the Prevention and Punishment of Genocide since the Holocaust*, Rowman & Littlefield, Lanham MD.

Rosecrance, R. (1986) *The Rise of the Trading State: Commerce and Conquest in the Modern World*, Basic Books, New York.

Rosegrant, M.W., and S.A. Cline (2004) 'Global Food Security: Challenges and Policies,' *Science*, vol. 302, no. 5652.

Rosenau, J. (1995) 'Governance in the Twenty-First Century,' in T.J. Sinclair, ed., *Global Governance: Critical Concepts in Political Science*, Routledge, London.

Rousseau, J.-J. (1997) 'Discourse on Plolitical Economy,' in *The Social Contract and later Political Writings*, ed. Victor Gourevitch, Cambridge University Press, Cambridge.

Rousseau, J.-J. (1917) 'Fragments of an Essay on the State of War,' in *A Lasting Peace through the Federation of Europe and the State of War*, trans. C.E. Vaughan, Constable, London.

Rubinstein, W. D. (2004) *Genocide: A History*, Longman Pearson, London.

Rummel, R.J. (2000) *Death by Government: Genocide and Mass Murder since 1900*, Transaction Publishers, London.

Ryan, C.R. (1999) 'Taking War Seriously,' University of Utah Philosophy Colloquium.

Ryan C.R. (1996) 'War and the State,' in *For and Against the State: New Philosophical Readings*, ed. J. Narveson and J. Sanders, Rowman & Littlefield, Lanham MD.

Said, E. (1978) *Orientalism*, Vintage Books, New York.

Salter, S. (1999) 'Our "Economic" Sanctions Are Killing the Children of Iraq,' *San Francisco Examiner*, January 10, www.sfgate.com/cgi-bin/article.cgi?f=/e/a/1999/01/10/EDITORIAL12925.dtl; accessed January 1, 2008.

Sargent, L.T. (1995) *Extremism in America*, New York University Press, New York.

Savage, T.M. (2004) 'Europe and Islam: Crescent Waxing, Cultures Clashing,' *Washington Quaterly*, vol. 27, no. 3, Summer.

Scheffer, D.J. (1992) 'Challenges Confronting Collective Security: Humanitarian Intervention,' in D.J. Scheffer, R.N. Gardner, and G.B. Helman, eds., *Post Gulf-War Challenges to the U.N. Collective Security System: Three View on the Issue of Humanitarian Intervention*, United States Institute for Peace, Washington DC.

Schelling, T.C. (1967) *Arms and Influence*, Yale University Press, New Haven CT.

Schermers, H.G. (1991) 'The Obligation to Intervene in the Domestic Affairs of States,' in A.J.M. Delissen and G.J. Tanja, eds., *Humanitarian Law of Armed Conflict: Challenges Ahead*, London: Martinus Nijhoff, London.

Schmid, A.P., and A.J. Jongman (2006) *Political Terrorism*, Transaction, New Brunswick.

Schmidt, B.C. (2002) 'Together Again: Reuniting Political Theory and International Relations Theory,' *British Journal of Politics and International Relations*, vol. 4, no. 1.

Schmidt, W.E. (1994a) 'Terror Convulses Rwandan Capital as Tribes Battle,' *New York Times*, April 9.

Schmidt, W.E. (1994b) 'Troops Rampage in Rwanda; Dead Said to Include Premier,' *New York Times*, April 8.

Searle, J. (1995) *The Construction of Social Reality*, Penguin Books, London.

Selden, Z. (1999) *Economic Sanctions as Instruments of American Foreign Policy*, Praeger, Westport CT.

Seliger, M. (1963) 'Locke's Theory of Revolutionary Action,' *Western Political Quarterly*, vol. 16, no. 3, September.

Shannon, U. (2002) 'Private Armies and the Decline of the State,' in K. Worcester, S.A. Bermanzohn and M. Ungar, eds., *Violence and Politics: Globalization's Paradox*, Routledge, New York.

Sharp, J.M.O. (1994) 'Appeasement, Intervention, and the Future of Europe,' in L. Freedman, ed., *Military Intervention in European Conflicts*, Blackwell, Oxford.

Sharpe, T.T. (2000) 'The Identity Christian Movement: Ideology of Domestic Terrorism,' *Journal of Black Studies*, vol. 30, no. 4.

Shaw, M. (2001) 'Return of the Good War?' www.theglobasite.ac.uk.

Shultz, T.R., and M.R. Lepper (1996) 'Cognitive Dissonance Reduction as Constraint Satisfaction,' *Psychological Review* 103.

Simmons, J.A. (1979) *Moral Principles and Political Obligations*, Princeton University Press, Princeton NJ.

Simons, G.L. (1998) *The Scourging of Iraq: Sanctions, Law, and Natural Justice*, Palgrave Macmillan, London.

Singer, P.W. (2005) 'Outsourcing War,' *Foreign Affairs*, vol. 84, no. 2.

Singer, P.W. (2003) *Corporate Warriors: The Rise of the Privatized Military Industry*, Cornell Studies in Security Affairs, Cornell University Press, Ithaca NY.

Singer, P.W. (2002) 'AIDS and International Security,' *Survival*, vol. 44, no. 1.

Singer, P.W. (2001) 'Corporate Warriors: The Rise of the Privatized Military Industry and its Ramifications for International Security,' *International Security*, vol. 26, no. 3.

Sjoberg, L. (2006) *Gender, Justice, and the Wars in Iraq*, Rowman & Littlefield, Lanham MD.

Sjoberg, L. (2002) 'Is Iraq a Threat to International Peace and Security?' annual symposium of Women in International Security, Washington DC.

Sjoberg, L., and C.E. Gentry (2007) *Mothers, Monsters, Whores: Women's Violence in Global Politics*, Zed Books, London.

Slovic, P., B. Fischhoff and S. Lichtenstein (1980) 'Facts and Fears: Understanding Perceived Risk,' in R.C. Schwing and W.A. Albers, eds., *Societal Risk Assessment: How Safe is Safe Enough?*, Plenum, New York.

Smith, A. (1937) *An Inquiry into the Nature and Causes of the Wealth of Nations*, ed. Edwin Canner, Random House, New York.

Smith, D. (1974) 'The Volunteer Army,' *Atlantic Monthly*, vol. 234, no. 1, July.

Smith, J.W. (2007) 'Augustine and the Limits of Preemptive and Preventive War,' *Journal of Religious Ethics*, vol. 35, no. 1.

Smith, K. (1996) *Environmental Hazards: Assessing Risks and Reducing Disaster*, Routledge, London.

Snyder, R.C., H.W. Bruck, and B. Sapin (1962) *Foreign Policy Decision Making: An Approach to the Study of International Politics*, Free Press, New York.

Spearin, C. (2004) 'The Emperor's Leased Clothes: Military Contractors and Their Implications in Combating International Terrorism,' *International Politics* 41.

Spearin, C. (2003) 'American Hegemony Incorporated: The Importance and Implications of Military Contractors in Iraq,' *Contemporary Security Policy*, vol. 24, no. 3.

Sperling, C. (2006) 'Mother of All Atrocities: Pauline Nyiramusuhuko's Role in the Rwandan Genocide', *Fordham Urban Law Journal* 33.

Spresser, M. (2007) 'War Seems So Distant To Me and My Peers,' *Eugene Register-Guard*, July 16, http://rgweb.registerguard.com/news/2007/07/16/pl.20 bspresser.0716.p1.php?section=opinion; accessed March 14, 2008.

Spruyt, H. (1994) *The Sovereign State and its Competitors, Princeton Studies in International History and Politics*, Princeton University Press, Princeton NJ.

Stairs, D. (1998) 'Of Medium Powers and Middling Roles,' in K. Booth, ed., *Statecraft and Security: the Cold War and Beyond*, Cambridge University Press, Cambridge.

Staub, E. (1989) *The Roots of Evil: The Origins of Genocide and Other Group Violence*, Cambridge University Press, Cambridge.

Stephenson, I. (2006) 'H5N1 Vaccines: How Prepared Are We for a Pandemic?' *The Lancet*, vol. 368, no. 9540.

Stern, A.M., and H. Markel (2004) 'International Efforts to Control Infectious Diseases, 1851 to the Present,' *Journal of the American Medical Association*, vol. 292, no. 12.

Stern, J. (2003) *Terror in the Name of God: Why Religious Militants Kill*, HarperCollins, New York.

Stern, J. (2002) 'Dreaded Risks and the Control of Biological Weapons,' *International Security*, vol. 27, no. 3.

Stöhr, K., and M. Esveld (2004) 'Will Vaccines Be Available for the Next Influenza Pandemic?' *Science*, vol. 306, no. 5705.

Storr, A. (1991) *Human Destructiveness: The Roots of Genocide and Human Cruelty*, Routledge, London.

Strauss, L. (2000 [1963]) *On Tyranny*, University of Chicago Press, Chicago.

Strayer, J.R., and D.C Munro (1959) *The Middle Ages*, Appleton-Century-Crofts, New York.

Sun Tzu (1963) *The Art of War*, trans. Samuel B. Griffith, Oxford University Press, London.

Szreter, S. (2003) 'Health and Security in Historical Perspective,' in L. Chen, J. Leaning, and V. Narasimhan, eds., *Global Health Challenges for Human Security*, Global Equity Initiative, Asia Center, Harvard University, Cambridge MA.

Takeuchi, K. (2002) 'Floods and Society: A Never-ending Evolutional Relation,' keynote lecture at Second International Symposium on Flood Defence, Beijing, September 10–13, published in *Flood Defense*, vol. I, Beijing.

Takeyh, R., and N. Gvosdev (2002) 'Do Terrorist Networks Need a Home?,' *Washington Quarterly*, Summer.

Talbot, S. (2001) 'America Abroad,' *Time*, June 24.

Tamil Eelam (2008) Tamil Eelam Homepage, www.eelam.com; accessed July 20, 2008.

Tendler, S. (2005) 'Flu Doctors to be Given Police Guards,' *The Times*, November 2, www.timesonline.co.uk/article/0,25149–1853843,00.html; accessed December 23, 2005.

Thomas, C. (2001) 'Global Governance, Development, and Human Security: Exploring the Links,' *Third World Quarterly*, vol. 22, no. 2.

Thompson, D.F. (1980) 'Moral Responsibility of Public Officials: The Problem of Many Hands,' *American Political Science Review*, vol. 74, no. 12, December.

Thomson, J.E. (1995) 'State Sovereignty in International Relations: Bridging the Gap between Theory and Empirical Research,' *International Studies Quarterly*, vol. 39, no. 2.

Thomson, J.E. (1994) *Mercenaries, Pirates, and Sovereigns: State-Building and Extraterritorial Violence in Early Modern Europe*, Princeton University Press, Princeton NJ.

Thucydides (1998) *The Peloponnesian War*, trans. Steven Lattimore, Hackett, New York.

Thucydides (1910) *The Peloponnesian War*, trans. J.M. Dent, E.P. Dutton, New York.

Tickner, J.A. (2001) *Gendering World Politics*, Columbia University Press, New York.

Tickner, J.A. (1992) *Gender in International Relations: Feminist Perspectives on Achieving Global Security*, Columbia University Press, New York.

Tilly, C. (1990) *Coercion, Capital, and European States*, Basil Blackwell, Cambridge MA.

Time (1931) 'First Lady and Lindberghs,' October 5.

Turse, N. (2005) 'An Army of (No) One: An Inside Look at the Military's Internet Recruiting War,' TomDispatch.com, July 13.

Tweeten, L. (1999) 'The Economics of Global Food Security,' *Review of Agricultural Economics*, vol. 21, no. 2.

Ullman, R. (1983) 'Redefining Security,' *International Security*, vol. 8, no. 1.

UN (2004) *A More Secure World: Our Shared Responsibility*, Report of the High-Level Panel on Threats, Challenges and Change, United Nations, New York.

Useem, M. (1973) *Conscription, Protest and Social Conflict*, John Wiley, New York.

Vattel, Emmerich de (1883 [1758]) *The Law of Nations*, trans. Joseph Chitty, T. & J.W. Johnson, Philadelphia.

Waever, O. (1995) 'Securitization and Desecuritization,' in R.D. Lipschutz, ed., *On Security*, Columbia University Press, New York.

Walker, R.B.J. (2006) 'Lines of Insecurity: International, Imperial, Exceptional,' *Security Dialogue*, vol. 37, no. 1.

Walker, R.B.J. (2005) 'The Double Outside of the Modern International,' *Ephmera: Theory and Politics in Organization*, vol. 6, no. 1.

Walker, R.B.J. (1997) 'The Subject of Security,' in K. Krause and M.C. Williams, eds., *Critical Security Studies*, University of Minnesota Press, Minneapolis.

Walker, R.B.J. (1993) *Inside/Outside: International Relations as Political Theory*, Cambridge University Press, Cambridge.

Wallensteen, P. (2000) 'A Century of Economic Sanctions: A Field Revisited,' Uppsala Peace Research Papers no. 1, Department of Peace and Conflict Research, Uppsala University, www.peace.uu.se; accessed January 1, 2008.

Wallensteen, P. (1968) 'Characteristics of Economic Sanctions,' *Journal of Peace Research*, vol. 5, no. 3.

Walsh, W.H. (1970) 'Pride, Shame, and Responsibility,' *Philosophical Quarterly*, vol. 20, no. 78.

Walt, S.M. (1991) 'The Renaissance of Security Studies,' *International Studies Quarterly*, vol. 35, no. 2.

Walt, S. (1987) *The Origins of Alliances*, Cornell University Press, Ithaca NY.

Walter, B.F. (2004) 'The Critical Barrier to Civil War Settlement,' in R.J. Art. and K.N. Waltz, eds., *The Use of Force: Military Power and International Ethics*, Rowman & Littlefield, New York.

Waltz, K.N. (1986) 'Anarchic Orders and Balances of Power,' in R.O. Keohane, ed., *Neorealism and Its Critics*, Columbia University Press, New York.

Waltz, K.N. (1979) *Theory of International Politics*, McGraw-Hill, New York.

Walzer, M. (2004) *Arguing about War*, Yale University Press, New Haven.

Walzer, M. (2000) *Just and Unjust Wars: A Moral Argument with Historical Illustrations*, Basic Books, New York.

Walzer, M. (1995) 'The Politics of Rescue,' *Social Research*, vol. 62, no. 1.

Walzer, M. (1992) *Just and Unjust Wars*, 2nd edn, Basic Books, New York.

Ward, L. (2006) 'Locke on the Moral Basis of International Relations,' *American Journal of Political Science*, vol. 50, no. 3, July.

Washburn, D. (2004) 'Many Iraq Interpreters Unskilled, Soldiers Say; Contractor Titan's Hiring Faulted,' *San Diego Union–Tribune*, May 21.

Watts, J. (2005) 'Vietnam Needs Cash to Stave Off Future Outbreaks of Bird Flu,' *The Lancet*, vol. 365, no. 9473.

Webb, S. (2002) 'A Threat to Humanity: Bush's New Military Doctrine,' *People's Weekly World*, October 19, www.pww.org/article/view/2192/1/114.

Weber, M. (1964) *The Theory of Social and Economic Organization*, trans. A.M. Henderson and T. Parsons, Free Press, New York.

Weiss, T., D. Cortright, G. Lopez, and L. Minear (1997) *Political Gain and Civilian Pain: Humanitarian Impacts of Economic Sanctions*, Rowman & Littlefield, Lanham MD.

Wenar, L. (2002) 'The Legitimacy of Peoples,' in P. de Grieff and C. Cronin, eds., *Global Politics and Transnational Justice*, MIT Press, Cambrige MA.

Wendt, A. (1999) *Social Theory of International Politics*, Cambridge University Press, Cambridge.

Wheeler, N. (2000) *Saving Strangers: Humanitarian Intervention in International Relations*, Oxford University Press, Oxford.

Whittle, R. (2005) 'Army Battling Decline in Black Recruits,' *Dallas Morning News*, August 5.

WHO (2009) 'Confirmed Human Cases of Avian Influenza A (H5N1),' World Health Organization, January 7, www.who.int/csr/disease/avian_influenza/country/en; accessed January 8, 2009.

WHO (2007a) 'Confirmed Human Cases of Avian Influenza A (H5N1),' World Health Organization, November 12, www.who.int/csr/disease/avian_influenza/country/en/; accessed November 30, 2007.

WHO (2007b) *Invest in Health, Build a Safer Future*, World Health Organization, Geneva.

WHO (2007c) 'Projected Supply of Pandemic Influenza Vaccine Sharply Increases,' World Health Organization, October 23, www.who.int/media centre/news/releases/2007/pr60/en/index.html; accessed November 19, 2007.

WHO (2007d) *A Safer Future: Global Public Health Security in the 21st Century, World Health Report 2007*, World Health Organization, Geneva.

WHO (2007e) 'World Health Assembly Closes,' World Health Organization, 23 May, www.who.int/mediacentre/news/releases/2007/wha02/en/index.html; accessed May 24, 2007.

WHO (2006) *Global Pandemic Influenza Action Plan to Increase Vaccine Supply*, World Health Organization, Geneva.

WHO (2005) 'Ten Things You Need to Know about Pandemic Influenza,' WHO, October 14, www.who.int/csr/disease/influenza/pandemic 10things/en/index.html; accessed July 25, 2007.

WHO (2002) *Reducing Risks, Promoting Healthy Life: World Health Report 2002*, World Health Organization, Geneva.

WHO (1983) *International Health Regulations (1969)*, World Health Organization, Geneva.

WHO (1946) *Constitution*, World Health Organization, www.who.int/entity/governance/eb/who_constitution_en.pdf.

WHO Writing Group (2006a) 'Nonpharmaceutical Interventions for Pandemic Influenza, International Measures,' *Emerging Infectious Diseases*, vol. 12, no. 1.

WHO Writing Group (2006b) 'Nonpharmaceutical Interventions for Pandemic Influenza, National and Community Measures,' *Emerging Infectious Diseases*, vol. 12, no. 1.

Wight, M. (1966) 'Why Is There No International Theory?' in H. Butterfield and M. Wight, eds., *Diplomatic Investigations: Essays in the Theory of International Politics*, Allen & Unwin, London.

Wilkinson, P. (2000) *Terrorism versus Democracy: The Liberal State Response*, Frank Cass, London.

Winfield, P.H. (1922) 'The History of Intervention in International Law,' *British YBIL*, vol. 130, no. 3.

Winkler, A. (1999) 'Just Sanctions,' *Human Rights Quarterly*, vol. 21, no. 1.

Woods, J.M., and J.M. Donovan (2005) '"Anticipatory Self-Defense" and Other Stories,' *Kansas Journal of Law and Public Policy*, vol. 14, no. 2.

Woodward, D., and R. Smith (2003) 'Global Public Goods and Health: Concepts and Issues,' in R. Smith, R. Beaglehole, D. Woodward and N. Drager, eds., *Global Public Goods for Health: Health Economic and Public Health Perspectives*, Oxford University Press, New York.

Wright, L. (2006) *The Looming Tower: Al-Qaeda and the Road to 9/11*, Vintage Books, New York.

Wyman, D.S. (1984) *The Abandonment of the Jews: America and the Holocaust, 1941–1945*, Pantheon Books, New York.

Zacher, M.W. (1999) 'Global Epidemiological Surveillance: International Co-operation to Monitor Infectious Diseases,' in I. Kaul, I. Grunberg, and M. Stern, eds., *Global Public Goods: International Cooperation in the 21st Century*, Oxford University Press, New York.

Zalewski, M. (1996) '"All These Theories Yet the Bodies Keep Piling Up": Theorists, Theories, and Theorizing,' in S. Smith, K. Booth, and M. Zalewski, eds., *International Relations: Positivism and Beyond*, Cambridge University Press, Cambridge.

Zaller, R. (1993) 'The Figure of the Tyrant in English Revolutionary Thought,' *Journal of the History of Ideas* 54.

Zartman, W., ed. (1995) *Collapsed States: The Disintegration and Restoration of Legitimate Authority*, Lynne Rienner, London.

Zartman, W., and M. Berman (1982) *The Practical Negotiator*, Yale University Press, New Haven CT.

Notes on Contributors

Lisa Burke is a Ph.D. candidate at the Graduate School of International Studies. Her dissertation is entitled 'The Profit of Humanitarian Relief.' Research interests include theories of sovereignty, violence, theories of space and time, and contemporary social theories.

Christian Enemark is Lecturer at the Center for International Security Studies at the University of Sydney. He has a Ph.D. in international relations from the Australian National University and his thesis was published as *Disease and Security: Natural Plagues and Biological Weapons in East Asia* (2007). Christian specializes in infectious disease threats to security, ranging from biological weapons, through naturally occurring disease outbreaks, to the risks associated with pathogen research. He is an appointed member of the National Consultative Group on International Security Issues (Australian Department of Foreign Affairs and Trade) and a visiting fellow at the John Curtin School of Medical Research, Australian National University.

Caron E. Gentry is Assistant Professor of Political Science at Abilene Christian University. She is a graduate of Mount Holyoke College. She received her Ph.D. in International Relations from the University of St Andrews. Caron's work is published in *Terrorism and Political Violence*, *International Relations*, and *International Feminist Journal of Politics* (forthcoming). She has co-authored (with Laura Sjoberg), *Mothers, Monsters, Whores: Women's Violence in Global Politics* (2007). Caron has presented at the

International Studies Association Conference multiple times as well as at the Southwestern Political Science Association Conference and at the UK Women's Studies Network Conference. She was an invited speaker at Pepperdine Law School's Human Rights Week (2006) and spoke at the Jebsen Center for Counter-terrorism Studies at Tufts University and Women in International Security's 'Women and Al Qaeda' Conference (2007). Her work focuses on female terrorists but she is also interested in gender and security.

Rebecca Glazier is Assistant Professor at the University of Arkansas, Little Rock. Her work generally concerns issues of religion in international relations, and has appeared in the *American Journal of Islamic Social Sciences* and *Genocide, War Crimes, and Crimes against Humanity*. She is the recipient of the University of California, Santa Barbara's Dean's Fellowship, and has given invited talks at Pepperdine University, Georgetown University, and the University of California, Santa Barbara.

Frances V. Harbour is Associate Professor of Government at George Mason University. She is a founding member and past president of the International Ethics Section of the International Studies Association and a former Social Science Research Council/John D. and Catherine T. MacArthur Fellow in International Peace and Security Studies. She is author of *Thinking about International Ethics: Moral Theory and Cases from American Foreign Policy* (1998), along with several other influential articles in international ethics, human rights, and international security.

Jennifer M. Ramos is Assistant Professor in Political Science at Loyola Marymount University. She received her Ph.D. from the University of California, Davis, in 2008. Her research focuses on understanding the causes and consequences of political change, with an emphasis on the role of ideas, norms, and identity. Her work has appeared in the *Journal of Politics* and *Public Opinion Quarterly*.

Cheyney Ryan is Professor of Philosophy and a founder of the program in Conflict Resolution at the University of Oregon Law School. His chapter was written while he was a senior research fellow at Merton College Oxford, where he was working with Oxford's program on the changing character of war. His principal area of interest is political philosophy, but he also works on issues of philosophy of law, ethical theory, and philosophy of film. His book *The Chickenhawk Syndrome: War, Sacrifice, and Personal Responsibility* (2009) deals with many of the issues touched on in his chapter. He is currently completing a book on non-violence and the critique of modernity for Zed Books. His work has appeared in *Ethics, Ethics and International Affairs* and most of the major philosophy journals. He has written numerous editorials for newspapers and other periodicals on matters of contemporary politics, mainly dealing with race and war.

Yannis A. Stivachtis is Director of the International Studies Program at Virginia Tech and Head of the Politics and International Affairs Research Unit of the Athens Institute for Education and Research (ATINER). He holds a Ph.D. in Politics and International Relations and an M.A. in International Relations and Strategic Studies from Lancaster University; and a Postgraduate Certificate in International Law and a B.A. in International Studies from Panteion University. He is the author of *Cooperative Security and Non-Offensive Defense in the Zone of War* (2001) and *The Enlargement of International Society* (1998); co-author of *Non-Offensive Defense in the Middle East* (1998); editor of *The State of European Integration* (2007), *International Order in a Globalizing World* (2007), *International Governance and International Security* (2005), *Current Issues in European Integration* (2004); and co-editor of *Understanding EU's Mediterranean Enlargement* (2002), and *Turkey–European Union Relations: Dilemmas, Opportunities, and Constraints* (2008). He has written several chapters and articles published in edited volumes and journals.

Index

Abu Ghraib 40, 58, 141, 148–49, 153;
see also Iraq War, Taguba Report
Afghanistan 17, 27, 28, 37, 40, 56, 57, 58, 64,
90, 92, 96, 102, 103, 104, 105, 108, 109, 110,
111, 112, 158, 165, 169, 185; *see also* war,
'war on terror'
Agamben, Giorgio 212, 215, 216, 227
Albright, Madeleine 106, 181
al-Qaeda 8, 22–25, 27–33, 36–45, 59, 69,
104, 156; *see also* bin Laden, September
11 attacks, terrorism
Angell, Norman 160
Aquinas, Thomas 71, 72, 127, 131; *see also*
Just War
Aristotle 131, 146
Aryan Nations 26, 27, 32, 170
see also terrorism
Assassins 24, 27, 28, 29, 33, 43
see also terrorism
Austria 30

Barry, Christian 115
Beitz, Charles 10
Belgium 86
Bentham, Jeremy 20, 174, 178, 186–91, 234,
244
bin Laden, Osama 28, 37, 38, 42, 104, 162;
see also al-Qaeda, September 11
attacks, terrorism
Blackwater 153, 163; *see also* private
military companies

Blair, Tony 2
Bonaparte, Napoleon 8
Brown, Chris 10
Bush Doctrine 2, 3, 4, 16, 53
Bush, George H.W. 47
Bush, George W. 1, 2, 11, 13, 14, 16, 22, 23,
26, 37–38, 41, 45, 52, 58, 59, 68, 108, 183,
196, 206
Afghanistan policy 104
economic sanctions policies 183, 193
National Security Strategy (NSS) 1,
48–50, 51, 52, 54, 57, 58, 60, 63, 64,
67, 68, 69
see also 'war on terror'
Buzan, Barry 5, 6, 196, 197, 198, 232

Carr, E.H. 8
Chechnya 26, 40, 44, 95, 158
Chiang Kai-Shek 226
China 2, 94, 95, 96, 179, 194, 199, 203,
205–6, 225–6
Churchill, Winston 116
civilians 19, 25, 36, 44, 87, 116, 120, 122, 129,
133, 134, 135, 148, 149, 150, 161, 163, 175, 185;
see also Just War
Clausewitz, Carl von 14, 19, 178, 181, 182,
183, 184, 185, 186, 191
Clinton, Bill 74, 86, 87, 158
cognitive dissonance 17, 90, 91, 99, 100,
101, 102, 105, 110, 233; *see also* psychology
Cold War 3, 4, 17, 19, 46, 7, 89, 93, 96, 103,

105, 106, 109, 140, 141, 154, 155, 156, 162,
   173, 174, 179, 180, 182, 191, 221, 222, 224
conscription 19, 157, 158, 160, 162, 164, 171,
   172; *see also* soldier
constructivism 4, 98, 176, 177, 187, 196
   and language 4, 177
   see also International Relations
Cox, Robert 11
Cuba 47, 179, 183, 185
Czechoslovakia 122

Darfur 17, 70, 138, 191; *see also* Sudan
Democratic Republic of Congo 70
DynCorp 138, 150; *see also* private military
   companies

Economic Community of West African
   States (ECOWAS) 144
economic sanctions 15, 19–20, 84, 173–92;
   see also sanctions
economics 6, 8, 11, 15, 20, 42, 64, 79, 223, 225
   development 218, 221
   and military privatization 144
   and pandemic influenza 195, 210
   public goods 193, 202, 203, 204, 207,
      210, 231
   and state behavior 97
   and terrorism 32
   see also economic sanctions, security,
      World Trade Organization
English School 189–90; *see also*
   International Relations
environment 6, 7, 8, 220, 223, 226, 231;
   see also security
Erskine, Tony 115
ethnicity 17, 26, 70, 74, 76, 79, 85, 88, 96
European Union (EU) 97, 206
Executive Outcomes 138, 140; *see also*
   private military companies

fortuna 21, 213, 214–15, 224, 227; *see also*
   Machiavelli
Foucault, Michel 212, 218, 219
France 24, 29, 42, 64, 77, 86, 88, 139, 146–7,
   157, 230
Fukuyama, Francis 155
Fullinwider, Robert 129

gender 6, 14
   and security 7
   men 28, 32, 33, 35, 48, 53, 56, 81, 158, 164,
      166, 169, 215
   rape 74

sexism 6
   women 28, 150, 164, 219
genocide 3, 7, 15, 17, 70–89, 93, 94, 96, 124,
   132, 134, 157, 175; *see also* Darfur,
   Holocaust, Rwanda, Sudan
Genocide Convention 74, 75, 76, 87
Germany 26, 29, 30, 42, 46, 120, 122, 124,
   126, 133, 169, 179
Grotius, Hugo 65, 127
Guantánamo Bay 58; *see also* Iraq War
Gulf War 37, 47, 66, 141, 143, 156, 169, 184;
   see also Iraq War

H5N1 influenza strain 20, 194, 195, 198,
   205, 206, 208, 210; *see also* health,
   influenza
Hamas 184; *see also* Palestine, terrorism
health 6, 7, 20, 168, 185, 187, 193, 194, 198,
   199, 200, 202, 203, 204, 205, 206, 208,
   210, 211, 224, 229, 231, 232; *see also* H5N1,
   HIV/AIDS, influenza, security,
   vaccine, World Health Organization
Hitler, Adolf 8, 32
HIV/AIDS 196; *see also* health
Hobbes, Thomas 33, 157
Holocaust 74, 86, 94, 175; *see also* genocide
Hoover, Herbert 226
humanitarian intervention 15, 19, 81, 89,
   95, 101, 141, 156, 157, 158, 159, 163, 213, 226
Hume, David 202
Hundred Years War 146
Huntington, Samuel 4
Hurricane Katrina 3, 211
Hussein, Saddam 47, 66, 67, 68, 116, 183,
   185; *see also* Gulf War, Iraq, Kuwait

imperialism 6
Indonesia 40, 206, 208
influenza 20, 193–210; *see also* H5N1,
   health
international law 3, 49, 50, 91, 92, 96, 105,
   109, 150, 175, 189
International Relations (IR) 5, 10, 13, 89,
   96, 136, 137, 151, 175, 176, 177, 189, 190, 196,
   217; *see also* constructivism, English
   School, liberalism, realism
Iran 26, 67, 173, 175, 181, 183, 185, 189
Iran–Iraq War 116
Iraq 23, 26, 41, 44, 45, 46, 64, 67, 95, 143,
   173, 175, 181, 182, 183, 184
Iraq War 38, 40, 45, 56, 58, 67, 68, 99, 113,
   120, 124, 125, 127, 143, 148, 149, 152, 153,
   165, 169, 171; *see also* Abu Ghraib, Gulf

War, 'war on terror'
Irish Republican Army (IRA) 26
Israel 27, 40, 43, 44, 46, 47, 67, 184; see also
Palestine, Six Day War

Japan 2, 3, 47, 158, 179, 226
Jiang Zemin 94, 95
Jones, Chris 115
Just War 16, 17, 19, 35, 47, 49, 50–51, 53, 54,
58, 60, 65, 66, 69, 71, 72, 73–84, 88, 89,
112, 130, 131, 135, 137, 138, 140, 146–51, 152,
153, 154
    discrimination 113, 120, 124, 125, 129, 132,
    133, 134, 148
    double effect 18, 113, 114, 115, 117, 118, 119,
    120, 121, 122, 123, 124, 127, 128–33, 134,
    135
    jus ad bellum 17, 55, 72, 113, 117, 118, 120,
    122, 123, 124, 125, 127, 128, 129, 133, 147,
    148, 152, 153
    jus ad pacem 80
    jus in bello 55, 72, 113, 118, 119, 124, 125,
    128, 132, 141, 147, 148, 152
    jus post bellum 72
    last resort 50, 72, 83, 84, 88, 120, 123,
    124, 125
    proportionality 18, 62, 67, 72, 80, 81, 82,
    87, 113, 119, 120, 121, 122, 124, 125, 127,
    132, 133, 134, 148, 152
    reasonable chance of success 72, 82–3,
    87, 88 , 120, 121, 122, 123, 124, 125, 126,
    127, 133, 141, 152, 154
    right authority 72, 75, 76, 85, 86, 120,
    124, 124, 125, 133, 147
    see also Saint Augustine, civilians,
    Walzer

Kaldor, Mary 3, 44, 159–160
Kant, Immanuel 52, 116, 132, 135
Kashmir 27, 40, 44
Keith, Toby 4
Kenya 106
King Philip's War 60
Kosovo 95, 96, 113, 120, 124, 125, 126, 133; see
    also Yugoslavia
Kuwait 47, 67, 95, 143, 156, 183, 156, 158;
    see also Gulf War

League of Nations 179
Lebanon 183
liberalism 31, 97, 142, 158, 176, 177, 189;
    see also International Relations
Liberation Tigers of Tamil Eelam 32–3;
    see also Sri Lanka, terrorism
Libya 106
Lindbergh, Charles 226
Linklater, Andrew 11
Locke, John 15, 16, 23, 24, 34–6, 36–7, 38,
    39, 41, 42, 43, 44, 45, 234

Machiavelli, Niccolò 14, 21, 178, 212, 213,
    214, 227; see also fortuna, virtù
Mandela, Nelson 26; see also South
    Africa
Mao Tse-tung 55
mercenary 19, 136, 139, 140, 141, 157, 158, 163,
    164; see also soldier
Military Professional Resources
    Incorporated (MPRI) 144; see also
    private military companies
Milosevic, Slobodan 32; see also Kosovo,
    Yugoslavia
modernity 171, 214, 217, 218, 220, 221, 223
Morgenthau, Hans 12, 96; see also realism
Mozambique 95
Myanmar 183

Napoleonic Wars 161, 179
Nixon, Richard 160
North Atlantic Treaty Organization
    (NATO) 104, 124, 189
North Korea 2, 183, 184, 185, 193

Onuf, Nicholas 4, 12

Palestine 31, 40, 41, 42, 43, 44, 184; see also
    Israel
Peloponnesian War 178
performativity 4
Peterson, V. Spike 14
Pol Pot 32
private military companies (PMCs)
    18–19, 58, 136, 137, 138, 140–46, 149–54,
    230; see also Blackwater, Dyncorp,
    Executive Outcomes, Military
    Professional Resources Incorporated
    (MPRI), Triple Canopy
'propaganda of the deed' 23, 29, 30, 39
psychology 10, 21, 91, 100; see also
    cognitive dissonance
public–private divide 145, 151–4

race 39, 74, 221
    and US military recruiting 164, 165,
    166, 167, 169
racism 6; see also ethnicity, genocide

realism 96, 97, 176, 189, 231; *see also* International Relations
Rice, Condoleezza 95
Rome 31, 59, 61, 62, 63, 138, 146, 158
Rousseau, Jean-Jacques 19, 155, 156, 158, 212, 234
Runyan, Anne S. 14
Russia 1, 2, 30, 94, 95, 96, 158; *see also* Soviet Union
Rwanda 3, 17, 70, 71, 74, 77, 83, 84–8, 94, 96, 156

Saint Augustine of Hippo 8, 12, 16, 49, 54, 58–64, 66, 68, 69, 71, 72, 78, 81, 127; *see also* Just War
sanctions 109, 174, 186, 187
   moral 188, 189, 190, 191
   political 188, 189, 190
   see also economic sanctions
SARS (Severe Acute Respiratory Syndrome) 199, 200, 201, 203, 204
Saudi Arabia 26, 37, 38
security 5, 8, 11, 15, 36, 39, 47, 65, 77, 94, 96–7, 100, 105, 141, 201, 210, 212, 213, 222, 223, 228, 232
   airport 109
   definition of 5–6, 8, 12, 13, 62, 229
   discourses about 4, 12, 13, 14, 174
   economic sanctions and 20, 173, 174, 175, 177, 178, 192
   economic security 6
   environmental 6, 7
   food 6, 7
   gender and 7
   health 6, 7, 202, 203, 205, 206, 210
   human 7, 8, 225, 231, 232
   and influenza 193, 195–200, 201
   and natural disasters 211
   newness of 21st century 4, 9 , 12, 43, 90, 174, 186, 192, 231
   and non-state actors 8, 137, 142, 143, 145, 164
   and political theory 11, 13, 233, 234
   states seeking 77, 96–97, 210, 231
   and terrorism 36, 47, 49
   see also Department of Homeland Security, George W. Bush, National Security Strategy, securitization, United Nations Security Council
securitization 12, 196, 197, 198, 202, 211
September 11 attacks 3, 7, 8, 15, 22, 23, 24, 28, 29, 30, 31, 37, 39, 43, 44, 47, 48, 53,

59, 67, 69, 96, 104, 105, 107, 108, 110, 162, 163, 164, 165, 181, 232; *see also* al-Qaeda, bin Laden, terrorism
Sierra Leone 138, 145
Six Day War 46; *see also* Israel
Smith, Adam 202
soldier 18, 112, 113, 121, 133, 135, 157, 160, 164, 166, 169, 170, 172, 182
   and dirty hands 129
   officer 120, 121, 123, 125, 126, 127, 148, 168
   see also conscription, mercenary
Somalia 27, 70, 96, 111
South Africa 20, 26, 140, 141, 173, 177, 179, 185, 189; *see also* Mandela
South Korea 193
sovereignty 7, 17, 21, 33, 50, 51, 59, 90, 91, 93, 96, 97, 99, 100, 101, 103, 106, 108, 156, 157, 158, 190, 213, 215, 216, 217, 218, 221, 225, 226
   absolute 92, 94, 95, 109, 111
   as a paradox 212, 214
   as a variable 98, 109
   contingent 102, 105, 110
   popular 23, 33, 42, 45
   see also Westphalia
Soviet Union 3, 26, 27, 37, 141, 156; *see also* Russia
Spain 27, 64, 161, 194
Sri Lanka 44; *see also* Liberation Tigers of Tamil Eelam
Stalin, Josef 26, 32
Sudan 28, 88, 106, 113, 120, 124, 126, 191; *see also* Darfur, genocide
Sun Tzu 16, 49, 53–58, 59, 63, 66, 68, 69, 178, 233
Syria 183, 185, 189

Taguba Report 148–49; *see also* Abu Ghraib
Taliban 28, 104, 107, 185
Tanzania 106
terrorism 3, 7, 15–16, 17, 22, 30, 36, 41, 42, 43, 60, 67, 94, 103, 110, 163, 182, 229, 232
   battle against 2, 23, 41, 48, 107, 110
   counterterrorism 17, 90, 100, 101, 103, 105, 108–10
   definition 25
   eras of 23, 24, 43
   global 23, 24, 31, 32
   Lockerbie 103, 106
   and pre-emption 52, 53
   religious 23, 27
   state 26, 32, 107, 108, 181

terrorisme 24
and the UN 26, 103
see also al-Qaeda, Assassins,
    September 11 attacks
Thirty Years War 161
Tickner, J. Ann 6, 232
Triple Canopy 150; *see also* private
    military companies
tsunami 3, 211, 225, 226, 227
tyranny 23, 33, 34, 35, 37, 38, 39, 42, 43, 44,
    45, 52, 53, 60, 67

UNBISnet 103
United Kingdom 7, 33, 47, 95, 96, 104, 126,
    158, 199
United Nations 3, 26, 47, 75, 83, 96, 144,
    179, 185, 196, 205, 222, 223, 224
    as a government, 189–190
    Commission on Human Rights 70
    inspections in Iraq 67
    and Iran 175
    and Israel 46–7
    Security Council 7, 94, 103, 141, 173,
        175, 181, 183, 185, 196, 205, 222
    troops in Rwanda 87, 88
    see also UNBISnet
usurpation 23, 34, 35, 37, 38, 39, 43, 44, 45

vaccine 193, 200, 201, 204, 207–10; *see also*
    health, influenza
Vattel, Emmerich 16, 49, 53, 54, 64–8, 69,
    157
Vietnam War 112, 140, 157, 159, 163
virtù 21, 214–15, 224; *see also* Machiavelli

Wahhabism 32
Walt, Stephen 6, 7, 12; *see also* realism
Waltz, Kenneth 96, 136, 213; *see also*
    realism
Walzer, Michael 47, 50, 80, 113, 114, 129, 137,
    159; *see also* Just War
war 6, 7, 19, 20, 24, 33, 35, 38, 43, 46, 55, 61,
    112, 114, 116, 119, 121, 138, 152, 153, 156, 160,
    171, 191, 197, 231
    in Afghanistan 37, 56, 103, 104, 105, 108,
        109, 110, 165, 169
    alienated 19, 170, 171, 172, 230
    between Rome and Carthage 62
    civil 93, 133, 140, 156
    and civilian deaths 44
    Clausewitzian definition of 19, 178,

182–3
    ethnic 17, 134
    frequency of 161
    new 17, 160
    obligatory 71, 77, 79, 80, 82, 84 , 85, 87,
        89
    pre-emptive 47, 51
    pre-modern 19, 55, 59, 178
    preventive 16, 17, 46–69, 230
    and private actors 8, 18, 72, 117, 118,
        136–54, 164
    propaganda 40
    resource 231
    and the right of revolution 35, 36
    sanctions as 173–86, 229
    virtual 21
    see also Afghanistan, Cold War,
        economic sanctions Gulf War,
        Hundred Years War, Iran–Iraq
        War, Iraq War, Just War, King
        Philip's War, Napoleonic Wars,
        Six Day War, Sudan, Thirty
        Years War, Vietnam War, War of
        Spanish Succession, 'war on
        terror, 'World War I, World War
        II
War of Spanish Succession 161
'war on terror' 15, 17, 22, 23, 32, 40, 41, 43,
    45, 47, 48, 56, 57, 58, 59, 60, 63, 66, 92,
    102, 103–5, 108, 109, 111, 112, 162, 165, 181
    see also Afghanistan, al-Qaeda, Iraq
        War, Terrorism
Weber, Max 18, 136, 139
Wendt, Alexander 213
Westphalia 49, 59, 92, 136–7, 139, 140, 143,
    145, 148, 229
    see also sovereignty
Wight, Martin 10
Wilson, Woodrow 47, 179, 180
World Health Organization (WHO) 194,
    198, 201, 202, 203, 205, 208, 209, 226
    see also health
World Trade Organization 93, 175;
    see also economics
World War I 46, 160, 162, 170, 179
World War II 46, 47, 82, 98, 113, 120 , 122,
    124, 126, 133, 161, 162, 169, 179

Yugoslavia 70, 95, 189; *see also* Kosovo

Zimbabwe 183